UNDERTOW PRESS

VOICES FROM THE DEEP

The British Raj & Battle of the Atlantic in World War II

Edited By
Sean A. Kingsley

The Postal Museum

MARITIME HERITAGE FOUNDATION

Published by The Undertow Press, London
with sponsorship from The Maritime Heritage Foundation

First published 2018

A CIP catalogue record for this book is available from the British Library

ISBN 978-1-78808-002-6

Printed by Barnwell Print Ltd. Aylsham, Norfolk. Est. 1840
Norfolk's first Carbon Balanced Publication Printer

WORLD
LAND
TRUST™
www.carbonbalancedpaper.com
CBP001326003137601

By using Carbon Balanced Paper
through the World Land Trust on this
publication we have offset 617kg of
Carbon & preserved 432sqm of
critically threatened tropical forests.

Carbon Balanced Paper. One of the most sustainable forms of communication that
will reduce your carbon foot print and promote CSR. www.carbonbalancedpaper.com

To the crew of the SS *Gairsoppa*,
who made the ultimate sacrifice for
the freedom of Britain and the world

CONTRIBUTORS

Editor: Sean A. Kingsley

Andrew Craig, Director of Marine Operations, Odyssey Marine Exploration, Tampa, Florida

Neil Cunningham Dobson, Director, ROVARCH, St Andrews, Scotland

Gretel Evans, AOC Archaeology, Edinburgh

Ellen Gerth, former Curator, Odyssey Marine Exploration, Tampa, Florida

Dr Sean A. Kingsley, Director, Wreck Watch Int., London

Natalie Mitchell, AOC Archaeology, Edinburgh

Chris Taft, Head of Collections, The Postal Museum, London

Ernie Tapanes, Project Manager, Odyssey Marine Exploration, Tampa, Florida

CONTENTS

FOREWORD

By The Rt Hon The Lord Lingfield,
Chairman, The Maritime Heritage Foundation

Britain, as an island nation, has been defined by the sea throughout its history.

Anything made or grown by the hand of man has sailed from producer to buyer on the high seas. Where reward went, risk followed and, unsurprisingly, our coasts are scattered with the remains of a vast number of shipwrecks – by some estimates 6,000 off the UK, 10,000 off Ireland and many more outside territorial waters.

The British India Steam Navigation Co. Ltd's SS *Gairsoppa*, built in Tyne and Wear in 1919 and lost on 16 February 1941, is just one of many hundreds of shipwrecks increasingly discovered in deep seas. This steamer, travelling from Calcutta to London with essential war goods, was sunk by a German U-boat during the Second World War.

Alongside the gleaming silver bars found by the American pioneers of deep-sea research, Odyssey Marine Exploration, other astonishing finds take us back to the Battle of the Atlantic. Dated to very tight moments in time, shipwrecks can be extraordinary resources for history and education. The *Gairsoppa* is no different. Without the silver, tea, iron and vital imports carried by the ship and similar convoys, the war economy would have crumbled. The small finds once used by the crew – from the ship's telephone to wallets, shoes, bottled beer and even a lady's compact being brought home for a sailor's sweetheart – add colour to the photos of this rusting hull.

The greatest historical treasure, however, is a cache of some 700 letters miraculously preserved at a depth of 4,700 metres, the largest such collection found at sea. *Voices From The Deep* presents a microcosm of World War II India: from soldiers to teachers, missionaries and businessmen, reminding us of a fading time when communicating required patience and perseverance. Most of the letter writers were replying to mail that had taken two to three months to reach India.

This lost post, back from the deep after 75 years, is a wonderful reminder of days gone by and an Indian Empire that few now remember.

The Maritime Heritage Foundation is proud to be associated with this project and it is with great pleasure that I write this Foreword to *Voices From The Deep*, its pages dedicated to the brave sailors of the *Gairsoppa* who made the ultimate sacrifice in the defence of freedom.

Robert Lingfield

ACKNOWLEDGEMENTS

This book owes a vast debt of gratitude to the very broad shoulders on which is stands. The logistics that go into a deep-sea shipwreck project are staggering. The salvage operations were conducted under contract with the UK Department for Transport. Special thanks are reserved for Odyssey Marine Exploration for taking due care with unexpected finds and especially for sponsoring the stabilisation of the *Gairsoppa*'s letters.

Deepest thanks are extended to Greg Stemm, Mark Gordon, John Longley, Laura Barton, John Oppermann, Alice Copeland, Liz Shows, Aladar Nesser, Kathy Evans, Mark Mussett, Alan Bosel (artefact photographs) and Chad Morris and Eric Tate (artefact dimensions) and of course the hard work of all the Odyssey offshore team and the crew at Swire Seabed. Without their diligence, research and support, this book would not have been possible. A very special tipping of the hat is reserved for Andrew Craig and Ernie Tapanes, project managers, who successfully oversaw the offshore logistics under extremely complex circumstances.

Conservation of the finds for Odyssey was overseen by Fred Van de Walle, who diligently made sure the as-yet unidentified letters ended up in safe hands. Gretel Evans and Natalie Mitchell at AOC Archaeology in Edinburgh patiently took on the daunting task of opening and stabilising the 1,256 items that ultimately made up the *Gairsoppa* postal archive.

Extensive post-recovery historical and finds research was conducted by Neil Cunningham Dobson and Ellen Gerth, co-contributors to this book, with whom it has always been a pleasure to collaborate and bounce ideas around.

I am extremely grateful to Mike Carabini, Greg Stemm and Laura Barton for facilitating and supporting my work and I extend great appreciation to Lord Lingfield and the Maritime Heritage Foundation for sponsoring the design and printing of this book.

Preparation of this work coincided with the transfer of the *Gairsoppa* postal archive to The Postal Museum in London, which was quick to recognise its social importance. Developing themes and ideas with co-contributor Chris Taft, as well as Emma Harper, Andy Richmond, Nick Bell and Nick Coombe has been memorable and enjoyable. Kind thanks to Alison Kentuck, the UK Receiver of Wreck, who worked swiftly to transfer legal title to the letters to the museum.

Julian and Lincoln Barnwell have been very generous with their time advising on optimum printing and design preferences and with other forms of support. Many thanks to Jason Williams of JWM Productions for kindly sharing source material on Richard Ayres and to the fine eye of Elias Kupfermann for helping identify some letter writers. Madeleine Kingsley most kindly proofread the letters chapters.

On a personal note, as ever, special thanks and love to Lexia Deng and Madeleine, Andrew and Sally Kingsley for putting up with me disappearing down the hole that opens up during the writing of a book like this.

Sean Kingsley, London, November 2017

1

INTRODUCTION. MOMENTS IN TIME

SEAN KINGSLEY

Into the Deep

From the dockside, the steamship that glided out of Calcutta on 5 December 1940 looked nothing out of the ordinary. The SS *Gairsoppa* was a latecomer to the war at sea. The Ministry of Shipping had already commandeered most of her sister ships from the British India Steam Navigation Co. Ltd fleet. Vessel and cargo were on their way to rendezvous at Freetown in Sierra Leone, where sixty-three convoys had already crossed the 'Atlantic Rubicon' carrying essentials for the front line and British homes. Sadly, the ship's loss to an enemy U-boat on 16 February 1941, 300 miles southwest of Ireland, after losing contact with convoy S.L. 64, was a not uncommon tragedy in these dangerous times. Even the *Gairsoppa*'s silver, tea and iron cargo were far from unique. India's mints had been riding the silver tiger for her British masters since World War I.

What makes the story of the *Gairsoppa* exceptional is her discovery by Odyssey Marine Exploration and the recovery of intriguing cargo and finds used by the British and Lascar crew. The sinking of her 2,817 Bombay Mint silver bars, the heaviest loss during World War II, certainly catch the headlines. Yet it is the stories of the unexpected from this shipwreck, not recorded in any manifest, that bring the risks of the Battle of the Atlantic into focus, adding a new layer of knowledge to history. It is these tangible remains from the deep, echoes of a drowned ship's brave crew and life in British India, that are the subject of this book.

A lesser known treasure of the *Gairsoppa* are over 700 personal and business letters and Christmas cards that surfaced from the 4,700 metre-deep oxygen-depleted darkness. The lost mail was heading from India to southern England, Scotland and America as the close of 1940 fast approached. Thoughts of families and loved ones were on all the writers' minds as Britain prepared for its second Christmas at war. Over several years the letters were painstakingly opened and stabilised in the laboratories of AOC Archaeology in Scotland and then transcribed and transferred to The Postal Museum in London,[1] where they find the perfect home today. There the mail will remain permanently accessible for research in its rich archives.

Alongside shoes, wallets, samples of silk, teapots and portholes, the letters showcase the gift of the sea to preserve historical and archaeological finds to an extent typically unmatched on land beyond the most arid of desert environments, such as the Dead Sea Scrolls or the Cairo Genizah. The discovery is timely. The first-person sad and humorous voices laced through the mail bear witness to the ever-fading memory of World War II. The letters are a reminder of a slower age, when the world seemed far larger. Sending news to loved ones or negotiating business took two to three months for a single communication.

In our 24/7 fast and furious age, a generation has grown up unfamiliar with the art and beauty of letter writing and how, throughout the majority of history and antiquity, ships were civilisations' only means of efficient mass communication – the worldwide web, text and Instagram of the past. Despite this obvious reality, and the tens of millions of letters that crossed the oceans down the centuries, the *Gairsoppa*'s lost mail is the only significant cache recovered from the bottom of the sea from any moment in time.

Backdrop 1940

When the *Gairsoppa* left Calcutta on 5 December 1940 to cross the Indian Ocean and rendezvous with convoy S.L. 64 at Freetown and steam escorted – safety in numbers – to London, neutral America was a year away from entering the war. The Soviet Union was belligerent to the Allies through Stalin's non-aggression pact with Nazi Germany. Since May, Winston Churchill was Prime Minister.

1.1. The British India Steam Navigation Co. Ltd ship the SS *Gairsoppa*.

The Führer was described as having turned from a Jack-in-the-Box into a Frankenstein, the terror of Europe.[2] On 9 April 1940, Germany invaded Denmark and Norway and on 10 May marched into Holland, Belgium and Luxembourg. At the end of May and early June, British forces were forced to retreat from the beaches of Dunkirk. Paris fell on 14 June and a week later northern France and its Atlantic Coast lay in Nazi hands. As the last voyage of the *Gairsoppa* so vividly shows, shipping through the English Channel was not only now severely restricted, but sailing anywhere approaching Britain from the west was extremely dangerous. Meanwhile, Italy invaded Africa on 13 September and Mussolini marched into Greece on 27 October.

The aerial Blitz and Battle of Britain, or what Major-General J.E. Chaney of the US Army Air Corps called "one of the world's decisive military engagements… bracketed in history with Marathon and Waterloo", had been raging since 8 August.[3] London was hit for the first time on Saturday 7 September and the capital hardly saw a peaceful night until the all-clear sounded on 11 May a year later. Families lived amid streets thick with broken glass and homes reduced to smoking piles of rubble. Nowhere was sacred. On 13 September Buckingham Palace was hit. Blazing London promised to become as historic as the Great Fire.

By the time the bombs fell silent in May 1941, in London alone 1.15 million houses had been damaged. In Hull only 6,000 out of 93,000 homes escaped destruction. Nearly one house in four was put out of action in Plymouth. Enemy air raids ultimately killed 60,595 civilians across Britain, while 86,182 people were seriously injured. 1940 saw lemons vanish from the high street, eggs become scarce and the 350 varieties of biscuits on sale pre-war drop to twenty varieties. A housewife in Staines baked a cake containing so few ingredients – flour, custard powder and dried egg – that it was christened 'The Nothing Cake'.[4]

A Moment In Time

On the day the *Gairsoppa* left Calcutta, Thursday 5 December 1940, *The Times* newspaper gave a fine impression of the world at war. The night before, its pages reported, German planes had attacked London and the Midlands. Rescue parties were searching through the capital's rubble for survivors in a ruined convent where eighty to ninety people were trapped. A school for incurable children was hit. Schools, churches, a cinema, police station, houses and shops took most of the heat in Birmingham.

The German news agency claimed that "Making full use of the bad weather, the *Luftwaffe* penetrated to the lowest layer of the clouds and attacked their targets with great precision", also setting fire and derailing a troop transport train travelling towards the Midlands from southern England. In return, and despite thick cloud cover, RAF bombs had been dropped on enemy aerodromes in northern France and the port of Dunkirk, while goods yards were attacked in Ludwigshafen and Mannheim and a blast furnace plant was targeted in Essen.

1.2. A Remotely-Operated Vehicle (ROV) used to dive on and record the wreck.

1.3. Bundles of letters from the *Gairsoppa's* mail room.

News from Romania reported that Jewish property was being confiscated, owners turned out at one day's notice and forced to sell their businesses at ridiculously low prices to Germans or relatives of the Iron Guard. An old rabbi was made to draw a cart and his son to drive and whip his father. In Haifa, 1,771 Jewish immigrants heading for Palestine were intercepted at sea and preparing to be sent to a British Colony detention camp for the duration of the war.

The German press announced that in Poland, based on the Nazi ideology that the weak must serve the strong, the death penalty was about to be introduced for violence against German citizens, for damaging public monuments, disobedience against German decrees, conspiracy, possessing arms or unregistered wireless receivers, owning gold or for profiteering. Greek troops countering Mussolini's invasion had taken the heights of Pogradets, Mount Ostravitza and Premeti after severe fighting and entered the port town of Santi Quaranta. Italians were seen evacuating from the harbours of Argyrokastro and Premeti.

Back home, Anthony Eden, the Secretary of State for War, confirmed that 44,000 British men would spend Christmas 1940 in German prison camps. Major Lloyd George, the Parliamentary Secretary for the Board of Trade, refused to give assurances that the price of Christmas turkeys could be controlled because they were not general commodities. Sir A. Southby begged the Government, before it was too late, to find a way to stop the German menace to seaborne trade by protecting the vital western approaches to the British Isles.

In St Albans Consistory Court, the Reverend William Henry Hopkin was found guilty of forty-three immoral acts of drinking, resorting to taverns and accosting females. A.F. Pollard of Milford-on-sea wrote a letter to *The Times* questioning the causes behind the loss of Henry VIII's as yet undiscovered *Mary Rose*. Charlie Chaplin's new film *The*

Great Dictator reached the shores of Britain on the day the *Gairsoppa* sailed forth from Calcutta.

Indian Summers

Far removed from the theatre of war, soldiers, teachers, engineers and missionaries in India were starved of news. The trickle of British newspapers that made it to the Raj deliberately left the names of damaged towns and cities off its pages, while the British India news sheets were equally ambiguous or gung ho. "Although London at present is a storm centre, owing to air raids", readers learnt from *The Sunday Statesman* of 1 September 1940, "the Thames is enjoying the most prosperous season within memory". Goering's bombs had failed to destroy the harvest, Britons in India read.

As exotic as British workers and soldiers found India, society retained a rather Victorian way of life dictated by strict rules of behaviour and etiquette.[5] Some families sailed for the Raj fearful of an imminent invasion of England after Dunkirk. Soldiers were dispatched to the lawless North-west Frontier of modern Pakistan to fight the border tribes. At the fort of Razmak, "Europeans of the Raj were hugely concerned to adopt nothing that was Indian, or should I say native. We ate curry on Sundays, but that was just about the only concession we made to Indian culture. Never did we wear Indian clothes – our shirts were always tucked *inside* our trousers – *pukka* Europeans never knew any Indian language, and we never mixed socially with Indians."[6]

Other expats, such as Dorothy Margaret Baker, attending Bishop Cotton Girls' High School in Bangalore, had a very different experience. "Due to the war, the school provided a social melting-pot with children of various races, colours and creeds", she recalled, "all living and learning together. It set the seal on lingering notions of racial or social superiority that I retained, and I count myself fortunate to have had friends from such varied backgrounds."[7]

Some British residents were amazed by exotic grey Langur monkeys leaping around house rooves, men chasing snakes and having to tip out shoes before putting them on in case of scorpions. Social life was lively in wartime India. People played hard. In the largely men-only clubs, members enjoyed swimming, tennis, golf and drinks parties. In this life of privilege and other worldliness, many families retained servants for every purpose: to clean clothes, run baths and squeeze toothpaste onto brushes.[8]

Most of these themes – from Hitler's progress, the invasion of Greece, the Blitz and limited food supplies in Britain to the privileges of life in India and fighting the northern tribes – turn up loud and clear in the shipwrecked letters. The discovered wreck of the *Gairsoppa*, its cargo and mail are equally an homage to the people of India's role propping up Britain's essentials from silver to the steel and iron turned into the planes and ships that won the war.

No other Allied country before America joined the fray made such a deep contribution to keeping the enemy at bay. This book is as much a tale of Indian industry and brotherhood in the waning years of the Raj as it is about Britain's fading colonial life and wartime history. On 2 September 1940, a headline emblazoned across the front page of the British India newspaper *The Statesman* read "The show must go on." Indian sweat and muscle played a vital role in keeping that show alive throughout World War II.

Notes

1. See: www.postalmuseum.org.
2. Jog, 1941: 140.
3. *The Times*, Thursday 5 December 1940.
4. Longmate, 1973: 133-34, 140, 145, 148, 259.
5. Fleming, 2004: 54.
6. Reported by Robert Baker in Fleming, 2004: 24.
7. Fleming, 2004: 26.
8. Fleming, 2004: 27, 38, 48.

2

BRITISH INDIA STEAM POWER: ROADS TO MANDALAY & WORLD WAR II

NEIL CUNNINGHAM DOBSON,
SEAN KINGSLEY, ANDREW CRAIG
& ERNIE TAPANES

Introduction

When the SS *Gairsoppa* began her final voyage in December 1940 the phoney war was over. Merchant convoys were zigzagging across the seas to keep Britain's war machine turning. Materials were at the limits for almost everything imaginable from food to munitions as the Battle of the Atlantic raged across four million square miles of ocean. The waters from South Africa to Britain were red hot with Kriegsmarine

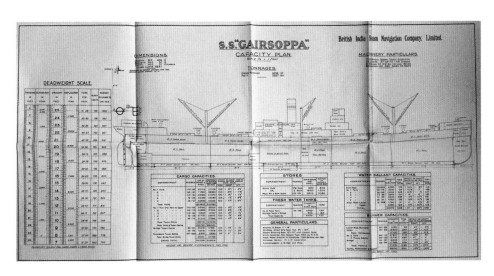

2.1. Capacity plans of the *Gairsoppa*.

raiders and submarines seeking prey. Britain's merchant marine found itself in the thick of it from the very beginning. Between September 1939 and the end of that year alone, 215 merchant vessels of 748,000 tons were lost.[1]

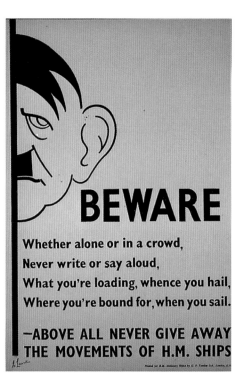

Now France was occupied, the Nazi naval bases along the Atlantic coast brought the war and threat of invasion closer to home. As the *Gairsoppa* slipped out of Calcutta and headed across the Indian Ocean, German U-boats were gloating at their success in the months of 'Die Glückliche Zeit', the Happy Time. By 1945 the war at sea took a terrible toll on man and machine. Over 36,000 Allied sailors perished and 2,500 British merchant vessels amounting to some 12 million tons were destroyed, 69% sunk by submarines.[2] On the Axis side, more than 30,000 Kriegsmarine U-boat crewmen died and 757 German submarines were lost in a failed attempt to sever Britain's maritime highway.[3]

The final voyage and sinking of the *Gairsoppa* reflects nearly every facet of the Battle of the Atlantic: the Government's far-flung requisition of shipping liners, the transport of mass agricultural and industrial goods over vast distances, the cat and mouse engagement between merchantmen and Kriegsmarine firepower, and tragic losses of life. For war-torn Britain, the *Gairsoppa*'s Indian tea and iron was equally as essential as its silver to keep the economy afloat. Little wonder Winston Churchill later recalled that "The only thing that ever really frightened me during the war was the U-boat peril."[4] The sea was Britain's lifeline.

Into India

The *Gairsoppa*'s last voyage is not just a story of Britain's desperation for agricultural and industrial resources during the Battle of the Atlantic or about a lost cargo of precious silver. It is equally a memory of the fortunes of one of the world's great ocean liners, the British India Steam Navigation Company Ltd. (BISN), from humble beginnings to world leader. The BISN Co. was one of the world's most successful cargo and passenger lines, whose services stretched from Japan to London by way of Africa and the Persian Gulf by the start of World War II.[5] The *Gairsoppa* was an ordinary cargo ship commissioned to fit seamlessly into the Company's workhorse fleet.

In business timing is everything and in 1847 Mackinnon, Mackenzie & Co. started chartering ships sailing from Glasgow and Liverpool to Calcutta, Australia and China to serve the fast-growing colonies. As Robert Mackenzie's observed on 15 April 1853 in a letter posted from Australia, where he was selling off company cargo, "Bear in mind that ships from England are bringing no cargo, and that consequently the Colonies are quite bare of all descriptions of English goods, particularly liquids". In a twist of fate, Mackenzie died in a shipwreck off Cape Howe a month later on the way to Calcutta and did not live to see the company's riches just around the corner.[6]

Mackenzie left behind strong foundations and in 1856 his associate, the Scotsman William Mackinnon, set up the Calcutta and Burmah Steam Navigation Company after winning a Government contract to carry mail between Calcutta and Rangoon. With a guaranteed revenue and a prestigious deal rubber stamped, Mackinnon opened offices in Glasgow and Liverpool two years later as the partner correctly predicted the opportunity to build a profitable passenger line to run hand in hand with the mail.[7]

2.4. German submarine *U-101* sank the *Gairsoppa* on 16 February 1941.

2.5. 2nd Mate Richard Ayres, the only survivor from the *Gairsoppa*'s last voyage.

The concern quickly prospered into one of the largest global shipping companies. By 1862, Mackinnon, Mackenzie & Co. was running mail twice a month between Bombay and Karachi and eight times a year up and down the Persian Gulf. In the same year the firm changed its name to the British India Steam Navigation Co., Ltd., which was registered in Scotland on 28 October 1862 with a capital of £400,000. By 1863 the company had nine ships of 860 to 1,050 tons. A decade later the BISN's thirty-one fleet ships were covering over 1.1 million miles of ocean a year.[8] The mail contracts remained the company's backbone well into World War II.

In the early 1880s, W. Mackinnon & Co. moved from Glasgow to London. Trade grew and early on the firm enjoyed a virtual monopoly in the British colony of Rangoon, a terminal for lucrative sea routes and ports of call radiating out to China and Japan by way of Penang and Singapore. Into the 1930s the Company's ships made over 500 annual calls to Rangoon.[9]

The island's charm and seafaring had an inspirational effect on a young Rudyard Kipling, who spent a few days there in 1889 when sailing from Calcutta to San Francisco by way of Penang. The writer arrived on the BISN ship the SS *Madura*, which he called the 'Mutton Mail' because it carried post and sheep,[10] while in his famous poem of 1889, 'Mandalay', he reminisced "Can't you 'ear their paddles chunkin' from Rangoon to Mandalay?" His 1927 poem 'Such As In Ships' equally captured the flavour of BISN trade of the period:

> Such as in Ships and brittle Barks
> Into the Seas descend
> Shall learn how wholly on those Arks
> Our Victuals do depend.
> For, when a Man would bite or sup,
> Or buy him Goods or Gear,
> He needs must call the Oceans up,
> And move an Hemisphere.
>
> Consider, now, that Indian Weed
> Which groweth o'er the Main,
> With Teas and Cottons for our Need,
> And Sugar of the Cane –
> Their Comings We no more regard
> Than daily Corn or Oil:
> Yet, when Men waft Them Englandward,
> How infinite the Toil!

After the mail service started up in the Persian Gulf in 1862, the BISN Co. expanded its regular services to the Gulf ports. By 1894 the fleet had grown to eighty-eight ships, the largest sailing under the British flag. The line was about to go truly global, however. After many years of close association and mutual profit, the Peninsular and Oriental Steam Navigation Company and the BISN Company merged in 1914 to dominate the main lines from the UK and Mediterranean to Australia and the East. The British India Steam Navigation Co. now commanded 126 ships of 570,243 gross tons.[11]

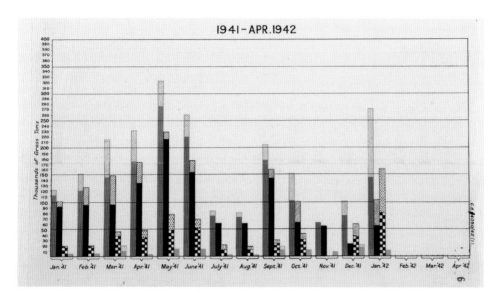

1941 – APR.1942

2.6. Monthly merchant shipping losses from U-boats, 1941 to 1942.

BISN timetables display a complex web of services well established by World War II. The 779-mile weekly Calcutta to Rangoon service took two days to sail. Another weekly line covered the 1,921 miles to Rangoon, Penang, Port Swettenham and Singapore in twelve days. The twice-monthly 5,773-mile Apcar Line from Calcutta to Osaka in Japan took a month and a day to Kobe by way of Rangoon, Penang, Singapore, Hong Kong, Amoy, Shanghai and Moji. A Calcutta to Sydney route ran 6,335 miles via Freemantle, Adelaide, and Melbourne. The service from Bombay to Basrah in the Persian Gulf via Bunder Abbas and other stops took fifteen days, running the 1,590-mile leg four to five times a month. The BISN's East African Coast service headed to Mombasa, Zanzibar and other ports twice monthly.[12]

From 1881 the BISN Co. ran a London-Calcutta fortnightly Home Line service.[13] By 1939 a joint service with P&O to London by way of Malta, Port Said, Suez, Aden, Cochin, Tuticorin, Colombo, Madras, Vizagapatam and Calcutta covered 8,556 miles per leg twice a month. London was also reached by way of a 7,923-mile monthly service stopping at Beira, D'salaam, Zanzibar, Tanga, Mombasa, Aden, Port Sudan, Suez, Port Said, Malta and Marseille. As 1940 unravelled, the war interrupted crossings to Europe so that BISN Company timetables to London had no alternative but to offer no precise schedules beyond the assurance that "Sailings Will Be Maintained as Regularly as Circumstances Permit."[14]

All the time a Calcutta, Coast Ports, Bombay and Karachi service tramped once a month the 2,995-mile seaway from Calcutta to Vizagapatam, Cocanada, Madras, Pondicherry, Cuddalore, Tirumalaivasal, Negapatam, Galle, Colombo, Tuticorin, Alleppey, Cochin, Calicut, Tellicherry, Cannanore, Mangalore, Bombay and Karachi.[15]

Going to War

By the time the *Gairsoppa* was launched in 1919, the British India Steam Navigation Company had been fighting wars for over half a century. From 1857 to 1863 its ships transported the 35th Regiment of Foot during the Abyssinian War. BISN ships took part in the Russo-Turkish War of 1878, the Zulu War of 1879, the Transvaal War of 1881, the Uganda Rising in 1897, the South African War of 1899 and the Boxer Rebellion of 1900 to 1901. During World War I, 120 company ships saw active service, carrying troops and supplies, acting as hospital ships and being converted into armed merchant cruisers.[16] The war to end all wars destroyed twenty-one BISN vessels.[17]

The path to the Second World War started early for the BISN Co. when Her Majesty's Government requisitioned ten British India ships for possible troop movements in

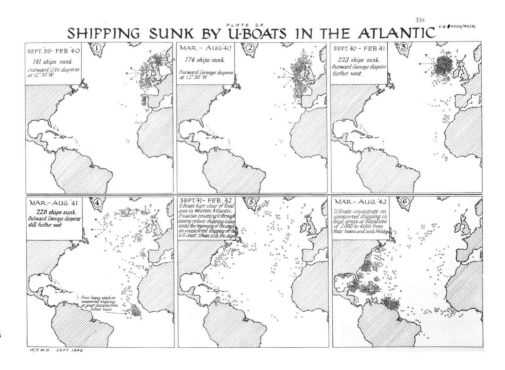

2.7. Shipping sunk by U-boats in the Atlantic, 1939-1942. Note the large losses in 1939-1941 in the Northwest Approaches southwest of Ireland.

VOICES FROM THE DEEP

late September 1938. A Directors meeting held at 122 Leadenhall Street, London, on 26 September acknowledged that "These temporary requisitions must have occasioned very serious distraction of the Company's mail and passenger services in an around India, the full extent of which has not yet been advised us."[18] Three more steamers were chartered for trooping and store ships on 26 April 1939. By the middle of September that year, eleven BISN vessels had been taken up under the Chatfield Scheme for moving troops to Singapore and Egypt and as a fleet auxiliary, hospital ship, store transport and a commissioned mercantile.[19] On the last day of January 1940 the Company was advised of the general acquisition of its fleet through a Liner Requisition Scheme under the Defence Regulations.[20]

Merciless casualties came swiftly from October 1939, when the *Dilawara* was damaged in convoy.[21] The Directors were informed that German aircraft attacked the MS *Domala*, built at a cost of £689,657, in the English Channel on 2 March 1940 during a voyage from Antwerp to India via Southampton. The captain, eighteen European personnel, thirty-six Indian crew and forty-five passengers died, including Indians being repatriated after serving on German steamers and finding themselves interred when the war broke out.[22]

By early October 1940, only nine BISN passenger ships were left on the coast of India from the thirty-nine vessels normally working these waters. A month earlier, Company equipment stored in the Royal Albert Docks was hit during bombing raids on London.[23] In a meeting held in Leadenhall Street on 5 March 1941, the Directors finally learnt the sad news of the "SS Gairsoppa. Reported with regret the loss of this vessel by enemy action on or about 16th February. At the moment only one of the ship's personnel is known to have been saved, Mr. R.H. Ayres, 2nd Officer and there is unfortunately little likelihood that there may be other survivors."[24]

All in all, the British India Steam Navigation Co. and its merchant marines served with fierce bravery and distinction during World War II, with the *Neuralia* representing the Company off Normandy on D-Day. Inevitably the Company's ships were lost everywhere from the coast of Greece, Cyrenaica, Algeria and Sicily to Atabia, Malaya, Burma and India, culminating in the sinking off North Africa of 1,150 troops and 120 crew on the *Rohna* in November 1943.[25]

Life & Times of the *Gairsoppa*

The SS *Gairsoppa* was built at the Hebburn yard along the River Tyne in northern England by Palmers Shipbuilding & Iron Co. Ltd. and named after Gairsoppa Falls, a breathtaking set of waterfalls in southwest India. The Lord Bishop of Madras, George Trevor Spencer, considered them in 1844 to be "indescribable by pen, and I should

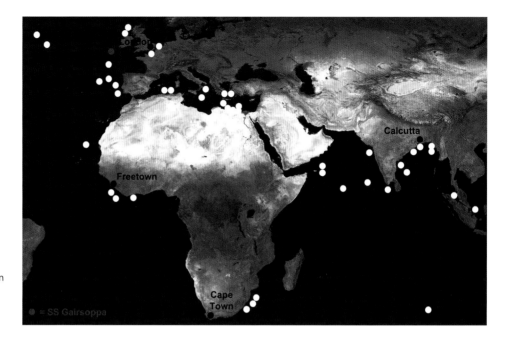

2.8. British India Steam Navigation Co. ships lost to enemy action during World War II.

think, by pencil also". Dr John Wilson of Bombay called the waterfall one of the three greatest wonders of India alongside the Himalayas and Taj Mahal.[26] The new steamship was 399 feet long and 52 feet wide with a depth of 28.5 feet (125.5 x 15.9 x 8.6 metres) and 5,236 gross tonnage. A 3,000 horsepower, triple-expansion steam engine fed by three single ended boilers, 15 feet 6 inches in diameter, drove a single screw. The ship made 11.7 knots in sea trials.[27]

The *Gairsoppa* – practical and anything but a beauty – was designed with five cargo holds, two forward of the amidships superstructure, one between the bridge and accommodation cabins and a final two holds aft of the accommodations superstructure. She could typically take a crew of seventy-three and four passengers. Installed on the deck were four 27-foot steel lifeboats and one 20-foot boat. A distinct funnel painted black with two white bands and the figure of Britannia backed by a lion with one paw on the globe identified her as a BISN vessel.[28] The ship was launched on 12 August 1919 and delivered into the hands of the British India Steam Navigation Company five days later.[29] Mrs Gowan, the wife of the managing director of Palmers Company, christened the *Gairsoppa*. At the time, her husband told reporters that the ship was being specially fitted up for the BISN's Far East trade.[30]

The newly launched cargo ship spent most of her life sailing the trade routes around India with the occasional foray into Western Europe. From the start she regularly carried mail, as Lloyds Mail News published in the British papers confirms, mostly across Asia, but reaching Marseille, Gravesend and London in March 1920 before heading to Karachi by way of Gibraltar.[31] In September 1920 she was back in Gravesend and returning to India with mail via Port Said in Egypt and on to Beira in Mozambique.[32]

August 1925 found the steamship leaving Hong Kong for the Japanese port of Moji and, as Mail Despatches published in the *Singapore Free Press and Mercantile Advertiser* suggest, with post from Singapore.[33] In late November 1934 the *Gairsoppa* was expected in Singapore.[34] On 1 January 1937 she arrived in Dundee from Calcutta via Colombo, Port Said, Hamburg and Antwerp with 13,407 bales of jute in what the local British newspapers dubbed one of the biggest 'jute rushes' in the port's history.[35]

In the 1930s and 1940s, India and especially eastern Bengal enjoyed a near monopoly in the production of jute, turning out 97% of the world's supply for everything from low cost and durable wrapping materials to ropes, carpets, tents, sailcloth and even parachutes. More than a billion jute sandbags were exported from Bengal to the trenches during World War I. The BISN Company specialized in shipping raw jute to Dundee's sixty mills from the late nineteenth century.[36] On the way back from Dundee the *Gairsoppa* picked up mail in London and steamed for Bombay via Busreh in Iran and Aden in the Yemen by way of the Suez Canal.[37] In May 1938 the steamer was on a passage to Galle in southwest Sri Lanka and in July 1939 left Mauritius for Calcutta.[38]

When war broke out the *Gairsoppa* was plying her usual trade around Indian waters and managed to keep away from requisition deep into 1940. She spent June and July 1939 routing from Calcutta to Mauritius and October to November sailing from Bombay, Calcutta and Karachi to Rangoon and back again via Tuticorin in southern India, Colombo and Jaffna in Sri Lanka, and Bassein (modern Vasai) and Beypore on India's west coast. In August 1939 she left Calcutta for Karachi to participate in militia training.[39]

Her movements in 1940 were much the same, sailing short haul from Bombay, Sri Lanka and Calcutta to Rangoon, but in addition stopping at Cochin (modern Kochi), Madras and Masulipatam. The August run to Rangoon included mail transport.[40] December 1940 found the *Gairsoppa* in Calcutta, where she was requisitioned for the UK Government. She left port on 5 December, stopped at Colombo on 12 December and on New Year's Eve was in Durban.[41]

The Last Voyage

There was little special about the *Gairsoppa*'s choice for convoy service and a secret silver cargo (see Chapter 4) – she merely found herself in a useful place at the wrong time. In December 1940 the lottery of war caught up with her. The ship was chosen to join S.L. 64, a UK bound convoy sailing from Sierra Leone (hence the abbreviated letters SL). The ship's declared destination was Oban in western Scotland, her sailing destination Methil d.g. on the east coast of Scotland, with London journey's end.

The British Admiralty had learned a bloody lesson during World War I, when German U-boats initially successfully picked off lone steamers before Britain re-introduced trans-oceanic convoying for merchant ships in June 1917. As the Austrian submarine commander Georg von Trapp – father of the family singers of *The Sound of Music* fame – recalled in his memoirs of the First World War, "Suddenly the U-boats came, the most dreadful pirates of all time. And then the steamers travel just like the silver ships of times past. They don't risk going alone anymore and select the old established means, the convoy."[42]

2.9. Examining the *Gairsoppa's* brass navigation lamp and a silver ingot.

Before departing, the fleet was divided into a regular and slower convoy designated S.L.S 64. Only ships that could steam between 9 and 14.9 knots were placed in convoy, but as the need for supplies became desperate in late 1940 a slow North Atlantic convoy for ships of 7.5-9 knots was added. Ships too slow for even those convoys had a life expectancy of less than a year.[43] The *Gairsoppa* and her crew of eighty-six men sailed with the faster S.L. 64 convoy.[44]

The twenty-eight ships in S.L. 64 carried a typical cross-section of Indian, African and Southeast Asian produce – copper, iron, manganese ore and tanker parts alongside cereals, frozen goods, grain, ground nuts, maize, seeds, sugar, tea and general East Indian and West African produce – for final destinations in Avonmouth, Cardiff, Glasgow, Greenock, Hull, Liverpool, London, Manchester, Middlesbrough and Swansea (Table 2.1). The *Gairsoppa* was expected to leave the port of Freetown on 31 January 1941, take up a position sixteenth in the convoy's line and reach its destination on 17 February.[45] Confidential Admiralty transmissions simply described the ship as carrying a 'general cargo',[46] a deliberate smokescreen that concealed 2,600 tons of pig iron, 1,765 tons of tea, 2,817 bars of silver and 2,369 tons of general cargo (Chapter 4).[47]

Ship	Cargo	Tonnage (Gross)	Declared Destination	Sailing Destination	Final Destination
Amstelkerk	West Africa Produce	4457	----------	Hull	Hull
Antilochus	Grain	9082	----------	Liverpool	Liverpool
Bengkalis	Iron, Ground Nuts	6548	----------	Hull	Hull
Benvenue	Rubber, Tea	5920	Oban	London	Returned to Freetown
Berwickshire	Sugar, Copra	7464	----------	Belfast f.c.	London
Bradford City	Seeds	4953	----------	Greenock	Greenock
Chr. Th. Boe. (Nor.)	Tanker B.	6192	----------	Clyde f.c.	Swansea
City of Lille	Seeds, General	6588	----------	Liverpool	Avonmouth
City of Newcastle	General	6921	----------	London	London
Clan Ross	Iron, Tea, General	5897	Oban	Glasgow	London
Darina	Tanker W.D.		----------	Manchester	Manchester
Fresno Star	Frozen	7998	Clyde	Clyde f.c.	Liverpool
Gairsoppa	Iron, Tea, General	5237	Oban	Methil d.g. then London	London
Gleniffer	General	9559	----------	Liverpool	Liverpool
Gogra	Iron, Tea	5190	Oban	Methil d.g. then London	Manchester
Halizones	Iron, Tea	5298	Oban	London	London
Hamla	Iron Ore	4416	------------	Middlesbrough	Middlesbrough
Hartlebury	Cereals	5082	Oban	Hull	London
Japan	Iron, Tea	5239	Oban	London	Liverpool
Marcella	Manganese Ore	4592	------------	Hull	Manchester
Oakbank	Maize	5154	------------	Oban	London
P.L.M. 17	Iron Ore	4008	------------	Cardiff	Cardiff
River Lugar	Iron Ore	5423	Glasgow	Glasgow	Glasgow

Table 2.1. Merchant ships in convoy S.L. 64 sent from Sierra Leone to the UK on 31 January 1941 (from National Archives, Kew, ADM 199/2186).

Ship	Cargo	Tonnage (Gross)	Declared Destination	Sailing Destination	Final Destination
Phrontis	East Indian Produce	6181	Liverpool	Liverpool	Liverpool
Simaloer	Sugar, General	6535	Oban	London	London
Simnia	Tanker W.D.	6197	------------	Manchester	Manchester
Terkoelei	Copper, General	5158	Oban	London	London
Thursobank	Seeds, Cake, General	5575	------------	London	London

While assembling at Freetown, the capital of Sierra Leone and since the fifteenth century a free town for slaves, a fatal logistical mistake was made. The African port was little more than a glorified large natural anchorage with no artificial harbour. Cargo had to be ferried to and from shore on small lighters and landed on the beach. Storage space ashore was limited because the land rose sharply up to the hills. Disease was endemic and the climate atrocious. Pickpockets worked the streets and lifted personal property from barracks.[48]

At the start of the war, oil and coal supplies had to be stored afloat. Coal was freighted in from Nigeria or the UK. Up to 200 cargo and military vessels were moored in Freetown at peak times. For an unknown reason, presumably the rush to turn convoys around, several ships in S.L. 64 left port without topping up their coal bunkers. So at 0830 on 31 January 1941 the convoy headed north in nine to twelve columns steaming four cables (800 yards) apart.[49] HMS *Arawa* took up its position astern as fleet escort. By day, and for most of the night, the convoy followed an evasive steering pattern as the moon shone brightly.

The thoughts, hopes and fears of the crew during the *Gairsoppa*'s final voyage will forever remain unknown. Convoys sailed under blackout conditions at night, so port-holes and deadlights were closed down. Ships were painted grey as camouflage, while their names and the distinctive company funnel colours were blacked out. Bad weather was an endemic issue in the Atlantic. In really bad conditions a convoy would disperse, making ships easy targets.

The British India Steam Navigation Company was one of the top shipping companies and officers enjoyed high standards of accommodation. Each officer had his own cabin turned out in a beautiful wood finish and the luxury of a hand basin and bath. A cabin steward cleaned his rooms and did the laundry. Food was excellent. Even though war was raging, decorum had to be upheld. Officers were expected to dress in uniform when in the saloon for meals and were not allowed to start eating until the captain sat down, even if he was an hour late.[50]

The main accommodation on the *Gairsoppa* lay in the central amidships section above the boiler room. The radio operator's cabins lay on the lower bridge deck next to the captain's rooms. The deck officers, engineering officers, chief steward, apprentices, the saloon and pantry were all on the bridge deck. Down aft were the accommodation and mess rooms for the bosun, carpenter, the seamen, firemen and gunners. On the lower decks, where up to eight ratings might share one glory hole with two-tier iron-framed bunks, the portholes could not be opened and the suffocating air was as thick and foul as in a submarine.[51] On some ships mattresses were not even provided: crews made do with a cover filled with straw known as a 'donkey's breakfast'.

The BISN Company had a tradition of using Indian ratings on their ships, mainly Lascars recruited from the Chittagong region of modern east Pakistan and Bombay and for cabin and table stewards Goanese from India's west coast. The Indian crews followed the cast system and many did not mix. It was also common for the BISN to hire Chinese ratings, which explains the presence of Leong Kong as the carpenter during the *Gairsoppa*'s final voyage.[52]

Under war conditions, crews were required to sleep in their clothes, their lifejackets kept to hand night and day. At times, crew and officers on convoy worked double

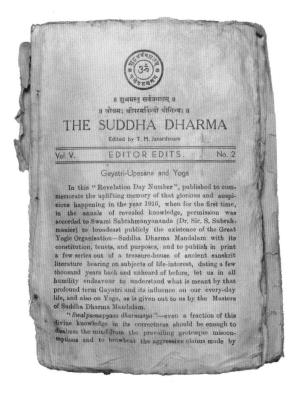

2.10. A copy of the *Suddha Dharma* Buddhist teachings went down on the *Gairsoppa* (TUR-13-00056, 12.5 x 17.5cm).

2.11. Crew's Indian copper coins (TUR-13-00064-05, TUR-13-00064-08, Diameters 2.0cm).

watches. Fear of torpedo was omnipresent and lifeboats were often kept swung out ready to launch. It was not just the living conditions that were poor for the ratings. Able Seamen were paid £12 a month on British merchant marine ships, less than half their American counterparts. Whereas the US Government insured the life of every American seaman for $5,000 and paid out $2,000 for disablement, British merchant seamen had to cover any insurance themselves.

In the UK overtime did not exist, whereas the American Merchant Marine paid 85 cents for every hour worked over a forty-four-hour week and added war bonus payments of 100% for service in the North Atlantic or Mediterranean. British Seamen made do with a War Risk Bonus of £10 a month.[53] Should disaster strike, before the May 1941 Essential Work Order for the Merchant Navy was passed, seamen forced to abandon ship and float for days in lifeboats were technically judged to be off pay from the moment of a sinking.[54]

The timing of the *Gairsoppa*'s last voyage was not fortuitous. The twelve months between June 1940 and May 1941 went down in history as the worst in the war at sea: 806 vessels were lost at a rate of over two a day, the majority to U-boat action in the North Atlantic.[55] December 1940 saw the worst ship losses to date. The *Gairsoppa* was sailing into a ferocious danger zone.

2.12. The ship's Alfred Graham & Co. navy phone (TUR-12-90515-UN, H. 38.0cm).

2.13. The ship's counter bell (TUR-12-90562-UN, Diameter 11.2cm).

Much uncertainty accompanied convoy S.L. 64's movements. None of the original ports listed in Admiralty correspondence ended up being the vessels' final destinations (Table 2.1). Was this a reaction to fast-changing enemy movements at sea or a deliberate smokescreen? Certainly rumour had it that one of the convoy captains lost a copy of the sailing orders in a local bar in Freetown,[56] a massive security breach for a

2.14. A porcelain cup with the BISN logo. Made by the Bakewell Bros. Ltd. of Hanley, England (TUR-12-90608-CR, H. 7.4cm).

2.15. A porcelain milk or water jug with the BISN logo. Made by the Bakewell Bros. Ltd. of Hanley, England (TUR-12-90610-CR, H. 18.6cm).

nation constantly being bombarded with adverts warning people to keep silent about ship movements – 'That Kind Of Talk Sinks Ships' – or as America more iconically put it, 'Loose Lips Sink Ships'.

The *Gairsoppa*'s movements were kept off the books as far as possible. BISN Directors' meeting minutes always listed which of its ships were requisitioned for the war every month, yet the *Gairsoppa* is curiously absent from its pages. The same was true for the Company's mail transport lists, which again carefully excluded any mention of Captain Hyland's ship. Whether by design or not, on the night of 31 January the Admiralty abruptly signalled for S.L. 64 to alter its route and track eastwards of Cape Verde, the Canary Islands and the Azores. Was this yet another measure to keep the enemy second guessing its plans?

In the end, the combination of concerns about coal stocks and bad weather played havoc with S.L. 64's movements. Not till midday 19 February, when the convoy turned east towards the Northwest Approaches, was any favourable sea found. The convoy started out with visibility at 5-8 miles and sailing in columns four cables or 800 yards apart on 2 February 1941. The next day strong northeasterly trade winds slowed down progress from 8.5 to 6.8 knots. By the afternoon of 9 February, strong northwest winds and a heavy swell continued to roll until 14 February, reducing the convoy's speed further to between 5.6 and 6.2 knots.

The *Benvenue* was sent back to Sierra Leone on 30 January, its degaussing gear burnt out (a copper cable along the outer hull that projected a 'north pole up' field to neutralize a ship's magnetic signature and stop German mines going off). The *Hamla* was unable to keep up with the convoy on 2 February. On 13 February, a general fuel shortage became apparent and on checking levels the convoy commodore realised that six ships had left Freetown with just twenty-six and a half days' fuel, not enough of a buffer for any heavy seas met during the optimum eighteen-day voyage. On the same day, the Dutch ship the SS *Simaloer* was sent to Fayal (Azores) due to a lack of fuel and its dirty bottom increasing fuel consumption from 36 to 40 tons daily. By early morning on 13 February the *Halizones* had dropped out of the convoy, probably again to low coal stocks. At the same time the SS *Oakbank* at the head of the convoy column got ahead of its station and vanished over the horizon.[57]

On 14 February, the Admiralty wrote a confidential cypher message confirming that one group of S.L. 64 was "corrupt" and only able to travel at a speed of 5.5 knots.[58] The *Hartlebury* was sent to Pont Delgado in the Azores that day in search of fuel. On the 16th the *Gogra*'s engine air pump broke, reducing its speed to 3 knots. When the local escorts the *Wolverine*, *Harvester*, *Fleetwood*, *Arbutus*, *Erica* and *Camelia* met up with S.L. 64 at 1400 on 17 February, eight of the company's original fleet was nowhere to be seen.

Meanwhile, the slower moving S.L.S. 64 was heading straight for disaster, a history that highlights the dangers of these cruel waters.[59] The convoy sailed under escort for two days and then continued unprotected, but safe, until 11 February, when a mystery passenger ship came up astern of the convoy 300 miles east-southeast of the Azores. The convoy Commodore put up a signal "Attention is called to the bearing indicated" and turned smartly 40° to starboard. The mystery ship sheered off amid great concern about what intelligence it may have passed on. A day later S.L.S. 64 was attacked. At 0605 a ship thought to be the anticipated British battleship escort steered across the convoy's bows. The morning light was too dark to see what ensign she was flying. Suddenly and without warning the ship opened fire. What proved to be the German enemy raider the *Admiral Hipper* hailed fire down in ten to fifteen minute bursts. The convoy scattered in all directions.

The *Admiral Hipper* had left Brest on her second Atlantic mission on 1 February 1941 and Captain Wilhelm Meisel infiltrated convoy S.L.S 64 by posing as the anticipated HMS *Renown* using intelligence captured from the British ship the *Iceland*. Alongside the convoy the raider lowered its phony White Ensign and raised the German battle flag, running into the British ships at 31 knots. The enemy raked every ship from a range of 400 metres to 5.5 kilometres and discharged twelve torpedoes, sinking twelve steamers of estimated 78,000 tons capacity and leaving two afloat smouldering. German accounts described the attack as the greatest massacre ever witnessed at the hands of a single warship.[60]

In the chaos the chain of command collapsed on some ships. On the SS *Clunepark* travelling to Middlesbrough with 5,150 tons of iron ore, the captain ran off the bridge with the Chief Officer when the shelling started and ordered abandon ship. The *Volturno*, *Margo* and another vessel also abandoned ship. Shells may have been screeching overhead, but these vessels had not yet been hit. The *Clunepark*'s risk-averse captain also refused permission four times for the gunners to fire on the *Admiral Hipper* amid dread that the raider would target him instead.

With the captain gripped by fear, the crew took control. The 2nd Officer, V. Smith, collected the secret books from the chart room and threw them overboard from the machine gun nest. Alongside the 3rd Mate he let off a smoke float screen and got the stopped ship underway. Under the smoke cover both the *Clunepark* and *Blair Athol* escaped. The German cruiser eventually spotted a Greek straggler and steamed off at high speed after signalling to the steamer *Lornaston* 'Save the crews'.

From the bridge of the convoy's lead ship, the SS *Warlaby*, bound for Oban on the west coast of Scotland with 7,000 tons of cottonseed, the Commodore had immediately hoisted the flag ordering the convoy to disperse, which the raider swiftly shot to pieces. The enemy continued shelling the ship mercilessly, shattering most of the lifeboats. Despite the *Admiral Hipper* firing on any clusters of men, "pumping away with pom-poms and everything they had", unlike on the *Clunepark* the *Warlaby*'s crew stubbornly refused to leave their stations. Fires broke out in the No. 2 and 4 holds, the ship listed heavy to port and turned completely around before starting to roll over. The Captain and Second Mate were still on the bridge when a shell hit. Neither was ever seen again.

Far away and several days later, the SS *Nailsea Lass* was heading for Oban with a general cargo of 6,200 tons. She was just 60 miles southwest of Fastnet in southern Ireland having dropped out of the S.L.S 64 convoy after one day at sea. The ship missed the massacre at the hands of the *Admiral Hipper* and by 24 February was less than a day from home, and sailing at a speed of 6 knots, when "there was a heavy shock, the ship heeled over, and a second later a loud explosion... there was no flame, but

2.16. A pewter tray for carrying tea glasses around the ship (TUR-12-90569-UN, H. 21.0cm).

2.17. One of several pewter teapots on the ship (TUR-12-90570-UN, H. 21.5cm).

a lot of water was thrown up which came down on the bridge." A torpedo from *U-48* had struck the port side of the ship abreast of the foremast between the No. 1 and 2 holds, 60 feet from the bow. "The ship vibrated, then took a gradual list to port which steadily increased. No wireless message was sent out as the valves were broken by the explosion", M. Knight, the ship's 2nd Officer, later told the Admiralty.

2.18. A pewter tankard (TUR-12-90553-UN, Height 6.1cm).

2.19. A pewter serving dish (TUR-12-90580-UN, Diameter 29.3cm).

The *Nailsea Lass*'s confidential books and papers were thrown overboard in a weighted bag before she started to go down by the bow. The crew managed to pull clear in lifeboats. About a quarter of an hour after being hit, the ship sank. Once downed, *U-48* surfaced and a German commander addressed the survivors from the conning tower, enquiring if anyone was injured and replying that "we are not all bad Nazis, and I hope the war will soon finish." The German crew handed out two packs of cigarettes before steaming off. The survivors landed at Ballyoughtragh in Co. Kerry, Ireland, on 26 February. The description of the sinking of the *Nailsea Lass* provides comparative details about the *Gairsoppa*'s otherwise unknown final minutes.[61]

A Present for Hitler

In his report to the Admiralty about the fate of convoy S.L. 64, the captain of the escort ship HMS *Arawa* expressed in the clearest of terms the system's failure to load sufficient coal. "I do not know what arrangements exist for bunkering ships at Freetown or elsewhere", he reported, "but it seems wrong that ships should be allowed to leave Freetown on a roundabout voyage to England with only sufficient fuel to reach the Azores, even when the original route has been shortened." He advised that the speeds of merchant ships given by Masters to Naval Control Services Officer were in many cases highly fictitious and needed to be understood better because, if not, "The result is either the whole convoy is slowed down or the ships drop out and become a present to Hitler."[62]

With insufficient coal, the final voyage of the *Gairsoppa* became a gamble with the elements and, ultimately, just such a gift to Hitler. The ship had left Freetown in the swifter S.L. 64 convoy and all went well until the Spanish ships *Monte Gurugu* and *Uribitarte*, heading for Cape Verde from Buenos Aires, spotted the convoy on 4 and 5 February. A Spanish signal intercepted and encoded "Entire Convoy Pontio" spread fear that intelligence might have been leaked to enemy agents. Trouble was brewing.

The *Gairsoppa* had already been at sea for five weeks after leaving Calcutta on 5 December 1940. Unlike the slow moving S.L.S. 64, a German raider never ensnared the swifter mother convoy. As the commander of the escort ship HMS *Arawa* made clear, however, any convoy craft forced to sail solo was a sitting duck. As fate turned out, on 14 February 1941 Captain Gerald Hyland realised that the *Gairsoppa*'s coal reserves were too low to reach London. At 1630 hours the ship changed course for Galway at coordinates 45 degrees 6' North and 23 degrees 16' West, about 630 nautical miles southwest of Ireland.

Two days after the *Gairsoppa* broke away from the convoy, a German submarine took up a firing position in the evening of 16 February. HMS *Arawa* had already advised the Admiralty of an unknown aircraft circling the area.[63] The straggling BISN ship had been spotted. Commanded by Korvetten-Kapitan Ernst Mengersen, *U-101* was a Type VIIB U-boat launched in early 1939. The German submarine had already sailed on four war cruises and sunk fourteen ships. More than 700 Type VII submarines armed with five torpedo tubes and nine reloads, as well as an 88-millimetre deck gun, served as the workhorses of the Kriegsmarine during World War II. These U-boats displaced 857 tons submerged and were crewed by forty-four men.[64] Mengersen had built a distinguished career and received praise from Vice Admiral Karl Dönitz and Commander of the Submarines – later named Head of State in Hitler's will – for his sighting of a British convoy off Iceland on 1 December 1940, an attack that downed ten ships.[65]

At 21.30 on 16 February, Mengersen launched a two-torpedo spread at the *Gairsoppa*'s starboard midsection. Her 280-kilogram G7e explosive warheads, the best available to Type VIIB submarines, could travel 5 kilometres at 30 knots if pre-heated and 3 kilometres at 28 knots if not pre-heated. Heavy seas threw the torpedoes off course and the *Gairsoppa* found a momentary reprieve. Four minutes later Mengersen fired a single torpedo. A massive explosion ripped through the *Gairsoppa*'s No. 2 hold. The explosion probably toppled the foremast, in turn severing the main and emergency wireless antennae. All contact with the outside world would have been immediately cut off and with it any hope of eighteen-year-old Radio Officer Robert Hampshire sending out an emergency signal. The ship quickly took on water by the bow. Within an hour the *Gairsoppa* and its cargo plunged 4,700 metres to the bottom of the freezing North Atlantic. She was 300 miles southwest of Galway – three days from safety.[66]

Two of the launched lifeboats were never seen again and of the eight Europeans and twenty-three Indians in the third, just one man beat the cruel sea to shore. The ship's 2nd Mate, Richard Hamilton Ayres, endured thirteen gruelling days at sea to make landfall at Caerthillian Cove in Cornwall. For his efforts trying to save his crew, the First Sea Lord approved Ayres's appointment as a Member of the Most Excellent Order of the British Empire (MBE) "for good services when his ship was torpedoed and sank." His citation left behind the only surviving record of the horrors the *Gairsoppa*'s sailors endured.[67]

At dawn on the morning after the fateful attack, Ayres pointed the lifeboat eastwards. The violent motion of the boat had forced the bungs to work out from both water tanks, so half of the drinking water was already gone. The 2nd Mate fixed the water ration at two dippers a day and gave the Indians, who were least able to withstand the cold, the forward part of the boat under the canvas cover, where they desperately huddled to keep warm under blankets. The hood was rigged aft for the Europeans. In the absence of a rudder, Ayres steered by oar. The survivors often had to bale.

After the first day, the crew could no longer swallow their biscuit rations and the 2nd Mate had to resist frequent appeals for more water and threatening behaviour. In the end the Indians took to drinking salt water, which drove them mad. Fighting broke out. After seven days only seven men were still alive, the rest having given in to exposure or died after drinking from the sea. Hope looked desperate:

> As the Second Mate could not do without rest he divided the others into two watches and taught them how to handle the boat. By the eighth day the water had all gone, and their hands and feet were badly frostbitten. In the next few days two light showers of rain gave them some relief, but their strength was fast ebbing. One of them was delirious, and the rest had barely enough hope and heart to carry on.

> Suddenly, after thirteen days in which they had seen nothing, one of them croaked "Land". They feared it must be a cloud: but the boat was going well and they soon made out a lighthouse. As far as the eye could see there were breakers and steep surf running on to an ironbound coast; but the Second Mate reckoned the risks and thought it best to run into a rocky cove. There [sic] were too weak to use the oars; so they ran under shortened sail for the inhospitable shore. A comber broached them to and overturned the boat. All hands were thrown into the sea…

> The Second Mate recalls feeling that he was tired out and that the fight for life was not worthwhile. Then he heard the voices of children on the shore, shouting encouragement. So he made a last effort, saw a rope, grasped it and made it fast round his waist.

> When they hauled him ashore he was no more conscious. Undismayed by suffering and death he had kept a stout heart and done all a good man could to comfort his shipmates and bring them to safety. It was only the cruelty of the sea which cheated him of his labours.

Ayres was rushed to Helston Cottage Hospital. The Second Officer would later receive the Lloyd's War Medal for Bravery at Sea to add to his MBE. But Richard Ayres never again spoke about his ordeal on the *Gairsoppa* or journey to the rocky shore. Awards were clearly no comfort. The Secretary of the Honours and Awards Committee concluded in a note to Sir Robert Knox at the Treasury that "I think you will agree that this is one of the starker episodes of the war".[68]

 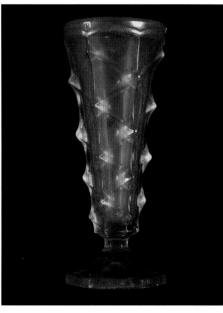

2.20. A glass drinking cup (TUR-12-90592-GL, H. 12.4cm).

2.21. A glass vase (TUR-12-90595-GL, H. 20.7cm).

Conclusion

The sinking of the *Gairsoppa* was tragic, but overall the January 1941 S.L. 64 convoy to the United Kingdom was a success. Whereas seven ships were lost from the slower S.L.S. 64, only the BISN ship ended up a casualty of the faster convoy. Although the wisdom of relying on a single 4.7-inch deck gun to fight off the enemy can be questioned in hindsight – compared to some ships in the two convoys armed with three – multiple arms are highly unlikely to have kept the U-boat at bay. In any case deck guns were only effective if a U-boat was on the surface; during a night attack a merchant ship was doubly helpless. Ultimately, it would be a basic lack of coal that forced the steamship to drop out of the convoy and cost the straggling *Gairsoppa* its life.

The problem was red flagged almost at once, headed by "A stricter check on the amount of fuel on board at Freetown… 5 ships of the convoy had not got 26½ days on board! Ships of a 'bare' or 'doubtful' 9 knots should not be included in 9 knot convoys". The Freetown to UK S.L. 64 convoy remained a mainstay of the war at sea, ending its service with a 178th crossing in November 1944.[69]

The merchant marine for whom the *Gairsoppa* sailed is rightly known as the Fourth Service. Numbering 120,000 officers and men, it was the size of eight Army divisions. By VE-Day in 1945, 22,490 British merchant seamen had lost their lives alongside nearly 4,000 Royal Navy gunners, 6,093 Indian Lascars, 2,023 Chinese and sailors drawn from America, Norway, Greece, the Netherlands, Denmark, Canada, Belgium, South Africa, Australia and New Zealand.[70] The men of the British India Steam Navigation Company paid a heavy price for their service. Of 105 vessels of 675,000 gross tons controlled by the firm in September 1939, fifty-one were lost by August 1945 – half the fleet wiped out alongside 1,083 officers and crew.[71]

The little that could be done for the families of the *Gairsoppa*'s brave men included looking into compensation for the dependants of twenty-eight of the India-based crew, such as a monthly pension of 12 rupees recommended for Ashraf Ali, the aged and rheumatic brother of the forty-four-year-old Indian trimmer Amin Rahman, because his financial position "is very bad and he has got no source of income to maintain his family." The wife of the Chinese carpenter Leong Kong was left stranded in Calcutta and sought money to return home. A stipend of just 2 rupees per month was agreed for his daughter, to be paid from 15 June 1941 until she reached fourteen years old.[72]

The bodies of four drowned men from the *Gairsoppa*'s lifeboat, Radio Officer Mr Hampshire, gunner Norman Haskell Thomas and two Lascar seamen, were recovered from the sea and buried in Wynwallow Church, Landewednack, on the Lizard in Cornwall beneath tombstones engraved 'A Sailor of the Second World War, S.S. GAIRSOPPA, 16th February 1941'. The Muslim Indians were buried at Richard Ayres's request in accordance with their religious rites, facing east-west towards Mecca. After nine months on a 100% disability pension, Ayres returned to sea with the British India Steam Navigation Company and later the Royal Navy Reserves. After the war he took a job as a cargo superintendent in India and Malaya.[73]

Of the SS *Gairsoppa*'s crew lost far out to sea, eleven are commemorated on the Tower Hill Memorial in London and seventy Lascars on the Bombay and Chittagong War

2.22. A Western style leather shoe (TUR-13-00067, Length 27cm).

2.23. An Indian style leather sandal (TUR-13-00066, Length 19.5cm)

Memorials in India. At a Directors meeting held at 122 Leadenhall Street in London on 10 December 1941, the Chairman read a proposal for building and financing an Indian Seaman's Home in Calcutta to accommodate three thousand seamen.[74] Echoes of the last voyage of the *Gairsoppa* resonate across land and sea.

Notes

1. Elphick, 1999: 11. Kaplan and Currie, 1998: 27.
2. Keegan, 1988: 265; Elphick, 1999: 11; Hague, 2000: 107; White, 2008: 2.
3. Niestlé, 1998: 4. For the impact of U-boats on the First and Second World War's Battle of the Atlantic, and the significance of their archaeological remains, see Cunningham Dobson, 2013.
4. Churchill, 1949: 529.
5. For the BISN history in general, see Laxon and Perry, 1994.
6. Blake, 1956: 13, 19-21.
7. Blake, 1956: 24-5, 27-8.
8. Blake, 1956: 32-4.
9. Blake, 1956: 89, 91.
10. Kipling, 1900: 213.
11. Blake, 1956: 100, 159, 174.
12. National Maritime Museum, Greenwich: BIS/29/4.
13. Laxon and Perry, 1994: 12.
14. National Maritime Museum, Greenwich: BIS/29/4.
15. National Maritime Museum, Greenwich: BIS/29/4.
16. St George Saunders, 1948: 22-3.
17. See: www.theshipslist.com/ships/lines/bisn.shtml. Accessed 11.9.17.
18. National Maritime Museum, Greenwich: BIS/1/21/160-161.
19. National Maritime Museum, Greenwich: BIS/1/21/206, BIS/1/21/239.
20. National Maritime Museum, Greenwich: BIS/1/21/266, BIS/1/21/276.
21. National Maritime Museum, Greenwich: BIS/1/21/252.
22. National Maritime Museum, Greenwich: BIS/1/21/285-286.
23. National Maritime Museum, Greenwich: BIS/1/22/15.
24. National Maritime Museum, Greenwich: BIS/1/22/53.
25. *BI. One Hundred Years of Trooping*; St George Saunders, 1948: 108, 160.
26. Spencer, 1845: 108; Smith, 2012: 276.
27. National Maritime Museum, Greenwich: BIS/13/9. Registry and Other certificates, British India Steam Navigation Company Ltd 1919-41. National Maritime Museum, Greenwich, BIS/13/9. See: www.poheritage.com/Upload/Mimsy/Media/factsheet/93198GAIRSOPPA-1919pdf.pdf. Accessed 2.9.17.
28. Blake, 1956: 46.
29. National Maritime Museum, Greenwich, BIS/13/9. See: www.poheritage.com/Upload/Mimsy/Media/factsheet/93198GAIRSOPPA-1919pdf.pdf. Accessed 2.9.17.
30. *Jarrow Express*, 15 August 1919.
31. *Western Daily Press*, 28 February 1920, 4 March 1920; *Yorkshire Post and Leeds Intelligencer*, 3 May 1920.
32. *Sheffield Daily Telegraph*, 9 September 1920, 24 September 1920.
33. *The Singapore Free Press and Mercantile Advertiser*, 14 August 1925; *Aberdeen Press and Journal*, 27 August 1925.
34. *Malaya Tribune*, 26 November 1934.
35. *Dundee Courier*, 3 December 1936, 15 December 1936; *Dundee Evening Telegraph*, 1 January 1937.

36. Chakrabarty, 1989: 8. See: www.verdant-works.com/exploration-article/what-is-jute. Accessed 9/9/17.
37. *Belfast News-Letter*, 22 February 1937.
38. *Sunderland Daily Echo and Shipping Gazette*, 5 May 1938; *Aberdeen Press and Journal*, 29 July 1939.
39. *Western Morning News*, 19 August 1939.
40. National Maritime Museum, Greenwich: BIS/7/115.
41. National Archives, Kew: BT 110/1229/12.
42. Von Trapp, 2007: 96.
43. Elphick, 1999: 19-20.
44. National Archives, Kew: ADM 199/2186/44. For the *Gairsoppa*'s crew-members, see: https://uboat.net/allies/merchants/crews/ship765.html. Accessed 1.11.17.
45. National Archives, Kew: ADM 199/2186/44.
46. National Archives, Kew: ADM 237/214.
47. Tennent, 2001: 36.
48. Hague, 2000: 138.
49. Hague, 2000: 26-7; Howard, 2015: 184-85, 196, 199.
50. Dobson, 1996: 3.
51. Kaplan and Currie, 1998: 25.
52. British Library, London: IOR/L/E/8/1537.
53. Kaplan and Currie, 1998: 27-8.
54. Elphick, 1999: 16.
55. Elphick, 1999: 13.
56. Edwards, 2001: 126.
57. National Archives, Kew: ADM 53/113594.
58. National Archives, Kew: ADM 237/214.
59. The following accounts of the attack on convoy S.L.S. 64 come from reports written for the Shipping Casualties Section – Trade Division, based on first-hand interviews with surviving crew: National Archives, Kew, ADM 237/214.
60. Koop and Schmolke, 2001: 47, 50.
61. National Archives, Kew: ADM 53/113594. Report of an Interview with Mr. Knight, 2nd Officer of the SS *Wailsea Lass*. Shipping Casualties Section. Trade Division.
62. National Archives, Kew: ADM 199/1143. M/02925/41. C.O. HMS Arawa. 20.2.41. Convoy S.L. 64. Report of Proceeding'.
63. National Archives, Kew: ADM 237/214.
64. Stern, 1998: 16, 21, 24.
65. Doenitz, 2002: 173-74.
66. National Archives, Kew: MT 9/3587. Report of Loss. Minute Sheet.
67. National Archives, Kew: ADM 1/11456.
68. British Library, London: ADM 1/11456.
69. See: www.convoyweb.org.uk/sl/index.html?sl064s.htm~slmain. Accessed 12 September 2017
70. Kaplan and Currie, 1998: 27.
71. Blake, 1956: 196.
72. British Library, London: IOR/L/E/8/1537.
73. See: www.bbc.co.uk/history/ww2peopleswar/stories/32/a3563732.shtml. Accessed 12 September 2017.
74. National Maritime Museum, Greenwich: BIS/1/22/112.

3

INTO THE DEEP.
DIVING THE GAIRSOPPA

NEIL CUNNINGHAM DOBSON

Introduction

Almost three miles below the cruel northeast Atlantic Ocean, and less than three days from home, the SS *Gairsoppa* collided with the seabed 300 miles southwest of Galway. The torpedo struck the port side hull, where surveys showed a 10 metre-wide hole opened up horizontally below the water line, 7.5 metres below the front of the bridge deck on the port side of the No. 2 hold. The force of the explosion almost certainly brought the foremast crashing down onto the deck. The ship would have started to fill with water very quickly. Soon the *Gairsoppa* disappeared under the waves bow first, the stern sticking out of the water like an ominous finger pointing heavenward.

Today the silt-dusted remains lie silently in the blackness of the 4,700 metre-deep Porcupine Abyssal Plain. Over seventy-one years, nature has stripped away the ship's once sturdy majesty. Her wooden veneer is largely gone, heavy metal-eating bacteria munch through the steel and strange marine creatures find a home in the organic-rich vessel. But for now she is visibly still the *Gairsoppa*: a 3D shell filled with cargo withstanding the cold deep-sea pressure and saltwater.

After German submarine *U-101*'s torpedo struck on the fateful night of 16 February 1941, the *Gairsoppa*'s end was rapid.[1] She plummeted through the water column for an estimated five and a half minutes at around 30 miles per hour before hitting the seabed with a force of some 8 x 107 newtons.[2] By nature of gravity and weight – the lading of the ship was intended to ensure an even keel when under sail – the 125 metre-long and 15 metre-wide vessel landed upright and relatively intact on a bearing of 95° with the bow facing east. The force of the collision buried the hull 4 metres deep, so today she lies in a large impact crater. In the chaos of her sinking anything not tied or

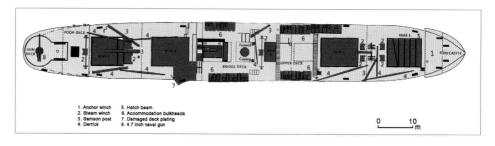

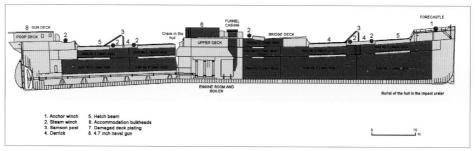

3.1. Plan of the *Gairsoppa's* key structural parts.

battened down would have been sucked out of the ship as the air escaped, landing 600 metres to the northwest of the stern in a debris field of assorted wreckage from crew's boots to an intact bath.

Shipwrecks are an oasis for marine life. At the *Gairsoppa's* resting place the temperature hovers around freezing. There is no sunlight, yet there is life. A surprising diversity of strange looking fish and weird 'squidgies' and 'cling-ons' – corals, crustaceans, jellyfishes, and worms – compete for food. The rattail or grenadier fish, *Macrouridae*, are the most common benthic fish of the deep, feeding on smaller prey and pelagic crustaceans such as shrimp, amphipods, cumaceans, cephalopods and lanternfish.

Various sea cucumbers live on and around the wreck, such as the purple *Psychropotes longicauda*, which can grow to 14-32 centimetres long and is found sifting for food with its tentacles in soft sediments. The opaque and spiky sea cucumber *Deima validium* is also prevalent. Another popular resident in huge numbers is the white coloured Galatheid crab, *Munidopsis crassa*. The organic cargoes and shipboard belongings made a welcome meal for the deep-sea marine life.

The whole of the wreck is coated in a light layer of sediment and all exposed steel surfaces and the open holds are covered in rusticles – icicle-like features formed as waste products from iron-eating bacteria. The rusticles have penetrated everywhere from the deck to the hold and from the skylight frames to the ship's gun. They cover all four bollards on the forecastle deck, the outsides of the steering gear house and poop deck structure and sides of the hull. Eventually these iron-eating bacteria will devour the wreck itself and all that will be left will be a brown crumbly stain on the seabed.

Surveying the Wreckage

The *Gairsoppa*'s bow is intact and undamaged with both the port and starboard stockless anchors secure in their hawse pipes, as would be expected for a long sea passage. At the summit of the wreck's stem sits the concreted remains of an otter gear cathead, a piece of equipment required in wartime by the Ministry of Shipping to facilitate the rigging and deployment of minesweeping gear. This type of paravane fitted to merchant vessels was called an 'otter' and was used to sweep for mines by diverting the ends of sweeps out to a ship's side.

Behind the otter gear cathead, the 9-inch diameter ventilation pipe from the bosun's store below still rises upwards. The forecastle's guardrails are mainly intact. The steam anchor windlass (a Clarke Chapman direct grip type) shows no signs of visible damage and rests on a bed of 4-inch pitched pine timbers. The port and starboard anchor cables run over the top of the windlass cable lifters' grooved drum. The two large windlass cogged wheels are intact, along with the two drum ends and brake controls. The anchor cables are stoppered off for sea voyage.

On the forecastle deck, six turns of wire rope are still tied to the port outboard set of 10-inch diameter bollards (two sets on port and starboard). On the port side of the anchor windlass a large pile of rigging has collapsed from the top of the mast onto the bow. The ladders that led to the forecastle deck are in one piece and the outline of the doors accessing the port side lamp locker and starboard side paint locker still stand.

Between the aft end of the forecastle and the forward end of the bridge are two cargo holds covering 30.7 x 15.8 metres of deck space. The forward hold No. 1 nearest the bows was accessible through a hatch opening of 10.8 x 6.1 metres.[3] Five evenly spaced steel king and sister hatch beams survive. (King beams are those onto which the ends of the hatch boards sit and sister beams support the centres of the hatch boards.) In turn, the wooden boards would have been covered with canvas sheets to form a

3.2. The bow with two anchors housed below the guard rails and fairleads.

3.3. View over the bow towards the anchor winch.

watertight cover and wedged tight. It was here that the silver and ship's mail, among other cargo, was carefully hauled into the holds.

The canvas covers of all four main holds are missing, blown out by escaping air pressure when the ship sank. In the other holds some hatch beams have fallen inside, where they are intermixed with cargo. No doubt the impact of the *Gairsoppa* colliding with the seabed caused this structural damage. Exploration of the No. 1 hold found it full to the top of the tween deck with sediment and a white and black spongy organic material in sacks (possibly bone meal for fertiliser). Silver bars were discovered below them, stacked along the bottom of the hold.

Situated in a 4.1 x 3-metre space between holds No. 1 and No. 2 are two 10.8 metre-high Samson posts (vertical metal posts from which derricks and tackle were rigged), each attached to two 5-ton steel derricks and four steam winches (with 17 x 30-centimetre drum ends). The port Samson post is bent towards the base and the starboard one is broken. Three of the four derricks are lying on the fore deck at the aft starboard side of the No. 1 hold. Derricks are spars used as a form of crane to hoist cargo and stores supported by masts or Samson posts. Their block and tackle lifting gear are powered by a winch.[4]

3.4. A crack on the port side of the midcastle formed when the ship went down by the bow.

3.5. The port derrick posts and derrick steam winches used to load cargo and stores.

All the hatch beams are missing from the 10.7 x 6.1-metre No. 2 hold. The bulk of its cargo was seemingly organic in nature and floated out as the *Gairsoppa* sank. Chests of tea were found in this space along with sacks containing another unknown organic material at the back of the lower hold tween deck. Tea is one of the most delicate cargoes to ship by sea. The greatest care is required in preparing holds for its stowage. All oil stains have to be removed, the bilge cleaned, disinfected and deodorized and the compartment thoroughly ventilated before any dunnage is laid. Even when secured in chests, tea can be tainted by all types of odorous cargoes, including Copra (dried coconut kernel), sugar, turmeric, cassia (bark of East Asian evergreen trees), oils of all

3.6. Creatures of the deep (top to bottom, left to right): sea cucumber (*Psychropotes longicauda*), sea cucumber (*Deima validium*), starfish, Galatheid crab (*Munidopsis crassa*), sea cucumbers and anenomes.

kinds, hides and paint, which should never be stowed in the same compartment or any other interconnected by ventilators.[5]

The ship's 35 x 16-metre centre island included the upper deck, bridge deck and lower bridge deck. The latter housed the bridge, chartroom, captain's cabin, radio room and radio officer's cabin. These four structures are missing, leaving the top of the forward section of the bridge deck exposed. The lost sections ended up in the wreck debris field having broken away when the ship plummeted towards the seabed.

The top of the upper deck is also exposed where the forward bridge section is missing. The outside bulkheads of the bridge deck accommodation lie flat on the upper deck. Remarkably, the wooden planking of the forward transverse walkway is mostly intact. Less than 1.5 metres from the aft end of the accommodation section is the No. 3 reserve hold. The 5.5 x 3.3-metre hatch opening includes a 0.6-metre high coaming. This hold was designed with three levels: at the bottom, the lower hold and above two tween decks used to store up to 1,582 tons of coal or cargo. Silver ingots were found stacked in the lower hold.

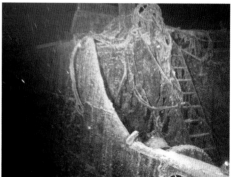

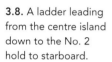

3.7. A porthole on the port side of the forecastle. Rusticles overgrow black painted hull plates.

3.8. A ladder leading from the centre island down to the No. 2 hold to starboard.

Two 6.5 metre-high Samson posts, each associated with a 5-ton steel derrick, lie 3.4 metres from the aft hatch coaming. Some 60 centimetres from the aft end of the No. 3 hold coaming is a steam winch (with 18.4 and 30-centimetre drum ends). Adjacent outboard of the Samson posts on both the port and starboard are 2.6 x 1.2-metre coal hatches for the 93-ton capacity lower side coal bunkers.

Covering a deck space of 16.8 x 5.5 metres just aft of the steam winch on top of the bridge deck are the funnel casing, officer accommodation and galley at the after end. The 7.7 metre-long and 2.5 metre-diameter funnel is missing and was again identified 45 metres north of the wreck in the debris field. A jagged edge in the casing, 2.4 metres above deck level, shows where the funnel tore away. Aft of the funnel casing on the bridge deck is a 1.4 metre-wide coal shoot that could hold 27 tons of coal. The overlying deck is again gone.

Aft of the coal shoot the base of a 53-centimetre diameter engine room vent can be seen to port side. The starboard equivalent is missing. Just aft of the vent is the engine room's skylight, its glass missing but the steel frame intact. Surrounding the engine room are sections of outboard port and starboard accommodation bulkheads; cut outs for doors and windows lie fallen on the bridge's deck. Most of the wooden decking on the bridge deck is preserved, albeit badly degraded.

Four steel lifeboats (each 8.4 x 2.6 x 1.1 metres) once hung to port and starboard on the bridge deck. Steel craft were safer than wooden clinker-built lifeboats, being much stronger and more proficient at negotiating steel plate edges and crashing wires when a listing ship needed to be abandoned. A fifth steel boat (6.1 x 2.0 x 0.8 metres) was once fitted on top of the poop deck.

From the start of the war the Ministry of Shipping (later the Ministry of War Transport formed in May 1941) was greatly concerned with safety and the survival of torpedoed seamen. New regulations and improvements in lifeboat design, manufacture and survival equipment were introduced. All deep-ocean ships had to carry at least one motor lifeboat. Aware that ship crews might spend days and weeks at sea before being rescued, the new measures made a significant difference to chances of survival.

For wartime lifeboats were pre-stored as standard with canvas hoods with side screens to provide shelter for the occupants, an automatic transmitting radio with an 80-mile radius, a wireless receiving set and bright yellow lifejackets with lights. Each boat held a dozen red flares, an electric torch suitable for Morse signalling, six hand rockets, four orange buoyant smoke signals and a signal pistol. The quantities of food and water were improved. Enough water was stored to sustain thirty-four people for a fortnight. Daily allowances of food and water per person stood at 112 ounces of fresh water and 14 ounces each of biscuits, chocolate, milk tablets and pemmican (or other approved meat extracts). Massage oil was added to first-aid kits to aid protection against frost-bite and trench foot.[6] No lifeboats were found on the wreck of the Gairsoppa, suggesting the whole crew escaped the doomed vessel.

A break in the hull aft of the centre island, just forward of the front hatch coaming of the No. 4 hold, is about 3 metres wide. A 2-3 metre section of deck plating is bent upwards. The crack reaches down the side of the hull to the seabed. Since the hull is buried in sediment by some 4 metres, whether the crack extends all the way to the

3.9. The poop deck steering house to starboard.

3.10. Wooden deck planking preserved near the engine room skylight on the bridge deck.

keel is not certain. To portside the corresponding crack is some 1 metre wide at the top and again goes all the way down to the level of the seabed. The crack runs horizontally from starboard to the port side at the forward end of the No. 4. Hold. This suggests the *Gairsoppa* went down by the bow, raising the stern out of the water and causing the hull to crack at the stress point impacted by the torpedo hit.

Two methods using a pistol device detonated torpedo warheads. Generally, torpedoes were fitted with both types and the U-boat captain selected his preference. One was contact-operated, the other magnetic. From the visual survey where the torpedo hit the *Gairsoppa* and blew the plates outward, it is safe to say that a contact operated torpedo was used, detonating as soon as it made contact.[7] The force of the explosion cracked the hull plates and forced them outwards due to the expansion of the explosives gases.

Between the aft end of the centre island and the forward poop deck are two cargo holds covering 30.7 x 15.8 metres of deck space. The forward No. 4 hold hatch opening measures 10.7 x 6.1 metres. All its access beams are missing. In its upper layer the hold again contained an unidentified organic cargo in sacks.

3.11. The derrick winch used to load goods into the No. 5 hold.

3.12. An upper deck toilet.

Between hold No. 4 and No. 5 in the bows are two more 10.8 metre-high Samson posts, each associated with two 5-ton steel derricks and four steam winches (18.4 centimetre and 30 centimetre drum ends). The starboard post lies broken parallel to the starboard aft bulwark. The port Samson post is bent, leaning over the open hatch of hold No. 5. Just outboard of the port and starboard Samson posts are 2.7 metre-diameter hold vents with their cowls missing. At the opening to hold No. 5's 8.5 x 6.1-metre aft hatch, all the beams but one were missing. An unidentified organic cargo in sacks was again stored in the upper hold.

Behind hold No. 5 were the well-preserved poop deck and gun deck housing, the rating's cabins, mess rooms, DEMS (Defensively Equipped Merchant Ship) gunner's accommodation and the steering gear house. The gun was operated by two dedicated gunners, military personnel from the Royal Navy and the Royal Artillery Maritime

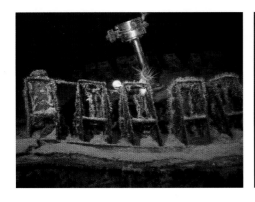

3.13. The poop deck steering indicator and 4-inch shell holders.

3.14. The *Gairsoppa's* Vickers BL 4-inch Mk IX British gun, made in 1918.

Regiment. Often DEMS personnel were ex Royal Marines or Royal Navy personnel called out of retirement. During convoy duties DEMS gunners worked a watch of four hours on and four hours off round the clock. On merchant ships where there were an Officers Mess and Seamen's Mess, DEMS crew were usually placed with the former.[8]

In 1941 Admiral Sir Frederick Dreyer, the inspector of Merchant Navy Gunnery, devised a special course to teach officers and men in the Merchant Navy how to shoot down aircraft.[9] Many Merchant Navy personnel attended machine gunner's courses, where they qualified for duty on DEM ships and learnt proficiency in the cleaning, oiling and firing of Oerlikon, Marlin, Hotchkiss and Lewis machine guns. It was common on merchant ships for the Second Mate to be designated as the Gunnery Officer if he had undergone a training course. Twenty-year-old Norman Thomas doubled up as a deck hand and gunner on the *Gairsoppa* alongside fifty-five-year-old Royal Marine William Price. Training drills were held weekly, and sometimes daily, onboard ship.

For ease of access the ammunition lockers for the deck gun, well preserved on the wreck of the *Gairsoppa*, were positioned under the poop deck. Two ladders port and starboard, the latter broken, lead up to the poop deck from the aft deck. A 18.4-centimetre and 30-centimetre steam winch with extended ends survives at the forward end of the poop deck for mooring lines and wires. Just aft of the steam winch a trunkway gave access to the firemen's and seamen's messes and crew cabins.

The gun deck above the poop deck covers 12 x 4 metres of the forward end and tapers to 8 metres diameter where the gun is mounted. The wooden deck planking is relatively intact. In the centre of the forward end of the gun deck stands an emergency brass steering indicator, slightly bent backwards towards the stern and its wheel missing. The aft steel ship's boat and davits are missing. On the port and starboard edges of the forward gun deck are a row of ten shell holders, which could hold 4-inch, 31-pound shells. One shell still stood housed in a holder on each side.

The deck gun itself, a Vickers BL 4-inch Mk IX British medium velocity naval weapon, still stands like a sentinel guarding the drowned ship, the barrel level and pointing out at 90°

to port side. Much of the iron is covered in rusticles and badly preserved, but all the brass fittings are in a good state, including the gun sights. The British Royal Navy introduced this gun type in 1916, based on the barrel of a QF 4-inch Mk V naval gun and fitted with a BL 4-inch Mk VIII breech mechanism.[10] Close-up photography of the *Gairsoppa*'s breech mechanism identified a date of 1918, proving that the steamship's protection was old stock. The gun's weight, including breech mechanism, is 2,154 kilograms, its total length 4.69 metres and its bore length 4.51 metres. At an elevation of 30° it had a range of 12,344 metres and was capable of firing ten to twelve rounds a minute.

3.15. A ladder leading into the ships hold, covered in rusticles.

3.16. The port corner of hold No. 5, its sides coated with rusticles.

Along the starboard side of the poop deck the guardrails are missing from the start of the deck to just before the starboard aft forward set of 25-centimetre diameter bollards. The wooden decking is intact, as are the portholes to starboard below the poop deck. Overall, the stern has suffered very little damage. The fantail rail is broken, bent and missing in sections, but the stern navigation light is intact. Both the port and starboard aft fairleads are in place along with the 25-centimetre port side bollards. The guardrail to port is mostly intact with a few bent and missing sections. There is no apparent damage to the counter stern. The ship's name and port of registry are not visible and only the top few metres of the rudder can be seen.

Extending up to 600 metres northwest of the stern is a debris field. At a distance of 30 metres from the port side of the wreck, the ship's funnel was discovered mostly intact. Sections of the outer accommodation bulkheads from the bridge deck (some still painted white) ended up some 45 metres north of the wreck. A mass of steel 'H' beams, wooden deck planks, ship's fittings, galley ceramics, a sink and a scatter of iron ingots spilt out of the ship as it sank and came to rest 500 metres northwest of the stern. Finally, at a distance of 600 metres northwest of the stern, the upturned bridge and associated accommodation structure ended up. This section of the ship housed the bridge, the captain's cabin, the radio room, radio officer's cabin and the officers' saloon. This complete section was severed at the bridge deck level.

All the signs show that the *Gairsoppa* sank bow first. After the stern pitched clear of the water, the ship plummeted downwards and the bridge and associated structures weakened by the force of the torpedo explosion broke off. At some point in the final descent seawater flooded the holds. The hatches quickly blew out as trapped air forced its way upwards. The hatch boards and upper top layer of organic cargo would have floated away and spilled out of the distorted vessel. When the ship became completely full of water, she would have levelled out and landed upright on the seabed in a vast plume of sediment, creating a large impact crater.

Conclusion

Physical, biological and chemical processes all play a part in the preservation of ship-wrecks, whether they settled in shallow or deep water. Every shipwreck is a relatively unique environment. However, extensive research carried out between the western English Channel, the Bay of Biscay and southwest of Ireland reveals a clear trend: while World War II ships lost in less than 100 metres have been largely flattened to two-dimensional features other than the lowest few metres of hull by fishing trawlers, depth charges and storm surges, the forces acting on a deep-water shipwreck like the *Gairsoppa* are far less destructive. Chemically, preservation is also far better in deep water due to its oxygen-depleted environment, low temperatures and low salinity. As is abundantly clear, the *Gairsoppa* is for now a three-dimensional entity.

The same high-level state of preservation extends to deep-sea wrecks of World War I, such as the 137.2 x 17.7-metre British India Steam Navigation Ltd. ship the SS *Mantola*, a 8,259 gross ton cargo and passenger ship bound from London to Calcutta with eigh-teen passengers, 165 crew and general cargo when she was hit by a German torpedo on 8 February 1917. The ship sits upright with a slight list to port and is relatively intact at a depth of 2,500 metres. Like the *Gairsoppa*, the exposed steel surfaces are ridden with rusticles. Beyond 600 metres impacts from fishing trawlers and scallop dredges decrease vastly, helping form the 'time capsules' that marine archaeologists not entirely accurately refer to in shallows.

All the exposed metallic surfaces on the wreck of the *Gairsoppa* are covered in rusticles formed by iron-eating bacteria. Studies of the 4,000 metre-deep RMS *Titanic* in the North Atlantic discovered that these growths are a complex network of structured microbial consortia formed by the layering of bio-accumulates (such as iron, manga-nese, calcium and silicon) around the cells and enabling water transfer through the structures leading to their growth and survival.[11] They get their orange-brown colour from their highly oxidized ferric iron content. At least on the *Titanic* a daily loss of iron from the wreck of between 0.13 and 0.20 tons per day has been calculated.[12]

Rusticles start to appear on parts of steel wrecks, such as lower hulls surveyed in the western English Channel and its Western Approaches, at 76 metres deep.[13] From 90 metres downwards they coat all parts of the wrecks.[14] Rusticles extend to German U-boats from 80 metres downwards.[15] Since no formal analyses examined the *Gairsoppa*'s rusticles, their rate of growth and hence the ship's curve of structural

3.17. Finds in the debris field (top to bottom, left to right): a sink and bath from the officer's accommodation, a vent cowl, twisted riveted plating, a sailor's boot and the ship's telegraph.

deterioration is impossible to predict. That said, it is a fair assumption that within the next century sites like these will be reduced to two-dimensional features and eventually, as the hungry bacteria continue their feasting, to a pile of rust.

Notes

1. The following survey is based on the review of Remotely-Operated Vehicle footage from the wreck and debris field, field notes and from detailed ship plans, ship particulars and capacity plans.
2. Pers. comm. Simon Shepherd, Professor of Computational Mathematics, University of Bradford, June 2009.
3. Feet dimensions taken from ships' plans have been converted into metres for this chapter.
4. Ransome-Wallis, 1957: 23, 25.
5. Thomas, 1945: 317.
6. *Life-saving Measures for Merchant Seamen in Time of War*, 1942: 35, 29.
7. Williamson, 2007: 37.
8. Halley, 1995: 271, 312.
9. See: www.iwm.org.uk/collections/item/object/205139464. Accessed 1.11.17.
10. Campbell, 1986: part 17.
11. Cullimore *et al.*, 2002: 117
12. Roy Cullimore and Lori Johnston, *Biodeterioration of the RMS Titanic*: www.encyclopedia-titanica.org/rms-titanic-bio-deterioration.html. Accessed 16.10.17.
13. Odyssey Marine Exploration Site T1M31b-5, early twentieth century.
14. Odyssey Marine Exploration Sites T3a35c-1, T3w67c-1, T3w67d-3, T3w33a-8, T3a5d-3, all twentieth century losses.
15. For submarine wrecks in the western English Channel and its Western Approaches, see Cunningham Dobson, 2013.

4

SILVER WAVES.
A WARTIME CARGO

SEAN KINGSLEY

The nature of the vast cargoes carried by British convoys throughout World War II were deliberately stripped bare of meaning in official paperwork to sound vague and humdrum – nothing to see here. Beneath the succinct notices lay a gargantuan web of raw materials desperately needed to turn the wheels of war. The *Gairsoppa*'s holds were no different, carefully balanced with crucial Indian goods: 2,600 tons of pig iron, 1,765 tons of tea, 2,817 silver bars and 2,369 tons of general cargo, a catch-all ambiguity seemingly including 420 tons of oil cake (either made from cotton, groundnut or linseed) used as cattle feed or fertiliser and 485 tons of bone, another plant fertiliser. Other sources add 150 cases of mica (used in aircraft and tank electronics) to the general cargo.[1]

Germany's main aim in the war at sea was to starve Britain into submission, as Hitler's Directive No. 23 made clear on 6 February 1941, ten days before the *Gairsoppa* sank: "the heaviest effect of our operations against the English war economy has lain in the high losses in merchant shipping inflicted by sea and air warfare." The Kriegsmarine had every expectation of breaking the UK's resistance in the foreseeable future.[2] The man on the street started whispering about a pending Nazi invasion of Britain.

Germany's war machine knew all too well from World War I how reliant Britain was on its colonies and Allies for arms and food. As the Right Honourable Oliver Lyttelton, Minister of Production, put it, "Victory in the War of 1939-45 was won not only on the battlefield, on the sea and in the air, but in the workshops and factories of the Allied Nations."[3] No country sweated so late into the night for the greater good as India.

By 1945 Britain owed its old colony a huge debt of gratitude. When hostilities broke out, virtually all the country's industries were redirected towards the war effort and the

4.1. Bone meal cargo spilt out of sacks in the *Gairsoppa's* No. 4 tween deck hold.

4.2. Bone meal in sacks in the No. 4 tween deck hold.

Raj became the largest contributor to the empire's struggle outside the UK, providing goods and services worth more than £2 billion – everything from heavy ordnance to 90% of desert tents, clothes, walking boots and dehydrated food.[4]

Around 40,000 tons of grain left India's ports every month by May 1942 alongside a tenth of the country's railway engines and carriages. The country's entire commercial timber, woollen textiles and leather goods, and three-quarters of its steel and cement were re-directed for the front line. Each year up to 18,000 tons of rubber were turned into ground sheets and tyres for aircraft and road vehicles.[5]

By the end of the war, 1,500 ordnance factories manned by 100,000 people – triple the peacetime number – were toiling beneath Indian skies for the Director-General of Munitions, turning out everything from field guns, howitzers and anti-aircraft gun parts to mines, depth charges and binoculars. The output of rifles shot up tenfold, light machine-guns twelvefold, bayonets seventeenfold, and gun ammunition twenty-sevenfold.[6] For war supplies, India was Britain's golden goose.

Silver Bullion

The *Gairsoppa* went down in history as the heaviest loss of silver bullion sent from India to Britain during World War II.[7] For a country with almost no natural reserves, how India came to control the largest stocks in the world, and Britain's deep reliance on its mints, was a defining part of the economic relationship between empire and colony. By 1941 the Royal Mint needed a million fine ounces of silver a month to cover the costs of Britain's swelling workforce, troops fighting abroad and to generally keep confidence alive on the high street.

By the start of 1941 the Bank of England was living hand to mouth as it waited for news of six million ounces of silver ordered on 27 November 1940 and sent from India on the *Gairsoppa* and the P&O ship the *Somali*.[8] If the silver failed to break through the German U-boat net, emergency steps would need triggering fast, including

Ingot Sizes

Elongated rectangular Type 1 bars:[82]

- Upper surface: Length 29.1cm, Width 9.2cm
- Bottom surface: Length 33cm, Width 12.0cm
- Height: 10.1cm
- Bombay stamp: Diameter 2.9cm
- Bar no. stamp: Length 7.5cm, Height 1.6cm
- Fineness stamp: Length 4.1cm, Height 0.9cm
- Fineness stamp: Length 5.5cm, Height 1.5cm
- Ounces stamp: Length 6.8cm, Height 1.5cm

Small rectangular Type 2 bars:[83]

- Upper surface: Length 26.8cm, Width 14.2cm
- Bottom surface: Length 28.8cm, Width 16.1.0cm
- Height 8.8cm
- Bar no. stamp: Length 2.9cm, Height 1.2cm
- Lot no. stamp: Length 1.6cm, Height 0.8 cm
- Fineness stamp: Length 6.8cm, Height 2.7cm
- Ounces stamp: Length 7.8cm, Height 1.9cm

taking control of the commercial silver market, issuing unpopular paper notes and turning to America for expensive loans or purchases. Britain's war economy stood on a cliff edge.

For no particular reason other than finding itself in the right place at the wrong time, the Ministry of War Transport requisitioned the *Gairsoppa* to carry three million ounces of silver in 2,817 bars under consignment from the Bombay Mint master to the Secretary of State for India in London. The precious cargo steamed out of Calcutta on 5 December 1940 in four bills of lading weighing 3.2 million gross ounces: 869 rupee standard bars, 1,009,485 ounces; 871 rupee standard bars, 1,009,127 ounces; 609 rupee standard bars, 708,928 ounces; and 468 fine silver bars, 500,059 gross ounces. The first and third batches were painted on both sides with red and white distinguishing marks.[9]

Beneath the sea the ingots were discovered on the wreck of the *Gairsoppa* stacked in two locations. Hold No. 1 in the bows held 1,574 silver bars: 463 elongated rectangular ingots (Type 1), all with a fineness of 999.3, while 1,111 were smaller rectangular bars of 917 fineness (Type 2). Hold No. 3 aft of the bridge and engine room secured another 1,218 bars, all of the smaller squat rectangular Type 2 shape: 1,162 had a fineness of 917 and fifty-six a fineness of 916.

The ingots were stowed upside down and predominantly lengthwise side to side. Four different stamps were imprinted on the top of the Type 1 bars (from top to bottom): a circular 'Mint Bombay' stamp, the ingot number, fineness and weight in ounces. The smaller squat Type 2 bars bore three sets of stamps: at top the bar number, at centre the fineness and at bottom the weight in ounces.

Sink of Precious Metals

How the world's largest reserves of silver ended up in India and then flowed out to Britain en masse was by the start of World War II a decades-old economic cycle. Rather than gold, India had relied on the silver standard since 1835 and thanks to the country's fast-paced growth had absorbed about 84% of the world production of silver by 1877.[10] The country was not blessed with significant natural reserves and so before 1917 relied chiefly on Chinese stocks that started life in the mines of America.

Out of a total of 211 million ounces of silver produced worldwide in 1914, 80% – 170 million ounces – came from North America, 13 million from South America, 15 million ounces from Europe and 6 million from Asia. After the Comstock Lode was struck in Nevada in 1859, the Anaconda Mine became the largest silver-producing pit on earth with a yearly output of 9 million ounces.[11]

American silver gravitated to India en masse via London, the banking capital of the world, to pay for British business. Through its strategic position as an agricultural and industrial heavyweight, silver piled up in India. The country's heavy war expenditure on behalf of the Home Government in World War I led in 1916 to Britain exporting over 104 million ounces to pay for Indian supplies – in excess of half the world's stocks. In the absence of an attractive buyer's market, and due to a cautious psychology, rural India took to hoarding.[12] Much of the country's wealth ended up sunk in the country-side as the *New York Times* somewhat patronisingly, but accurately, reported on 23 August 1918:

> Indian masses do not understand any modern currency systems. Numbers of
> them do not know what checks or paper money are. They want actual hard cash,
> and they have an incorrigible habit of taking silver and gold coins and beating
> them into bangles and other ornaments for their wives. This is one form of saving,
> but the results is that for years India has been known as the 'sink of precious metals'.

4.3-4.4. Stacked silver bars from the Bombay Mint, as discovered.

VOICES FROM THE DEEP

After the First World War ended, various schemes were brainstormed to unblock India's sink, including the Indian Currency Commission's recommendation to make a large proportion of Indian rupees illegal tender in 1927 in the hope locals would cash in their coins. Only a small fraction of the 400 million ounces of silver in Indian hoards nevertheless surfaced over the next ten years.[13]

Once hostilities broke out in World War II, Britain's silver reserves haemorrhaged fast. By the start of 1940 the question of how to maintain adequate supplies in the face of ever-rising armament needs and government spending, soaring employment and rising wages caused huge anxiety. The UK's expenditure skyrocketed from £40 million a week in May 1940 to £70 million a week in September of the same year.[14] Salaries alone rose from £264 million in the first quarter of 1940 to £300 million in the fourth quarter.[15]

Silver coin also headed overseas en masse to pay troop's salaries and on 26 July 1940 the Manager of Barclay's Bank in Birmingham warned that "the constant paying away of silver, with very little of it coming back, is a permanent feature".[16] Meanwhile, wartime hoarding hit the high street. As the Bank of England wrote in a letter to J.H. Craig, the Deputy Master and Comptroller at the Royal Mint, on 23 August 1940, "in the country recently I heard of a number of cases of people carrying anything up to £50 sewn in their underclothes or in bags hung around their necks and was told that people were doing this on advice from their bank managers, who were recommending that a fair sum of money should be kept handy in reserve in the event of invasion."[17]

The Bank of England had taken the prudent step of taking over the sale of India Government silver to the London market to guarantee constant low prices, set at 23½d per standard ounce in February 1941.[18] The private trade in silver was made illegal. Despite these checks and balances, by September 1940 silver coin stocks in the British Banking Department had dropped to a low of £436,145, while the Issue Department held silver coins worth just £11,451.[19] "The outlook for 1941 must necessarily be obscure", Messrs. Mocatta and Goldsmid told the *Financial Times* of 3 January 1941.

To help fill Britain's shortfall, the Secretary of State sent a secret cypher telegram to the Government of India on 27 November 1940 with a new order:[20]

> Please ship by first available British India Steam Navigation Company's steamer 3 million half of 6 million fine ounces of silver and consign to Secretary of State for India London... Of this, 2½ million half of 5 million should be in bars of rupee standard fineness and in two lots of 925,000 each and one of 650,000 separately invoiced and distinguished by bands of coloured paint on bars... Remaining half million (half of one million) should be in commercial bars of fine silver with distinguishing paint unless others readily distinguishable from rupee standard.

The *Gairsoppa*'s silver was intended to prop up Britain's on the ropes economy. The Royal Mint's minimum coin programme for 1941-1942 required about one million fine ounces of silver every month.[21] More broadly, the Mint was in dire need of between 7 and 7¼ million standard ounces, most by the end of January 1941 and the rest before the close of March. Some 4½ million ounces were designated for UK coin production and 2¾ million ounces for empire coinage, including Maria Theresa dollars used to pay foreign Allied troops at a rate of half a million pieces a month.[22]

As January 1941 drew to a close, the whereabouts of the Bombay silver at sea started to raise serious concerns. On 28 January, the India Office advised the Treasury in a secret communication that they had no information about when the *Gairsoppa* and *Somali* could be expected, adding cryptically that "it is not our practice to make enquiries on the point since we have considered that it is well that as little as possible should be said about the movement of steamers. In any event we are doubtful whether precise information could be obtained."[23] On 10 February Ernest Rowe-Dutton, the Treasury's chief exchange expert, pressed the India Office once more because "I begin to get anxious about the first of these believed to have left on 5th December, i.e., nearly ten weeks ago. If anything has happened to this silver, we may have to replace it urgently".[24]

Three days later the India Office blocked the sale of any more silver until the missing shipments on the high seas reached the Royal Mint.[25] Matters were getting desperate. The Bank of England judged that when their silver coins reached four weeks' worth of stock, reserves would have hit rock bottom. By 21 February just five weeks of reserves were left. Around 5 of the 6 million ounces of Indian silver on the North Atlantic highway were earmarked for coinage and 1 million for commercial purposes and strengthening India Office stocks, but even these large shipments were "merely hand to mouth provision and are below what prudence would dictate."[26] The Bank wrote prophetically that "We are, in fact, at the mercy of one or two sinkings. Should these occur, there would be literally no silver to fall back upon".[27]

Officials started thinking seriously about hitting the emergency button. A letter to Lord Catto, Director of the Bank of England, on 24 February 1941 set out reluctant plans to issue 5/- and 2/6d paper notes despite the risk of triggering inflation and to take control of the silver market by requisitioning all stocks as a last resort. The short-term position was seen to be acute "due to the virtual exhaustion of the India Office stock, and delay in the arrival of six million ounces shipped from India last December, and now expected daily in two ships". A round-the-world enquiry produced little immediate hope of extra large-scale silver.[28]

4.5. A *Gairsoppa* Type 1 silver bar (no. TUR-13-02408-SI, left and bottom). Type 2 silver bar (no. TUR-13-02403-SI, right).

Riding the Silver Tiger

While not catastrophic thanks to the safe arrival in London on 4 March 1941 of the second batch of 3,018 silver bars sent from the Calcutta Mint on the *Somali*,[29] the sinking of the *Gairsoppa*'s silver was part of a serious logistical breakdown. To cover the shortfall from the missing British India Steam Navigation Co. ship, Britain bought stock from America, an expensive measure due to high dollar conversion rates.[30] On

6 March 1941, Rowe-Dutton informed Sir George Lewis French Bolton, adviser to the governors of the Bank of England, that:[31]

> I fear that we must recognise that the presumed loss of our shipment of 3 million ounces of silver alters the whole position and lands us in serious difficulties. So far as I can see, Craig [J.H. Craig, Deputy Master and Comptroller, the Royal Mint] has already had ½ million ounces out of the 3 million which have just arrived [on the *Somali*], so that the total stock in the hands of the India Office is now 3 million ounces. What Craig has had should allow him to go on minting until, I think, 22nd March, when he would have to shut down unless he can be given further supplies… I fear this brings us again to the necessity of considering some further purchases in the United States…

The *Gairsoppa*'s 2,817 silver bars were insured under the Marine and War Risks scheme on behalf of the Governor-General of India in Council through Messrs. Hogg, Robinson and Capel-Cure Ltd. Insurance Brokers of Staple Hall, Bishopsgate in London, which generally covered steamers on war duty to a maximum of £1 million.[32] The War Risks Insurance Office paid out an insurance claim of £325,514 for the silver's loss on 18 March 1941 under the authorisation of Sir Stuart Brown, Under Secretary for State for India.[33]

The dangerous combination of three million ounces of silver sunk on the *Gairsoppa*, the dark grip of war and spiralling British demands marked the beginning of ever-growing Indian reluctance to hand over its precious metal at uncompetitive rates. Already in November 1940 the Government of India was looking for a way out, advising the Secretary of State for India that for any further exports "we would deprecate further appreciable depletion of stocks… We suggest possibilities of making other less uncertain arrangements for obtaining future supply for armament and industrial requirements may be considered by H.M.G., even though involving some expenditure of foreign exchange".[34] A secret note written by S.D. Waley of the Treasury admitted that "India is rather jealous, at present, of her reserve which is estimated at 100 million ounces." By February 1941 the Treasury was nevertheless again pushing India to sell 3 million ounces of silver each month.[35] On 27 March the Government of India advised the India Office in no uncertain terms that it was most reluctant to part with any more silver, which it needed to control the Bombay market.[36]

To liberate more metal the Indian Government triggered an enormous re-coinage programme, reducing the silver fineness of the rupee to free up millions of ounces of silver. Securing stocks from India through re-coinage, rather than being forced to buy from America and deal with high dollar exchange rates, was hoped to save Britain $20-25 million a year.[37] The following month, April 1941, India proposed sending future shipments to the UK in the form of cut coins, instead of bars, to free up its furnaces for more urgent war work, to save on the wear and tear of crucibles and reduce wharfage charges, an approach accepted by the Royal Mint.[38] The Ministry of Supply, meanwhile, started looking into salvaging waste silver from the film and photographic industry, including large stocks used by reconnaissance planes.[39]

The situation was still looking bleak. Buying silver from the USA was judged to be a highly unattractive last resort. On 29 September 1942, the Bank of England informed the Treasury that "On financial grounds alone we should be glad to discover a source of supply other than India but, as we have explained before, the political implications of the silver racket in Washington are so unpleasant that we would prefer to reject this alternative without further discussion."[40]

Within the space of a few months Britain was forced to change its thinking as India reduced its supplies and the danger of shipping across the Far Eastern theatre of war rose. Shipping silver through the Indian Ocean was becoming so precarious that warships started to be considered for precious cargoes. The reliance on India was not sustainable and London foresaw the silver bubble bursting. The market was in turmoil. By the end of March 1942, Mr Waley of the Coinage Programme and Small Notes Committee again proposed introducing a 5s paper note to replace the unreliable Indian silver shipments.

In all fairness, India was being stretched to breaking point as the Bombay Mint's output peaked at 686,962,550 coins in 1942-1943. The Master of the Mint explained bluntly in his annual statement that "Charity begins at home". Henceforth, foreign orders were to be "rigorously cut and future commitments refused".[41] This was no hollow threat. Britain had quarried India's reserve so deeply that by 8 September 1942 only 800 silver bars sat under lock and key in the Reserve Bank of India.[42]

A month later, G.H. Baxter of the India Office informed the Treasury on 20 October that:[43]

> I believe that the supply of silver from India… have proved valuable contribu-
> tions to the general war effort. In the early stages it was perhaps not unreasonable
> to act as though we were dealing with an exhaustible silver mine. Recent events,
> however, including the calling in of the remaining issues of standard silver rupees,
> have shown clearly that this is not so and that, indeed, we are within foreseeable
> distance of the time when we may be able to see the bottom of the 'mine'.

No longer a neutral bystander in the war against Hitler, America proved to be the long-term solution to Britain's silver worries as the Bank of England started seriously debating the merits of accepting an American lend-lease agreement first offered by Henry Morgenthau, US Secretary of the Treasury, in April 1942. Following sharp price increases in New York, India was no longer willing to ride the silver tiger for Britain's greater good by being forced to offer below market prices.

In its place America opened its vast vault to Britain: the 70 million of the world's 203 million ounces of silver the USA produced in 1942 made it the world leader.[44] With London seeking an estimated 1½ million ounces of silver a month to replace India's supplies, the Bank of England had no alternative but to accept Morgenthau's offer, based on ounce for ounce replacement after the war. The United States Senate Banking Committee signed off the immediate sale of 1,400 million ounces of US Treasury silver in December 1942 to further the war effort.[45] The following day a Government of India statement confirmed it would no longer sell any more silver to the UK or any other country.

Everything Stops for Tea

"Food is a munition of war. Don't waste it", Ministry of Food adverts cautioned Britain during World War II. Alongside mass silver and ordnance needs, hostilities soon started to pinch the Kitchen Front and in July 1940 rationing extended to tea. The two ounces a week handed out to most families did not last long. By the end of 1940, most British cupboards were almost bare.[46]

Early in the war a Home Morale Emergency Committee had been set up to counter "the danger of a break in morale".[47] In its own way the 1,765 tons of tea stowed on the *Gairsoppa*, enough to feed a small army, was as important as the ship's silver to boost Britain's wavering morale as convoy losses mounted during the Battle of the Atlantic.

The steamer's tea consignment was found excellently preserved in hold No. 2, between the bridge deck and forecastle, and in hold No. 5, just forward of the poop deck. The leaves were still sealed in packets of aluminium foil, which in turn were locked in large square wooden crates, some subdivided into six sub-units separated by wooden crossbeams. Brass border frames secured the wooden planking. 'Product of India' was stamped twice on the top and bottom of each crate.

Tightly bolted wooden cases lined with metal foil were essential for long-distance trade to seal the environmentally sensitive contents. The Ministry of Food required all exported tea to be packed in sound merchant chests weighing no more than 60 lbs, hoop-ironed and strapped with approved wiring. All chests had to be lined with aluminium or lead foil (with paper linings) of quality and gauge approved by the Tea Controller. Chests were marked with the estate producer's name and mark, an invoice number, tea grade, chest serial number, gross weight of chest and nett weight of content, the consignee's name (Minister of Food, London) and the country of origin (Produce of India).[48]

Typical chests were built from three-ply veneer wood and measured 24 x 19 x 19 inches with a capacity of about five cubic feet.[49] Several plywood factories along the

4.6. Tea stacked nine wooden chests high in the No. 2 hold.

4.7. Detail of a shipwrecked wooden tea chest.

southern coast outfitted the tea industry,[50] such as Colombo Commercial Co. Ltd. in modern Sri Lanka, which advertised 'Momi Chests, 3-Ply Chests and Packets' in *The Tea Quarterly* of 1940.[51] The Government made sufficient funds available for the industry to use the best chests and not cut corners to export inferior or second-hand crates. Special attention was paid to ensuring the wood was dried rapidly during seasoning to prevent attack by worm borers.[52]

Finding aluminium lining was an altogether tougher prospect. Problems arose towards the end of 1940 when wartime export restrictions prevented the lining being sold commercially in the UK and USA, which was replaced with lead foil. Tea chests headed to the UK were an exclusive exception where aluminium was acceptable. The Tea Research Institute's numerous tests on alternatives, such as Kraft paper, Pliofilm and Cellophen, ended in unsuccessful representations to the Ministry of Food.[53]

Where precisely the *Gairsoppa*'s tea originated is a great unknown. In December 1940, 2,100 tons of leaves in 357,000 chests were allotted for export from Calcutta and Chittagong. These included 59,322 Clan Buchanan and 25,000 Clan MacBrayne crates. The tea was insured by the seller until it went 'Free On Board' over the ship's rail, at which point Ministry of Food insurance took responsible for any loss or damage.[54]

Of the 6,474 plantations farmed for tea across 835,400 acres of India in 1941, 76% of the cultivated area lay in Assam (within Brahmaputra and the Surma Valleys) and in Darjeeling and Jalpaiguri in west Bengal. In the absence of markings identified on crate sides, it is a fair bet that the *Gairsoppa*'s tea originated somewhere in these provinces: of the 488 million pounds of black tea sold that year, 59% came from Assam and 25% from Bengal.[55]

A consignment of soggy tea superficially sounds trivial compared to the *Gairsoppa*'s silver wealth. Tea, however, was essential for the nation's morale. Butter and sugar were first rationed on 8 January 1940, soon followed by bacon, ham, cheese, tea, preserves, canned foods, cereals and biscuits. The British war effort relied on imports for half of the country's calories, so feeding the Kitchen Front was as deadly a business as fighting the front

Shipwrecked Tea Letters

Tea inevitably turns up in several letters recovered from the *Gairsoppa*'s mail room. An invoice for sixty-seven chests weighing 6,935 gross pounds produced by the Yellapatty Estate in Travancore was sent for the UK Government Food Controller's 1940 contract.[84]

As Managing Agents of the Rajahbhat Tea Company Ltd. and Bhatkawa Tea Company Ltd., McLeod & Co. of Calcutta mailed monthly reports to shareholder Roland M. Woods in Beer, S. Devon. Up to the end of October 1940, 559 men and 626 women had produced 7,620 maunds (626,364 lbs) for the Rajahbhat Tea Company Ltd. and "The bushes continue to flush freely and prospects are good. There are no blights & the garden is clean." At the Bhatkawa Tea Company Ltd., 899 men and 873 women had turned out 12,575 maunds (1,033,665 lbs) also by the end of October and "Pruning has started. There are no blights showing. 425 Mds was needed only to complete the crop."[85]

On 1 December 1940, the Darjeeling Consolidated Tea Co. Ltd. sent its Secretary, James F. Playfair in Exeter, Devon, the final crop figures for the year with the original pencil-written daily log. The Balasun Division yielded 2,462 maunds (202,376 lbs) and the Murmah Division 1,624 maunds (133,492 lbs), all dispatched from the factory.[86] A second letter to Mr Playfair compared Darjeeling's figures with previous years: 1940 was more productive than the 2,241 maunds turned out in 1938 and 3,038 maunds in 1939. The letter included a tea storage statement for November 1940.[87]

line. Inadequate food supplies during World War II eventually caused the overall death worldwide of at least 20 million people from starvation, malnutrition and related diseases.[56]

Britain's reputation as a bottomless consumer of cheap black tea was renowned by World War II. As Jack Buchanan sang in the 1935 comedy film *Come out of the Pantry*:

Every nation in creation has its favourite drink.
France is famous for its wine, it's beer in Germany.
Turkey has its coffee and they serve it blacker than ink.
Russians go for vodka and England loves its tea.

Oh, the factories may be roaring
With a boom-a-lacka, zoom-a-lacka, wee.
But there isn't any roar when the clock strikes four
Everything stops for tea…

It's a very good English custom
And a stimulant for the brain
When you feel a little weary, a cup'll make you cheery.
And it's cheaper than champagne.

A national stereotype was born. Britain's weekly tea ration was set at 2 ounces per adult during World War II. The *Gairsoppa*'s cargo, the equivalent of 63,257,842 ounces, was enough to sustain 65% of the entire population of Britain for a week or London's 8.6 million population for three and a half weeks.[57]

The *Gairsoppa*'s tea loss was a serious disappointment. Across the food chain the Battle of the Atlantic was taking a high toll. Imports reaching Britain fell from 68 million tons before the war to 26 million tons in 1941, largely due to U-boats strikes, but also because of a lack of British shipping and handling mismanagement in the ports. Overall, the autumn and winter of 1940-1941 was the worst period for British food supplies during the whole war.[58] The fall in production in world tea supplies to 700 million pounds between 1942 and 1945 was the lowest figure recorded since 1905-1909.[59]

Indian Tea

Tea first reached England in 1657, fetching £6 to £10 per pound, and in 1669 the East India Company started importing leaves.[60] In 1823 Robert Bruce discovered tea growing wild in the upper Brahmaputra Valley. Commercial cultivation started in 1874, when the first gardens appeared in Western Dooars in northeast India funded by London merchants.[61] Because of deteriorating trade relations between China and Britain in 1780, the East India Company investigated the feasibility of switching to India, as recommended by Sir Joseph Banks, President of the Royal Society.

Turning to India became attractive after the Chinese Government refused in 1833 to renew a grant giving the East India Company a monopoly for British trade. Soon after, tea was planted in Darjeeling in west Bengal in 1839, in Sylhet and Cachar (Assam) in 1855, Terai in 1862 and Dooars 1874. By 1871, some 295 estates were flourishing across India, whose 31,303 acres turned out 62.5 million pounds of tea.[62] Britain's thirst for the beverage was endemic. As William Gladstone, Prime Minister on and off from 1868 to 1894, put it, "If you are too hot it will cool you, if you are too cool it will warm you; if you are depressed it will cheer you; if you are too excited it will calm you."[63] Tea was all things to all men.

A few days after war was declared with Germany, the Ministry of Food took over existing tea stocks and closed the London market. All exports were now supervised and imports requisitioned. Tea was purchased from Indian growers through fixed price tendered contracts overseen by the UK's Tea Controller for India, a position held by

Y.N. Sukthankar during the early war years.[64] Around 90% of Britain's tea made its way into five hundred emergency warehouses lining London's Docks.[65]

India's role in putting soothing beverages on British kitchen tables cannot be under-estimated: the colony provided 95% of the UK's wartime tea requirements. As the managing agent for all tea purchases for the United Nations, the British Ministry of Food also equitably supplied the Allied and neutral countries.[66] Of 232 million pounds imported from India in 1939, 32 million were re-exported.[67]

In December 1940, the month when the *Gairsoppa* steamed out of Calcutta, the UK managed to import 45 million pounds of black tea from India out of the country's total 48 million pounds of stock.[68] Of that, 3.9 million pounds ended up sunk in the steamer's hold. All in all, Britain's love affair with its favourite hot drink never dimmed during the crisis years of World War II

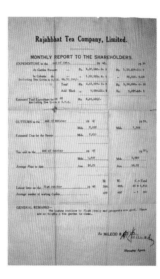
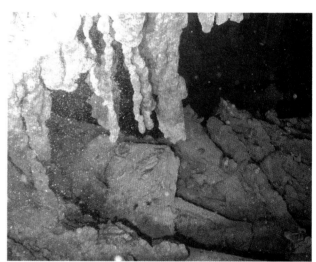

4.8. A monthly report to a shareholder in Devon from the Rajahbhat Tea Company (Letter TUR-13-00088-29).

4.9. Pig iron bars in the hold.

Iron, Planes & Trains

The 2,600 tons of pig iron shipped on the *Gairsoppa* played a dual purpose of lining the merchant vessel's hull with heavy ballast, plus the financial benefit of being sale-able at destination. The shipment coincided with a period of steel shortage as the British shipbuilding industry failed to respond adequately to the early challenges of war. Vessel loss rates accelerated as the Battle for the Atlantic raged, outpacing British shipbuilding by five to one between July 1940 and June 1941.[69]

India's rich iron reserves – estimated at over eight billion tonnes – are renowned as the largest and finest in Asia. An estimated 20,000 million tonnes are high-grade ores containing about 60% metallic iron. The modern steel industry emerged in India in 1874 when the short-lived Bengal Iron Works Company set up shop, only to close just two years later, heavily in debt. The firm was re-founded by British businessmen in 1889 as the Bengal Iron and Steel Company and a constant market was guaranteed after the Indian Government contracted in 1897 to purchase 10,000 tons of iron annually for ten years. The Indian Iron and Steel Company (IISCO) was set up in 1918 at Hirapur in Bengal, some 140 miles from Calcutta, exclusively to produce pig iron, mainly for export to the USA and Japan, and amalgamated with the Bengal Iron and Steel Company to form the Steel Corporation of Bengal in 1936.[70]

However, it was the Tata Iron and Steel Company (TISCO), established by Parsi entrepreneur J.N. Tata in 1907 at a large modern plant at Jamshedpur in Bihar, that put the country on the global map. The factory was built at the junction of the Subarnarekha and Khorkai Rivers, where iron ore could be shipped in from mines 40 miles away at Gorumashisani. Calcutta was conveniently accessible 156 miles to the southeast.[71]

TISCO's output was colossal. In 1913-1914 the company produced 155,000 tons of pig iron and 78,000 tons of steel, while throughout World War I some 1,500 miles of rails and 200,000 tons of steel were turned out. A major government-assisted expansion in 1924 more than tripled TISCO's annual steel output to over 420,000 tons. During the inter-war years, India became the world's cheapest producer of pig iron, undercutting the rest of the world at 75 cents per ton, compared to $8 in Pittsburgh. The Jamshedpur plant was now the largest integrated iron and steelwork's east of Suez. By the late 1930s, TISCO was manufacturing over 700,000 tons of finished steel every year.[72]

Keeping abundant pig iron (the raw material for steel making) and finished steel flowing as the springboard to develop ship and airplane technology was crucial for the war effort. Between 1909 and 1913 nearly 60% of the world's shipping tonnage had come out of Britain, a figure that had dwindled to 26% by 1932. As early as December 1936 the Admiralty informed the Cabinet Defence Policy and Requirements Committee that new warship construction was being stalled by delays in steel deliveries.

Britain only had six blast furnaces active with weekly capacities of 3,000 tons and another nine processing 2,500 to 3,000 tons.[73] The annual output per furnace was less than America's in 1910 and barely two-thirds of the German figure for 1929. The industry in America was helped by a wage rate double that of Britain and the UK was further handicapped by out-dated equipment and high transport costs. Only four mechanised grab transporters could be found in the country in 1938 to unload iron ore from ships, compared to twenty in Rotterdam alone, each double the UK capacity. British steel cost 30 shillings per ton more than foreign steel because of these inefficiencies.[74]

4.10. From Calcutta, Edward Melton advised H.P. Martin of the Acheson Graphite Corporation in New York of the Government's need to build up India's wartime steel industry (Letter TUR-13-00078-7-4-5).

4.11. S.N. Mitra from the Tata Iron & Steel Co. at Jamshedpur asks former colleague Paul F. Kohlhaas in New York for support in a promised promotion (Letter TUR-13-00079-40).

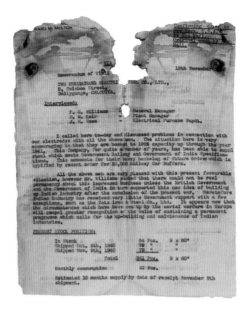
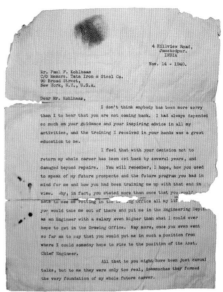

Once war broke out the situation had to improve and fast. Whitehall's planning estimate in 1939 for wartime production pointed to an annual need of around 1.2 million gross tons of merchant vessels and 370,000 tons standard displacement for naval ships. The backlog of damaged merchant vessels in Britain awaiting repair by March 1941 had surpassed 2.5 million tons as sinkings rose to 4.3 million tons that year.[75]

Britain needed more steel than it could produce, but the loss of swathes of Europe's supply chain and the west coast of Africa to the Nazi invasion deprived the UK of 35% of her iron ore imports. Before the war, total imported raw materials amounted to nearly 2.5 million tons a month on average, but fell to 600,000 tons a month during the Battle of the Atlantic. In response, home mining was expanded from 11 million tons in 1938 to 19.5 million tons in 1942. The Industrial Salvage Group Scheme inaugurated in late 1942 famously brought in 600,000 tons of iron railings from public parks and private frontages.[76] Everything that could be converted into scrap was fair game – derelict railways, disused bridges, tramlines and steel salvaged from bombed out buildings.[77]

The shipment of pig iron for steel conversion lay at the heart of the *Gairsoppa*'s cargo. Although unspecified in any manifest, the Tata Iron and Steel Company, which ran one of the largest plants in the British Empire, was its most probable source. Production boomed inside India between 1939 and 1949, when TISCO turned its focus to war supplies, even making armour plate for defence carriers and special alloy steels for high-speed tools.[78] Pig iron production in India peaked at 2 million tons in 1941.[79]

Iron & Steel Beneath the Waves

India's iron and steel industry features in the *Gairsoppa's* shipwrecked mail. In one part of the post the Tata Iron & Steel Co. at Jamshedpur asked its New York branch for a quote to ship a crane to the Noamundi Iron Mine for 31 January 1941 and enclosed an engineer's parts plan.[88]

A devastated S.N. Mitra working in Tata's Jamshedpur works sent Paul F. Kohlhaas, again in the company's New York office, a letter regretting the former Chief Engineer's relocation to America. Mitra had been trained by Kohlhaas and now his prospects were crushed and his whole career damaged beyond repair. The encouraging Chief Engineer had hated seeing Mitra rotting in the Drawing Office and promised to seek a promotion: "Nay more, once you even went so far as to say that you would put me in such a position from where I could someday hope to rise to the position of the Asst. Engineer". The abandoned man asked Kohlhaas to write a letter laying out the full plans he had for Mitra, "the position, the prospects, the salary and everything".[89]

A memorandum from Edward M. Melton to H.P. Martin of the Acheson Graphite Corporation in New York reported his visit to the Hakumchand Electrical Steel Co. Ltd. in Ballygunge, Calcutta, to discuss problems with electrodes. For years the firm had supplied steel to Government Railway & Government of India specifications, but "It appears now that the circumstances which have been set up by the aerial warfare in Europe will compel greater recognition of the value of sustaining a permanent programme which calls for the up-building and maintenance of Indian industries."[90] A second letter from Mr Melton asked E.W. Hill at the Carnegi-Illinois Steel Co. in Duquesne, America, for technical advice in installing a 25-ton open-hearth furnace.[91]

Britain depended on Indian steel for an abundance of heavy metal needs during the war, especially ordnance: the home production of almost 19 million tons of munitions from 1939-1945 was topped up with 2.2 million tons of imports in 1941.[80] The Tata Iron and Steel Company was India's only commercial firm equipped with the right combination of experienced personnel, equipment and research to satisfy Britain's evolving military needs.

TISCO established new Research and Control Laboratories a few years before the war and opened a 100-tonne blast furnace between 1939 and 1940. The firm turned out parachute snap fasteners, hand grenades and in the latter war years Signals Equipment for the Royal Air Force. In 1942 the company started manufacturing special bulletproof plate for armoured cars, popularly known as 'Tatanagars', alongside steel minesweepers, anti-submarine patrol and assault boats. A year later India manufactured 13,270 different items for the RAF. By the end the war the number of ordnance factories in India had tripled and its workforce expanded from 15,000 to 100,000 people. The Director-General of Munitions Production could call on 1,500 active engineering shops.[81]

As an advert placed by TATA in the English language Indian newspaper *The Statesman* told readers on 25 October 1940, "Steel is the factor on which economic freedom is based." It was the House of Tata's National Radio and Engineering Company that turned out the radio transmitters and receivers through which Winston Churchill and President Roosevelt's famous fire side chats boosted British and American morale as war waged across the world's oceans and skies. If the *Gairsoppa's* iron had made it safely to Britain, it may well have been converted into steel ships and sent back out onto the cruel sea.

Notes

1. For the *Gairsoppa's* cargo in general, see Tennent, 2001: 36. The oil cake and bone cargo is suggested by Lloyds War Losses. Some 18,815 tons of oil cake and 1,780 tons of bone meal were exported from India to the UK in December 1940: British Library IOR V/17/559, *Accounts Relating to the Sea-borne Trade and Navigation of British India. For December 1940* (Department of Commercial, Intelligence and Statistics, India), 217-18, 206.
2. Boog *et al.*, 2001: 304.
3. *British War Production 1939-1945. A Record* (London, 1945), vii.
4. *British War Production 1939-1945. A Record* (London, 1945), 192.
5. Mukerjee, 2010: 4-5, 46.
6. Ahluwalia, 1949: 115.
7. *Lloyd's War Losses*, 1989: 190.
8. British Library, London: IOR/L/F/7/735, F.3943/40.
9. British Library, London: IOR/L/F/5/15. Statistics of Unrefined Silver Shipments and Sales. IOR/L/F/7/735: Secret Telegram F.4061/40. From Governor of Bengal to the Secretary of State for India, Calcutta, 6 December 1940.
10. Rothermund, 1970: 93.
11. *Financial Times*, 9 March 1917.
12. *Financial Times*, 19 January 1917; 22 January 1917.
13. *Financial Times*, 10 September 1941.
14. National Archives, Kew: MINT 20/1793. Memorandum of Westminster Bank, 11 September 1940.
15. *An Analysis of the Sources of War Finance* (London, 1941), 10-11.
16. National Archives, Kew: MINT 20/1793.
17. National Archives, Kew: MINT 20/1793. Letter to J.H. Craig from Bank of England, 23 August 1940.
18. British Library, London: IOR L/F/7/732: F.17446.
19. *Financial Times*, 10 September 1941.
20. British Library, London: IOR/L/F/7/735, F.3943/40.
21. National Archives, Kew: T 236/76
22. National Archives, Kew: T 236/76. Copy of Note of Silver by Mr. G.H. Baxter of the India Office.
23. National Archives, Kew: T 236/76. Baxter, India Office, Whitehall, to E. Rowe-Dutton, Treasury, 28 January 1941.
24. National Archives, Kew: T 236/76. Rowe-Dutton To G.H. Baxter, India Office, 10 February 1941.
25. National Archives, Kew: T 236/76. Royal Mint to E. Rowe Dutton, Treasury, 17 February 1941.
26. National Archives, Kew: T 236/76. Royal Mint to Rowe Dutton, Treasury, 21 February 1941.
27. National Archives, Kew: T 236/76. 'Silver', 21 February 1941.
28. National Archives, Kew: T 236/76. Lord Catto, Silver, 24 February 1941.
29. British Library. London: IOR/L/F/5/13. Sales of Bombay Mint Refined Silver. Also

Account of Shipments from India & Stocks of Fine Silver Held in London, 1940-1941.

30. British Library IOR L/F/7/732: F.17446. Treasury to G.W. Baxter, India Office, 22 February 1941.
31. National Archives, Kew: T 236/76, F.17446.
32. British Library, London: IOR/L/F/7/1378. Insurance: Silver Storage and Shipments, 1936-1947.
33. British Library, London: IOR/L/F/7/735, F.817/4/19.
34. British Library, London: IOR/L/F/7/732. Decypher of Telegram, From Government of India, Finance Department, to Secretary of State for India, 23 November 1940.
35. British Library, London: IOR L/F/7/732, F.17446. Treasury to G.W. Baxter, India Office, 22 February 1941.
36. National Archives, Kew: T 236/76, F. 858/41. Baxter, India Office to Rowe-Dutton, 27 March 1941.
37. National Archives, Kew: T 236/76. G.H. Baxter, Financial Secretary, India Office, 25 March 1941.
38. National Archives, Kew: T 236/76, F. 1258/41. India Office to Rowe-Dutton, 11 April 1941.
39. National Archives, Kew: T 236/76. Ministry of Supply to Rowe-Dutton, 8 April 1941.
40. National Archives, Kew: T 236/77. Bank of England to Rowe-Dutton, 29 September 1942.
41. British Library, London: IOR/V/24/3061. India, Finance Department, Reports on the Administration of the Mints at Calcutta and Bombay with a Review.
42. National Archive, Kew: T 236/77, F.6328/42. Baxter, India Office, Whitehall to Rowe-Dutton, Treasury, 12 September 1942.
43. National Archive, Kew: T 236/77, F. 6602/42. Baxter, India Office, to S.D. Waley, Treasury, 20 October 1942.
44. *New York Times*, 29 March 1942.
45. *Financial Times*, 16 December 1942.
46. Longmate, 1973: 141, 153.
47. McLaine, 1979: 62.
48. British Library, London: IOR/L/E/9/1308. Scheme for the Control of Tea in Time of War, 1941-1942.
49. Wickizer, 1951: 184.
50. Griffiths, 1967: 207.
51. British Library, London: Mss Eur F174/763. *The Tea Quarterly* Vol. XIII, 1940.
52. British Library, London: Mss Eur F174/877. Ministry of Food. General Correspondence on Tea Control, May-December 1941.
53. British Library, London: Mss Eur F174/763. *The Tea Quarterly* Vol. XIII, 1940: 2.

54. British Library, London: IOR/L/E/9/1307. Scheme for Control of Tea in Time of War, 1938-1941.
55. British Library, London: IOR/V/14/273. *Indian Tea Statistics. 1941 and 1942* (1948): 1.
56. Collingham, 2011: 1, 105.
57. The 1941 national population density of 48,216,000 is based on Hicks and Allen, 1999. The population of London for 1939 is based on: www.demographia.com/dm-lon31.htm. Accessed 30.9.17.
58. Collingham, 2011: 102-103, 106.
59. Wickizer, 1951: 158.
60. Watson, 1936: 446.
61. Chaudhuri, 1995: 87.
62. Misra, 1986: 1, 2, 3, table 1.1.
63. Watson, 1936: 446-47.
64. Griffiths, 1967: 201-202.
65. Wickizer, 1951: 227.
66. Wickizer, 1951: 212, 213, 216-17.
67. British Library, London: IOR/V/14/273. *Indian Tea Statistics. 1941 and 1942* (1948): 5.
68. British Library, London: IOR V/17/559. *Accounts Relating to the Sea-borne Trade… For December 1940*: 230-33.
69. Smith, 2000: 155.
70. Rao, 1964: 3-4; Tomlinson, 1993: 128.
71. Datta, 1986: 7.
72. Rao, 1964: 2, 3; Datta, 1986: 7; Tomlinson, 1993: 129-31.
73. Barnett, 1986: 90, 107.
74. Barnett, 1986: 89-91, 111.
75. Barnett, 1986: 113.
76. *British War Production 1939-1945. A Record* (1945): 4, 22-24.
77. Weir, 2003: 13.
78. Datta, 1986: 7, 10.
79. Rao, 1964: 3, 4.
80. Weir, 2003: 10.
81. *British War Production 1939-1945. A Record* (London, 1945), 191; *Sands of Time. Tata Central Archives Newsletter* 9.2 (2010).
82. Based on bar no. JZ0470, shipwreck inv. no. TUR-13-02408-SI.
83. Based on bar no. 669, shipwreck inv. no. TUR-12-00403-SI.
84. Letter TUR-13-00069-09B. Yellapat Kanan Devan Hills Produce Co. Ltd consigned to Food Controller for the Season 1940.
85. Letter TUR-13-00071-57B-C. McLeod & Co., Managing Agents, Rajahbhat Tea Company Ltd., Calcutta to Roland M. Woods, The Croft, Beer, S. Devon.
86. TUR-13-00071-56, 1.12.40. Manager, The Darjeeling Consolidated Tea Co. Ld, Balasun & Murmah Divisions, Toong PO,

D.H. Ry to James F. Playfair Esq, Secretary, Darjeeling Consolidated Tea, 3 Palace Gate, Exeter, Devon.

87. Letter TUR-13-00088-37(2). Darjeeling Consolidates Tea Co. Ld., Ring Tong Hometown Division, Nagri Spur 11, Toong P.O. to James F. Playfair Esq., 3 Palace Gate, Exeter.

88. Letter TUR-13-00079-42. Tata Iron & Steel Co., Jamshedpur, Via Tatanagar, B. N. Ry. to Messrs. Tata Iron & Steel Co., 90 Broad Street, New York.

89. Letter TUR-13-00079-40, 14.11.40. S.N. Mitra, 4 Hillview Road, Jamshedpur to Mr Paul F. Kohlhaas, C/O Messrs. Tata Iron & Steel Co., 90 Broad Street, New York.

90. Letter TUR-13-00078-07(4), 18.11.40. Edward M. Melton, Hakumchand Electrical Steel Co. Ltd., 8 Swinhoe Street, Ballygunge, Calcutta to Mr H.P. Martin, Acheson Graphite Corporation, 30 East 42nd Street, New York.

91. Letter TUR-13-00078-07(8-9). Edward M. Melton, 93 Clive Street, Calcutta to Mr E.W. Hill, Open-Hearth Dept., Carnegi-Illinois Steel Co., Duquesne, Penna, USA.

5

MESSAGE IN A BOTTLE

ELLEN GERTH

Introduction

Before the age of plastic, when everything from medicines to perfumes, foodstuffs and alcohol were packaged in glass, the large number of bottles strewn across the storeroom above the No. 3 hold on the wreck of the *Gairsoppa* is no surprise. What they were doing there, however, is a curiosity that takes us back to a time when raw materials were running low and badly needed as the wear and tear of fighting World War II hit home. Piles of metal saucepans and railings torn down and heaped up across city streets for recycling into spitfires is a defining picture and metaphor of Britain's unbending will.

Some of the wrecked bottles' contents were enjoyed by the crew. The Heinz Tomato Ketchup, HP Sauce and Worcestershire Sauce containers that presumably originated in the galley, or were kept ready on the saloon table, were staple fare to enhance the monotony of food at sea. The pickled lemon was either added to the Indian crew's dishes as home comforts or was encouraged to keep scurvy at bay. Medicine bottles were once locked in the captain's quarters. Bottled beer and the odd spirits to toast

5.1-5.2. Glass bottles in the *Gairsoppa's* storeroom.

5.3. Glass bottles in the *Gairsoppa's* storeroom.

5.4. Glass bottles and wooden crates on the wreck of the *Mantola*, sunk off Ireland in 1917.

the king were kept in the bulk storeroom. All these spaces were located midship above the engine room.

The majority of bottles transported, by comparison, are best understood as empties heading back to the UK for reuse having once graced the sophisticated bars of British private members clubs in Bombay, Calcutta and other parts of India. The bottles are unlikely, but not definitely, to have originated in Indian homes. Inside the Raj excessive alcohol lowered esteem for the British in the eyes of the local Hindus, who detested drunkenness.[1] Temperance and the nationalist struggle went hand in hand: Indian freedom meant independence from both colonial administrators and the liquor they brought with them.[2] British establishments, such as the Bangalore Club, Bengal Club, Calcutta Club, Madras Club and United Service Club were havens for free-flowing alcohol of all varieties. In 1940 and 1941 India, Dewar's White Label Superior Whisky advertised itself as "The King of Clubs!" and Tennant's Beer advised customers to "Insist on it at the Club."[3]

Alongside metal and waste paper, back home shortfalls in glass were a recognised problem addressed through a Ministry of Commerce salvage campaign. The main culprit was milk bottles. Of 350 million used each year, 13 million went missing.[4] Lost and hoarded bottles extended to alcohol, partly caused by a spike in consumption. A whisky shortage triggered by increased employment and money in circulation enveloped Glasgow in March 1940, for instance, when publicans refused to sell the drink despite fights breaking out. "The result is that bottles are unobtainable and publicans are conserving their supplies to spread them over for regular customers in small quantities", the *Birmingham Daily Gazette* reported on 30 March 1940.

The Ministry's appeal for empty bottles was exploited by the Belfast Bottle Exchange Ltd., which promised that "a ready market will be found for Mineral Water Bottles at new and attractive rates. Every facility will be arranged for collection".[5] In Derry the same commercial opportunities extended to empty dark whisky and wine bottles.[6]

Drink/Food Type	Brand/ Glass Maker	Glass Colour	No. of Bottles	Dimensions
Beer. Guinness Stout, India Pale Ale?	AGW, FGC, PGC, CBC, P, SCGW	Green	115	H. 23.8, Diam. 6.3-6.5, Th. 0.5, 391-429gms
Beer	M6	Brown	1	H. 23.8, Diam. 6.5, Th. 0.5, 419-437gms
Beer	ABC: Aukland	Brown	1	H. 24.3, Diam. 6.8, Th. 0.5, Weight 471gms
Beer	Malayan Breweries	Olive Green	1	H. 23.4, Diam. 6.7, Th. 0.5, 463gms
Beer	South African Breweries	Amber	4	H. 23.2, Diam. 6.9, Th. 0.5, 451gms
Gin	Gordon's; UGB	Clear	2	-----------------------
Whisky	Johnnie Walker	Clear	3	-----------------------
Whisky?	Glenlivit ?	Clear	1	-----------------------
Soda	Unmarked	Yellow, Brown, Clear		H. 23-23.2, Diam. 6.5cm, Th. 0.5cm, 364-425 gms
Indian Tonic Water?	Schweppes; UGB	Clear	60	H. 18.9-22.3, Diam. 5.5-6.3, Th. 0.5, 316-391gms
Indian Tonic Water?	Schweppes; UGB, J L & Co.	Olive Green, Pale Green		H. 23.6, Diam. 6.3, Th. 0.5, 446gms
Wine (Hock)	Unmarked	Brown	9	H. 35.4, Diam. 7.0, Th. 0.6, 753gms
Ginger Beer	Josiah Russell Tower	Brown	13	H. 19.8, Diam. 7.4, Th. 0.5, 430gms
Martini	Martini	Green	1	H. 32.2, Diam. 8.6, Th. 0.5, 776gms
Cognac	Jas Hennessy	Pale Green/ Aqua	2	-----------------------
Vermouth?	Hybrid Bordeaux Style. Unmarked	Light Green	2	H. 28.9-32.2, Diam. 7.8- 8.9, Th. 0.5-0.7, 617-722gms. Cap H. 1.2, Cap Diam. 2.9
Lemon Pickle	Unmarked	Clear	7	H. 19.2, Diam. 7.6, Th. 0.6, 393gms
Gordon's Gin	UGB	Clear	2	-----------------------
Spirits (Whisky?)	Unmarked	Green	1	H. 28.5, Diam. 8, Th. 0.5, 764gms
Spirits	+ V On Base	Clear	1	H. 29.7, Diam. 8.0, Th. 0.6, 603gms
Worcestershire Sauce	Holbrook & Co. J L & Co.	Clear	1	H. 21, Diam. 6.7, Th. 0.4, 312gms
Club Sauce	JLC	Clear	4	H. 22.6, Diam. 6.1, Th. 0.5, 334gms

Table 5.1. Types, dimensions and numbers of glass bottles recovered from the wreck of the *Gairsoppa*.

Drink/Food Type	Brand/ Glass Maker	Glass Colour	No. of Bottles	Dimensions
Tomato Ketchup	Unmarked	Clear	2	H. 23.6, Diam. 6.8, Th. 0.5, 315gms
HP Sauce	Garton's	Clear	1	----------------------
Paregoric Elixir Poison ?	'Not To Be Taken'	Amber	1	H. 9.6, Diam. 6.0, Th. 0.6, 148gms
Medicine	Unmarked	Clear	2	H. 8.3, Diam. 3.7, Screw Top Diam. 2.2, Th. 0.4, 81gms

Table 5.1. Types, dimensions and numbers of glass bottles recovered from the wreck of the *Gairsoppa*.

Abbreviations:

ABC: Auckland Bottle Company; AGW: Alloa Glass Works;

FGC: Forsters Glass Company; J L & Co.: John Lumb & Co.;

PGC: Portland Glass Co.; SCGW: Unknown; UGB: United Glass Bottle Manufacturers Inc.

The Lord Mayor's appeal in Newcastle brought in thousands. Narrow necked glass bottles that once held a pint of liquid, such as whisky, gin, beer or spirits, were especially desirable.[7]

The Whitstable Times and Herne Bay Herald of 6 April 1940 advised readers to "Save bottles, labels and corks and save your pocket by having bottles re-filled. You can gain 10 per cent. to 15 per cent. in this way, therefore bring your own bottles – Gilman and Clarke, Chemists, Whitstable." One of the country's largest Nations Salvage Schemes was rolled out by Handsworth in Birmingham, in whose premises "All that is to be seen is a handful of men and women dealing with mountains of bottles." Handsworth's, a non-profit organisation, handled 12,000 bottles a day brought in from Aberdeen, Bournemouth, Norwich, Leeds and across Britain.[8]

The bottles discovered in the *Gairsoppa*'s hold, from which a representative sample was recovered, are too limited to be cargo and seem to be too extensive and eclectic to be crew's stores. As primarily British products, the majority are also sailing in the wrong direction. Surveys in the hold of the World War I steamship the *Mantola*, where bottles were densely stacked in labelled crates, show what a cargo of Boord's gin, Invalid sherry, Castle A sherry and French champagne from Reims looks like. The *Mantola* was lost to German torpedo fire on 8 February 1917, 143 miles off Fastnet in southwest Ireland, and bound for Calcutta. For this reason, combined with the stark need for glass empties back home, the majority of the *Gairsoppa*'s bottles are believed to have played a humble role in the British war effort.

The eroded letters embossed on many bottles, including the date 1938, and the presence of glass maker's marks that went out of use three years prior to the *Gairsoppa*'s final voyage (see John Lumb & Co. below), plus the apparent presence of Hock style

German wine bottles, further paint a picture of old containers assembled for the Ministry of Commerce salvage effort. Simultaneously, the wrecked bottles offer insights into the diversity of drinks available to British subjects frequenting largely male-only clubs in 1940 India.

Taking the Medicine[9]

Recoveries on the *Gairsoppa* brought up three small medicine bottles, one amber in colour and embossed 'Not to be Taken'.[10] In addition to its bold warning, narrow vertical ribbing served as a tangible reminder that the dangerous contents should be handled with caution. Similar poison bottles labelled 'Paregoric Elixir Poison' were manufactured in central England by E.E. Hall & Co. Chemists of Newbridge in Wolverhampton.

Paregoric was one of many opioid preparations commonly used by at least the early nineteenth century. Derived from tincture of camphor and opium, the elixir was among the most common opium of British pharmacopeia and while prescribed for various ailments in large doses it was also a recognised narcotic poison to be handled with caution. British India was a major source of opium manufacture, its cultivation and sale controlled at one time by the Opium Department.[11]

An 1812 *Treatise on the Prevention and Cure of Diseases* prescribed a teaspoonful of paregoric elixir added to a patient's drink twice a day to cure common coughs.[12] Paregoric treatment routinely managed diarrhoea brought about by dysentery and twenty drops every hour alleviated vomiting. The elixir was an accepted therapy for malarial fever.[13] While its contents are no longer preserved, if the *Gairsoppa's* ribbed

5.5. Left to right: a probable Paregoric Elixir Poison bottle, stamped 'Not To Be Taken' (TUR-12-90289-BE) and prescription bottles for medicinal use (TUR-12-90141-BE; TUR-12-90292-BE).

medicinal bottle once contained a British paregoric elixir, it would potentially have been a handy remedy for the crew, the ship having long sailed in malaria-ridden India, where the disease accounted for half of all deaths by the early twentieth century.[14]

The two other small medicine bottles are generically termed 'Narrow Mouth Round Prescription' bottles in twentieth-century glass company catalogues.[15] The name reflects the cylindrical shape, round in cross-section, and narrow mouth opening designed to aid dispensing. These bottles are associated with any number of medicinal products.

Condiments & Sauces

Club Sauce

In the *Gairsoppa*'s well-stocked galley were several condiment and sauce bottles for spicing up the crew's meals. Four clear glass containers are of the distinctive 'club sauce' shape: cylindrical, parallel vertical sides rise to a tall neck, often with a slight upward taper.[16] The bottle form typically held a Worcestershire sauce, although the shape also took a wider range of liquid food sauces.[17] The shape originated as a Lea & Perrins Worcestershire Sauce design, reportedly first used in the 1840s. The company's success inspired many companies to turn out a similar sauce marketed in imitation bottles, as is the case for the Holbrook & Co. bottles recovered from the shipwreck (see below).[18]

'Club sauce' bottles are topped with a distinctive three-part finish (a narrow rounded upper section, tall middle, flat and slightly rounded, leading to a narrow rounded lower collar), which is often called the Lea & Perrins style because of the company's common use of the design as early as 1850. One example was recovered from the wreck with its dark liquid preserved inside and a cork stopper lodged in the narrow neck.[19]

On the base of each bottle, barely visible, are the embossed letters 'JL' above a 'C', probably the maker's mark of John Lumb & Co. of Castleford in Yorkshire. Established in the 1870s, the firm became part of United Glass Ltd. in 1937, after which the company mark was replaced with the letters 'UGB' positioned above an 'L'. The *Gairsoppa* bottles with the earlier stamp are seemingly older containers produced by John Lumb & Co. before the takeover.[20] The wreck's Holbrook & Co. sauce bottles and the Schweppes bottles also bear the 'JLC' maker's mark.

Holbrook & Co. Worcestershire Sauce

One clear glass 'club sauce' bottle style is embossed with the Holbrook & Co. name and probably once contained its Worcestershire sauce product.[21] A 'J L & Co.' stamp

5.6. A Holbrook & Co. Worcestershire sauce bottle (TUR-12-90250-BE) and club sauce bottle (TUR-12-90252-BE). Both bases embossed 'J L & Co.' for the John Lumb & Co. UK glass factory.

on the base show that the bottle was again manufactured by the British firm John Lumb & Co.

The Holbrook & Co. brand was first sold in England in 1875 by the Birmingham Vinegar Brewery Company, fifty years after Lea & Perrins formulated their famous sauce in their chemist shop at 68 Broad Street in Worcester. By the late 1830s, cases of Lea & Perrins tangy sauce sailed as standard aboard all ocean liners in and out of British waters. The company paid ship stewards a fee to serve their product to passengers in the dining rooms. Word spread quickly and Lea & Perrins' Worcestershire Sauce rapidly gained a worldwide reputation.[22]

When the Birmingham Vinegar Brewery Company launched its product, Worcestershire Sauce was a household name. By January 1895, Holbrook & Co.'s alternative was a staunch competitor with its similarly shaped long-necked bottles sold in the United States for 35 cents a pint and 18 cents a half pint, compared to its older and more esteemed competitor selling for 45 cents and 25 cents respectively. Seeking to further popularize its recipe, the Birmingham Vinegar Brewery Company dazzled the public with flashy advertising at the 1897 Brussels International Exhibition, creatively building a pyramid of Holbrook's Worcestershire Sauce bottles 20 feet high and 20 feet square.[23]

The company's efforts paid off. By the early twentieth century its product was touted as being made in the world's largest Worcestershire Sauce factory and was frequently marketed as a savoury addition to otherwise dull soups.[24] By the time the *Gairsoppa* departed Calcutta in 1940, Holbrook's had captured an international market and its consumption aboard ship was a vital enhancement to a typically tedious diet.

Ketchup

Another distinctive condiment on the *Gairsoppa* was bottled in two clear glass bottles, each with eight moulded flat side panels running vertically down the lower half to the base – a typical design for ketchup bottles between around 1910 and at least the mid-twentieth century.[25] The neck and mouth incorporate an externally threaded finish designed to take a metal screw cap, which was the most common closure and finish combination for ketchup containers after the 1890s.

The use of ketchup in England dates back to at least the mid-1700s, when three types dominated British cooking: mushroom, walnut and fish ketchup.[26] The fish-based version probably reached Europe and Britain decades earlier via Dutch and English sailors and merchants returning home from Southeast Asia, where they were introduced to *ke-tchup*, a Chinese fermented fish sauce made in Fujian Province. Back in England an anchovy based recipe was first published in 1727.[27]

By the late eighteenth and early nineteenth century, the most popular ketchup recipes derived from tomatoes and in 1804 the first Anglo-American recipe for tomato sauce was published in Britain. In the early years ketchup was essential for preparing a number of dishes, including savoury pies, and was used as an ingredient for other sauces, as well as a basic serving condiment for meat, poultry and fish.[28]

The celebrated Heinz Tomato Ketchup was launched in the US in 1876. Henry Heinz's brand was introduced to the UK ten years later and quickly became the nation's favourite. The product was sold in long narrow-necked bottles to make the contents easier to pour and to reduce contact with air that darkened the sauce.[29] The eight-sided *Gairsoppa* example looks much like the iconic original that Heinz patented in 1882.

The production of Heinz Ketchup expanded into Britain by the 1920s, where 10,000 tons were produced in the first year. However, during the 1940s ingredients were in limited supply due to the strain of war and Heinz Ketchup vanished from British high-street shelves between 1939 until 1948.[30] Despite their tragic fate, in this regard the crew of the *Gairsoppa* fared better around their mess table than the average man on the street.

HP Sauce

Another taste popular for spicing up dishes on the *Gairsoppa* was 'Garton's HP Sauce', 'The Original Steak Sauce', as the wording on one shipwreck bottle with its contents preserved sold itself. The bottle shape is synonymous with the traditional HP Sauce bottle still in use today, the brand now owned and produced by the Heinz Company.[31]

The original recipe for HP Sauce was invented and developed in the late nineteenth century by Frederick Gibson Garton, a Nottingham grocer who ran a sauce and pickling business from home. Garton sold various sauces in small quantities to local residents by evening, making deliveries from his three-wheeled cart pushed around the streets. The initials HP are said to stand for 'Houses of Parliament' based on the rumour that the sauce was served in one of its restaurants. For many years the bottle's label bought into this excellent publicity by carrying a picture of the Houses of Parliament. For the sum of £150 and the settlement of substantial unpaid bills, in May 1899 Garton transferred his HP brand to Edwin Samson Moore, the founder of the Midlands Vinegar Company. Moore's malt vinegar was an essential ingredient of Garton's HP Sauce.[32]

Whereas Garton had peddled his sauce in limited quantities to local Nottingham customers, Moore planned world domination. Joined by his son Edwin Eastwood and

5.7. A ketchup bottle, possibly Heinz Tomato (TUR-12-90274-BE), a Garton's HP Sauce bottle with contents (TUR-12-90273-BE) and a lemon pickle bottle with contents (TUR-12-90279-BE).

his eldest daughter Minnie, who insisted she could work as effectively as any man, by 1903 Moore launched HP Sauce on a large scale. The original name Garton's HP Sauce was kept and proved an immediate success around the country. During World War I the British government signed large contracts with the Midland Vinegar Company to supply the troops, many of whom explained how "the sauce had livened up what had become the all too familiar diet of bully beef".[33]

The HP brand remained popular throughout the Depression and the turbulent years of World War II, once again benefitting British troops who were delighted to see the zesty sauce in their rations.[34] British expats in the Raj also bought the sauce enthusiastically. The rich, piquant and fruity product that went equally well with meat, fish, cheese or egg dishes was advertised in *The Sunday Statesman* as "For sunny meals in sunny climes. When you get that 'too-hot-to-eat' feeling, piquant H.P. Sauce brings back a real zest for your meals. H.P. is an enjoyable aid to digestion too."[35]

Lemon Pickle

One clear glass cylindrical container turned up with especially unusual contents preserved, one of six identical and otherwise empty containers.[36] Inside the bottle was what appeared to be lemon pickle or lemon in brine, a condiment common in Indian cuisine. The spice turmeric gives the contents a distinctive yellow colour, while red food inside the bottle may be hot chilli peppers, another common ingredient.[37] The other preserve bottles appear to have once held the same recipe since the glass's interior is stained yellow or yellow residue is visible within.[38]

This round container type, produced by many different glassmakers between the nineteenth and mid-twentieth century, was designed to hold bulky food products. The *Gairsoppa* preserve bottles are a narrower and taller successor to the earlier English Chow Chow types, which commonly held pickled and preserved products, including vegetables.[39] The shipwreck bottles' wide mouth bore was well designed for packing and extracting the solid food items within. These bottles were typically sealed with a cork stopper and wax.[40]

Europeans heartily embraced the spicy Indian lemon preserve ever since the German naturalist George Eberhard Rumphus spoke of a "delicious pickle" served with meats and curries in 1677. Lemon pickle captured the attention of the British too and remains a popular condiment in England today. As well as its culinary attributes, doctors in India's Punjab region recommended lemon pickle for its therapeutic value. Nineteenth-century records describe the consumption of thinly sliced lemons, layered with salt, ginger and caraway to treat a number of medical ailments, including an enlarged spleen.[41] Drinking lemon juice is still considered an effective deterrent for kidney stone prone patients.[42]

The lemon was the first citrus fruit known to prevent scurvy, a potentially life-threatening condition that induces bleeding gums, swollen joints and heart failure. In the late eighteenth century lemons were broadly prescribed to counteract the condition that took more British lives than enemy action.[43] The fruit proved so effective that in 1795 Britain issued lemon juice as part of the Navy's daily ration. By 1815 British sailors had consumed 1.5 million gallons of the stuff.[44]

Hard Drink

Beer – the Best Drink on Earth

The largest quantity of containers on the *Gairsoppa* were 115 unembossed green glass export beer bottles. This classic shape is typified by a slender body with straight sides and a rounded shoulder topped by a swollen neck.[45] The export style was crafted of thick glass to maintain the pressure of its carbonated contents and to withstand mass handling and re-use. A minority of darker green, taller and heavier bottles were also under transport.[46]

In the absence of preserved paper labels naming the beer's brands, the question of content remains open. While most of the *Gairsoppa* beer bottles lack embossments identifying brand names, several base stamp forms name their British glass manufacturers. The majority show the letters 'AGW', probably an abbreviation of the Alloa Glass Works in Scotland.[47] Established in 1750 by Lady Frances Erskine of Mar, this glass firm is the oldest in the world still operating on its original premises, now under the ownership of Owens-Illinois Inc. The AGW company mark is barely visible on several bases, possibly the result of overuse and worn metal moulds, which no longer produced a clear stamp.

The common 'FGC' stamp registered on some *Gairsoppa* beer bottle bases, in most cases accompanied by the embossment 'Bottle Made in England', points to production at the Forsters Glass Company in St Helens, Lancashire. FGC was in business from 1902 to 1966.[48] 'PGC' on at least one base was probably turned out by the Portland Glass Co., originally in Greenford, Middlesex. The company was in business from at least 1922 to 1956 and also ran a plant in Irvine, Scotland.[49] A small number of bottles combining the letters 'PGC' and 'Bottle Made in Scotland' were clearly produced in Irvine.

As well as present on the shipwreck's Schweppes bottles, the letters 'UGB' appear on a few beer containers, including a singular amber coloured example, mostly alongside the base embossment 'Bottle Made in England'. UGB or the United Glass Bottle

5.8. Over 100 green and brown export beer bottles were recovered from the wreck, including a variety with a curved neck (far right).

5.9. Most beer bottles are embossed on the base with the glass factory name 'AGW' for the Alloa Glass Works, Scotland. Many are stamped 'UGB' for United Glass Bottle Manufacturers Ltd. and 'Bottle Made in England'. A few curved neck bottles are stamped 'PGC' for the Portland Glass Company and 'FGC' for the Forsters Glass Company, St. Helens. Other initials are unknown, such as 'P' and 'SCGW', 'Made in England'.

Manufacturers Ltd. was a large conglomerate of five glass factories located in the UK (Raven Head Glass Works, Merseyside; Carrington Shaw & Co, Sherdley Glass Works, St Helens; Nuttall & Son, St Helens; Robert Candish & Son, Seaham Harbour, Co.

Durham; and Alfred Alexander & Co, Leeds and Southwick-on-wear),[50] which together formed a public company in 1913. By 1922, advertisements proclaimed the company to be Europe's largest bottle manufacturer with 250 million containers manufactured each year. The wares were touted as being accurate in capacity, uniform in height and shape, and the strongest bottles available.[51]

A few bottles are embossed with the initials of presumed British glass companies yet to be identified. The stamps 'SCGW' and 'CBC' (associated with a 'Made in England' clarification) are a case in point. A large letter 'P' appears on several examples, in some cases with the 'Bottle Made in England' stamp. Five *Gairsoppa* containers are embossed simply 'This Bottle is Made in Scotland'.

While the source of much of the *Gairsoppa* beer remains uncertain, these export styles of bottle were widely, yet not exclusively, used for lager.[52] Despite its absence from adverts placed in India in 1940 and 1941, it is also tempting to speculate whether some once held Guinness Stout, which from the 1840s onwards dominated the British Victorian home market and sales to the colonies. An Irish beer introduced by Arthur Guinness in the late eighteenth century, by 1890 Guinness was the largest brewery in the world. The drink's popularity was in part due to its proclaimed 'medicinal' value. Stouts and stronger ales had long been touted for their restorative qualities and were even prescribed by doctors for poor appetite, low spirits and pregnancy.[53]

During World War II the government appreciated the merits of beer to connect soldiers to a sense of home and boost spirits. Beer was said to be almost as important as bullets. At the request of the British army, Guinness set aside 5% of its production for the troops: it was shipped to the front, served at a discount to all men in uniform at home and distributed to hospitals free of charge.[54]

Another possible candidate for the unmarked *Gairsoppa* export bottles is one of the popular India Pale Ales (IPA), a brand originally made to cater to British troops in India.[55] To weather the months at sea from London to India, more hops were added to the recipe, instilling a deeper bitterness and aroma to the taste.[56] One example was the famous Bass India Pale Ale developed after 1823 by the British brewer William Bass.[57] Both Guinness and Bass India Pale Ale kept extremely well once bottled, enabling the many merchants based by the mid-1800s in Liverpool, London and Southampton to ship these beers over long distances and reach markets too far for other beers.[58]

Numerous brands advertised in the English language Indian newspaper *The Statesman*. Allsopp's lager was promoted in September 1940 as "The best drink on Earth" and was sold by Cutler Palmer & Co. of London, Bombay, Calcutta, Lahore, Madras and Colombo, who also oversaw the import and distribution of Gordon's Gin, Johnny

Walker whisky, Dry Monopole champagne, Invalid's Port, Exshaw Liqueur Brandies and Whiteways Cider.[59]

Whitbread's Light Beer was appreciated for its lightness, character and purity and, as the same newspaper explained, being "especially brewed for the tropics, has had a great reception throughout India."[60] Tennant's Beer adverts suggested the reader "Insist on it at the Club."[61] Red Tower Lager from northern England, made from pure water from Thirlmere in the Lake District, claimed to be the "best beer ever bottled".[62]

The beer most heavily advertised in *The Statesman* was EWO Beer, "British Brewed from Empire Malt & Hops. A Fine Light Pilsner Beer. Obtainable Everywhere. Quality + Economy. EWO Brewery Shanghai." EWO imports were managed by the trading company Jardine Skinner & Co. of Calcutta and the drink was distributed throughout India by Spencer & Co., Ltd.[63] A rarer brand seemingly manufactured in India told customers that "When it's your turn to call [at the bar] say EK Number. Premier No. 1 Beer".[64] Finally, British readers of *The Statesman* were directed on 25 October 1940 to Gold Ribbon Lager and Light Lion Pilsener Beer produced by the Murree Brewery Co. at Rawalpindi, Punjab, "The stuff for the troops, Major… and for you and me."

South African Brew

Four *Gairsoppa* beer bottles, two amber in colour, are embossed with the exotic title in uppercase letters 'Property of the South African Breweries Ltd'. Swedish businessman Jacob Lettersrtedt, who immigrated to the Cape in 1820, set up the Mariedal Brewery, which was later integrated with Ohlisson's Cape Breweries and subsequently merged with South African Breweries Ltd. (SAB). By 1895 SAB was floated on the London Stock Exchange as a British investment company and for the first half of the twentieth century its operations were based and registered in the UK.[65]

By the time the *Gairsoppa* set sail in December 1940, South African Breweries had incorporated hotels into a broader international diversification plan and prospered through the tied-house system whereby brewing companies fixed hotels, public houses and bars to contracts requiring a percentage of the brewing company's beer to be sold on their premises. This deal was instrumental to SAB's booming fortunes after World War II.[66]

New Zealand Beer

One foreign beer bottle, amber in colour, is embossed near the base with the letters 'ABC', an abbreviation of 'The Auckland Bottle Company'. Also legible is the wording 'This Bottle Is', 'Limited Auckland', plus the date '1938'. The Auckland Bottle Company, also known as the Auckland Bottle Works, was founded at Penrose near Auckland in New Zealand in 1922 by the Australian Manufacturers' Company.

Bottle shortage was a chronic problem in New Zealand, where numerous attempts to get successful bottle and glassworks off the ground failed due to the opposition of bottle importers, the pro-British lobby and a shortage in skilled glass labour. When establishing the Auckland Bottle Company, the Australian Glass Manufacturers' Company launched a successful public relations campaign, which won the support of British industrialists, while managing to bring in a contingency of skilled glass workers from Sydney. ABC remains the major supplier of bottles in New Zealand today.[67]

5.10. A brown glass beer bottle embossed 'Property of the South African Breweries Ltd.' and 'Talana' on the base for its factory location (TUR-12-90189-BE). A brown beer glass bottle embossed 'ABC' for the Auckland Bottle Company (TUR-12-90049-BE). A green beer glass bottle stamped 'Malayan Breweries Ltd.' (TUR-12-90120-BE).

Malayan Brew

Another singular beer bottle recovered from the depths of the North Atlantic, olive green in colour, is embossed with the words 'Malayan Breweries Ltd', founded in Singapore in 1931 by the British company Fraser and Neave Ltd. as a joint venture with the Dutch company Heineken to produce Tiger-brand beer. Prior to the launch of Malayan Breweries, large quantities of Japanese beer were imported into British Malaya. Colonial authorities' restrictions on imported beers soon protected the new local products. Within a year of the *Gairsoppa*'s sinking, the Japanese army invaded Malaya and Singapore and soon expropriated all of Fraser and Neave's brewing facilities for its own production.[68]

Soft Drinks

Ginger Beer

Historically, perhaps the *Gairsoppa*'s most interesting bottles are thirteen ginger beer containers embossed with an image of the Tower of London and the maker's name 'Josiah Russell Tower Brand'. A British company based in London, Josiah Russell launched his mineral water and soft drinks factory towards the end of the nineteenth century. From the beginning the bottle's shape was synonymous with ginger beer in the eyes of buyers because it imitated earlier stoneware ginger beer containers. The Josiah Russell Tower Brand is a classic example of a 1940s machine-made amber crown cork cap ginger beer bottle. The glass's dark colour helped prevent the contents being adversely affected by sunlight and shielded the at times cloudy and unappealing liquid from a customer's sight.[69]

Ginger beer originated in England in the mid-1700s and was typically safer to drink than the local water supply. The basic ingredients of ginger, lemon, sugar and yeast were often supplemented with extra flavouring, such as juniper, liquorice and even chilli to add an extra bite. As required by British Excise Regulations of 1855, the drink could not contain more than 2% alcohol, making the beverage popular among children and adults alike.[70]

Ginger beer was so popular in Britain that in World War I Londoners served it to German prisoners of war, as well as showering the enemy with cigars and fruit in the hope German civilians might extend the same courtesy to their own young soldiers should they end up in a similar fate.[71] For those British troops stationed overseas, ginger beer was considered essential for their contentment. An early twentieth-century report from British army commissioners and inspectors spoke of the benefits of stocking it in India's canteens. Each soldier was permitted three pints a day, one per meal. Providing the beer under a controlled environment in a limited capacity lessened intoxication.[72] Among India's British population, ginger ale was popular when mixed with Gordon's Orange and Lemon Gin, which created a beverage that was "Energising and exhilarating as an appetiser or cocktail, refreshing and invigorating as a long drink" in the words of *The Statesman*.[73]

Schweppes

The sixty Schweppes bottles recovered from the *Gairsoppa*'s hold have a body of moderate height with almost vertical parallel sides and a long, steep-sloping shoulder. Most of the shipwreck examples were manufactured in clear glass and two were of a smaller size. The remainder were olive green and two a paler green. The bulk feature the Schweppes company name embossed on the bases and replicated on two sides. On a few bottles, the Schweppes logo runs lengthwise along just one side,[74] while two display broader lettering.[75] The various containers were clearly manufactured in different moulds at different times.

5.11. Schweppes soda bottles (TUR-12-90091-BE, TUR-12-90212-BE) with 'UGB' (United Glass Bottle Manufacturers, Inc.) stamps on the base. Right: a Josiah Russell Tower Brand ginger beer bottle, its base embossed 'FGC' for the Forsters Glass Company (TUR-12-90085-BE).

The letters 'UGB' visible on the base again show the bottles were made by the United Glass Bottle Manufacturers Inc. conglomerate (see above). The embossment 'Made in England' encircles the underside base of several Schweppes bottles, but not all. In addition, 'J L & Co.' appears on at least a dozen bases, the company mark of glass-maker John Lumb & Co. of Castleford in Yorkshire, England. On a few Schweppes bottles the glass stamp is no longer visible, typically the result of moulds being used until they wore out.

The discovery of a large Schweppes bottle inventory on the *Gairsoppa* is not surprising given that the company was the leading manufacturer of soft drinks in Britain during World War II.[76] As the British Empire grew, Englishmen yearning for a taste of home brought Schweppes with them to distant countries and the company's products were promoted globally with advertisements claiming that "Schweppes' Table Waters were served exclusively in royal households, leading clubs, hotels, and steamship lines throughout the world."[77]

German-born Jean Jacob Schweppes formed the Schweppes Company in 1783 in Geneva to bottle carbonated water after developing a successful aerated water system, the Geneva System or Geneva Apparatus.[78] As with many early carbonated waters, particularly spa waters coming out of the Rhineland, Schweppes' products were originally promoted for medicinal purposes to cure kidney and bladder ailments, as well as for indigestion and gout.[79] Daily consumption of soda water and seltzers was supported by leading physicians, including Dr Erasmus Darwin, grandfather to Charles Darwin, who advocated Schweppes' carbonated water particularly to treat "Stone of the bladder".[80]

In 1792 Jean Jacob Schweppes set up a factory in London as a young entrepreneur in competition with numerous apothecaries and dispensers of aerated water prepared on simple machinery and hawked through the streets of London by cart. By 1851 Schweppes was the official drink at the Great Exhibition in London's Crystal Palace. In the 1870s Schweppes introduced two new product lines, ginger ale and Indian Tonic Water.[81] When the *Gairsoppa* sailed forth from Calcutta in 1940, Schweppes' ginger ale was well-established globally and was a favourite among British colonials.

Indian Tonic Water was inspired by the British colonial practice of consuming quinine as an effective anti-malarial antidote. For this reason, Schweppes was especially popular in India, where British subjects mixed the tonic with gin to mask the bitterness of quinine. From this practice the classic gin and tonic was born.[82] The *Gairsoppa* bottles stamped with the famous Schweppes name may have held any number of the company's popular carbonated beverages. While their contents remain a mystery, it is enticing to think that some of the inventory was perhaps Schweppes's famous Indian Tonic Water, a companion to the Gordon's gin bottles recovered from the shipwreck.

Spirits & Wine

Gordon's Gin

Two clear glass Gordon's Gin bottles recovered from the shipwreck again display the 'UGB' glass stamp on the base. Embossed above the factory glass stamp is a central embossed boar's head, the trademark of Gordon's Gin. After 1903 the product was packaged in both green and clear class bottles, the former intended for the home market and the latter for export,[83] a strategy consistent with the clear examples shipped aboard the *Gairsoppa*.

Alexander Gordon, a Londoner of Scottish descent, founded his distillery in the Southwark area of London in 1769 for the production of Gordon's London Dry Gin. The long associated boar's head symbol, according to legend, derived from a heroic

family feat in which a brave Gordon clan member saved the king of Scotland from a wild boar on a hunting expedition.[84] Gordon's no doubt also played on the medieval image of the boar's head as a symbol of feasting and rejoicing to forge a strong brand identity.[85]

Well before the launch of Gordon's product, gin had been a firm favourite in Holland, where its invention is generally credited to the professor of Medicine Dr Franciscus Sylvius, who supposedly created the formula at the University of Leiden in the mid-seventeenth century and promoted it as a medicinal beverage. English soldiers supporting the Netherlands during the Thirty Years' War (1618-1648) acquired a taste for this exotic drink and brought it back home, calling it 'Dutch Courage' based on the Dutch practice of taking a shot of gin before battle.[86]

By 1742, twenty million gallons of gin were distilled in England with an estimated 400,000 gin sippers in the London vicinity,[87] who could purchase their spirits from shops, market stalls, basements and street carts. By the mid-eighteenth century, gin-drinking in London reached epidemic proportions, as satirised in William Hogarth's infamous print of Gin Lane in 1751.

On the back of the British penchant for gin, within three decades of its launch Gordon's distilling business was selling half a million gallons a year.[88] The celebrated spirit soon spread far and wide as sailors in the British Navy and Merchant Marine carried it across the world.[89] By the twentieth century, Gordon's was the biggest selling gin worldwide as advertisements happily proclaimed: "Of all the Englishmen who drink gin, how many drink Gordon's? Most of them. And it's been that way for years. To be blunt about it, Gordon's is England's biggest selling gin – as it is America's and the world's".[90]

Gordon's was advertised in British India in 1940 on prime front-page placements in *The Statesman* as made from a secret formula of the House of Gordon, with no colouring and as "The Gin that has medicinal properties. If your value your health – insist on Gordon's."[91] The year the *Gairsoppa* sank, Gordon's Gin was awarded its second royal warrant from His Majesty King George VI.[92]

5.13. Two vermouth bottles (back: TUR-12-90283-BE, TUR-12-90137-BE) and two cognac bottles (front: TUR-12-90285-BE, TUR-12-90281-BE).

5.14. One cognac bottle was identified by its 'Jas Hennessy Cognac' stamp on the metal cork stopper (TUR-12-90281-BE).

Cognac

The shipwreck contained four plain, but distinctively shaped, spirit bottles often referred to as 'hybrid' due to a similarity to Bordeaux and Burgundy wine bottles. Two of the four shipwreck containers are pale green/aqua, with a slightly longer neck than the other two bottles and whose shape is often associated with cognac brandy.[93] One of these was recovered with liquid contents suggestive of cognac, golden yellow in colour and originally sealed with a flanged cork stopper.[94] In two bottles the cork stopper remained lodged inside.

The necks of both examples preserve traces of the original metal (aluminium?) protective wrapping that once covered and sealed the stopper. The cognac interpretation is supported by the bottle with intact contents: the top of its circular metal cork cover is inscribed 'Jas Hennessy Cognac' around the edge. Also visible is the iconic Hennessy trademark featuring a fist clutching a hatchet or battle-axe. This logo reportedly derived from the Hennessey family coat of arms in honour of the company's founder,

Irishman Richard Hennessy, the youngest son of Lord Ballymacmoy, and his twelve-year army career fighting with the Irish Brigade for King Louis XV of France.[95] Hennessy established his distillery in Cognac in 1765 and the business blossomed under his son James from whom the firm took its name in 1813.[96]

5.15. A Martini bottle (TUR-12-90134-BE). A Hock style wine bottle (TUR-12-90074-BE); one base is embossed 'Wiener Rathaus Keller' after the famous wine tavern in Vienna's City Hall and with a double-headed winged eagle bearing the Austrian coat of arms (TUR-12-90133-BE).

Vermouth & Martini

The two other hybrid bottles, light green in colour, are taller and broader than the Hennessey forms with longer and more slender necks, a shape commonly associated with vermouth.[97] A fifth green glass shipwreck container, again similar to the broader hybrid style, is embossed with the famous name 'Martini', an Italian vermouth founded in 1840. Vermouth is made from wine fortified with alcohol and flavoured with various herbs and roots. Its name derives from its principal ingredient, wormwood (*wermut* in German), a shrub-like perennial that grows throughout Europe and Asia.[98]

As early as 1678, vermouth was described as an aid to digestion, among other medicinal properties, including purifying the blood and 'rejoicing' the heart. The oldest vermouth house dates back to 1757, while the earliest named brand was credited to Antonio Benedetto Carpano in 1786, an apprentice to a merchant in Turin who infused Moscato wine with various botanicals. Carpano's vermouth achieved national popularity.[99]

Not until the nineteenth century was vermouth introduced to gin, launching the birth of the Martini, although the recipe's origin is steeped in folklore. Some sources claim the drink was invented in San Francisco by the legendary bartender 'Professor' Jerry Thomas, who named it the Martinez and brought it to New York City after the 1862 publication of his *Bar-tender's Guide*. Other New Yorkers attribute the recipe to Martini di Arma di Taggia, an Italian immigrant bartender working at the Knickerbocker Hotel before World War I, while the citizens of Martinez, California, claim it was invented there in 1870 by a San Francisco miner. Further afield, British legend lays claim to the drink too, perhaps named after the Martini & Henry rifle used by the British army between 1871 and 1891.[100]

Whatever its origins, by the turn of the twentieth century the word Martini was common in bars and clubs on both sides of the Atlantic. The recovery of the *Gairsoppa* vermouth bottles, along with the two Gordon's gin bottles, reflects the mixing on Indian shores of the now trendy Martini, which by the 1940s – the golden age of the cocktail – was popularized by glossy advertising linking the drink to social sophistication and economic success.[101]

Whisky

The *Gairsoppa* liquor bottles include three square-shouldered containers whose shape is typically associated with Scotch or Irish whisky.[102] The letters 'J W' are visible on the base of the shipwreck examples, confirming contents of the famous Johnny Walker Scotch brand founded in 1820 by John Walker, a Scottish grocer and wine and spirit merchant of the Royal Burgh of Kilmarnock. Later joined by his son Alexander, a man of "immense energy, vision and ability", the firm developed a successful wholesale and export business. Following Alexander's death in 1889, his two sons took the helm and by the early 1900s the rapidly expanding company acquired additional bottle factories.[103] English adverts advertised the whisky in India in 1940 as "Johnnie Walker. Famous for its finer flavour. Born 1820 – still going strong".[104]

A fourth clear glass spirits bottle is tall with a moderately slender bulging neck, a shape again strongly identified with Irish and Scotch whisky.[105] The bottle includes its cork stopper nestled inside and along the neck are remains of the original metal protective wrapping once sealing the stopper. The content's identity is unknown, but perhaps the bottle was once filled with the similarly shaped Glenlivet whisky brand, a product of the Scottish Glenlivet Distillery founded in 1824 by the Smiths of Banffshire.[106]

The singular *Gairsoppa* container may represent the last of the Glenlivet pre-wartime stock, since after 1941 whisky exports declined after the government imposed grain rationing during World War II.[107]

5.16. A whisky bottle identified by a 'J W' base stamp as Johnny Walker scotch (TUR-12-90286-B; base TUR-12-90125-BE). A Scotch or Irish whisky bottle embossed '+ V' on the base (TUR-12-90069-BE).

Wine For Unstrung Nerves

Finally, nine amber Hock style wine bottles turned up in the *Gairsoppa*'s hold – the only wine containers from the wreck. The graceful bottle shape with its seamless, long slender neck and body is largely associated with German red or white Rhine or Mosel wines. The name hock probably derived from the word Hockheim, a German village at the forefront of the wines' export to England.[108] The hock style shape dates back to the 1870s or 1880s and machine-made examples were introduced from the mid-to-late 1910s, as in the case of the *Gairsoppa* bottles.[109]

The base of one shipwreck bottle is embossed with the exotic name 'Wiener Rathaus Keller',[110] Vienna's famous restaurant and wine tavern established in 1899 in the cellar of Vienna's City Hall. The central double-headed winged eagle featuring the Austrian coat of arms was traditionally used to represent the Hapsburg royal family.

Notes

1. Collingham, 2001: 30.
2. Colvard, 2013: 264-65.
3. *The Statesman*, 24 October 1940; *The Statesman*, 22 March 1941.
4. *Lichfield Mercury*, 29 March 1940.
5. *Belfast News-Letter*, 6 May 1940.
6. *Derry Journal*, 18 December 1940.
7. *Newcastle Evening Chronicle*, 19 June 1940.
8. *Birmingham Mail*, 24 February 1940.
9. The bottle identification and history section relies heavily on the Historic Glass Bottle

Identification and Information Website (US Department of the Interior Bureau of Land Management/Society for Historical Archaeology): www.sha.org/bottle/typing.htm.

10. *Gairsoppa* inv. no. TUR-12-90289-BE.
11. *The British Almanac*, 1883: 32-4.
12. Buchan, 1812: 200-201.
13. *The Chemist and Druggist*, Vol. 41, 1892: 358; Hare and Martin, 1899: 236-7; McCallum, 2008: 216.
14. Youngerman, 2008: 87.
15. Pers. Comm. Bill Lindsey, 8 February 2015; see for example the Illinois Glass Company Catalog, 1926: 210.
16. See: www.sha.org/bottle/food.htm#-Club%20sauce.
17. Pers. comm. Bill Lindsey, 28 February 2015.
18. *See:* www.sha.org/bottle/food.htm#-Club%20sauce.
19. *Gairsoppa* Inv. no. TUR-12-90524-BE.
20. See 'Glass Bottle Marks' in: www.glassbottlemarks.com/bottlemarks-3.
21. *Gairsoppa* Inv. no. TUR-12-90250-BE.
22. Shurtleff and Aoyagi, 2012: 5, 8, 157.
23. Shurtleff and Aoyagi, 2012: 9, 63, 67.
24. Shurtleff and Aoyagi, 2012: 78, 90.
25. See: www.sha.org/bottle/food.htm#Catsup.
26. Lundy, 2006: 134; Shurtleff and Aoyagi, 2012: 174.
27. Lundy, 2006: 134; Jurafsky, 2014.
28. Smith, 2013: 502; Jurafsky, 2014.
29. Meyers and Gerstman, 2005: 28; Burkitt and Zealley, 2006: 14.
30. See: www.heinz.co.uk/Our-Company/About-Heinz/Heinz-Story.
31. Britton, 2013: 233.
32. Britton, 2013: 145, 161-63, 169, 171-72.
33. Britton, 2013: 182-83, 185, 199.
34. Britton, 2013: 217, 240.
35. *The Sunday Statesman*, 15 September 1940.
36. *Gairsoppa* inv. no. TUR-12-90279-BE.
37. Pers. comm., R. Charudattan 24 October 2014; Chynoweth and Woodson, 2003: 12.
38. *Gairsoppa* inv. nos. TUR-12-90138-BE, TUR-12-90139-BE, TUR-12-90140-BE, TUR-12-90141-BE, TUR-12-90076-BE, TUR-12-90095-BE.
39. Pers. comm. Bill Lindsey, 31 January 2015. See: www.sha.org/bottle/food.htm#Pickles & Preserved Foods.
40. See: www.sha.org/bottle/closures.htm#General Closure Types.
41. Chynoweth and Woodson, 2003: 12, 14.
42. Balch, 2006: 537.
43. Chynoweth and Woodson, 2003: 14.
44. Cumo, 2013: 568.
45. Lockhart, 2007: 53; www.sha.org/bottle/beer.htm#Export style.
46. See *Gairsoppa* bottle inv. no. TUR-12-90172-BE.
47. Pers. Comm. Bill Lindsey, 4 February 2015; Lockhart *et al.*, 2013: 522.
48. David Whitten, 'Glass Bottle Marks' in www.glassbottlemarks.com/bottlemarks-3.
49. Pers. comm. Bill Lockhart, 11 February 2015; Stephens-Adamson Mfg. Company, March 1922: 10.
50. See Inchicore Pressed Glass Works Private Museum: http://www.inchicore-pressedglass-museum.org/United%20Glass%20Bottle1.htm; http://www.gracesguide.co.uk/United_Glass_Bottle_Manufacturers.
51. See: www.gracesguide.co.uk/File:Im1922BIF-UnitedGlass1.jpg.
52. See: www.sha.org/bottle/beer.htm#Export style.
53. Hughes, 2006: 22, 88, 167.
54. Mansfield, 2009: 234.
55. Dunkling, 1992: 111.
56. Maiya, 2011: 1.
57. Hughes, 2006: 85.
58. Hughes, 2006: 88, 109.
59. *The Statesman*, 2 September 1940.
60. *The Statesman*, 6 September 1940.
61. *The Statesman*, 22 March 1941.
62. *The Statesman*, 5 March 1941.
63. *The Statesman*, 7 September 1940.
64. *The Statesman*, 11 March 1941.
65. Tucker, 1986: 89.
66. Tucker, 1986: 90.
67. Auckland Bottle Works New Zealand: www.glass.co.nz/NZglassbottles.htm.
68. Shimizu, 2008: 111.
69. Pers. comm. Mark Nightingale, 10 October 2014.
70. Madden, 2007: 1.
71. Neiberg, 2011: 192.
72. *Report of the Committee Appointed to Consider the Existing Conditions Under Which Canteens and Regimental Institute Are Conducted…*, 1903: 251-52.
73. *The Statesman*, 5 September 1940.
74. *Gairsoppa* inv. no. TUR-12-90026-BE.
75. *Gairsoppa* inv. nos. TUR-12-90078-BE, TUR-12-90256-BE.
76. Donovan, 2014: 19.
77. See: http://spiritschweppes.com/tag/history-schweppes.
78. Simmons, 1983: 16.
79. Smith, 2007: 80. See: Bottles and Bygones, http://mikesheridan.tripod.com/schweppes1.htm.
80. Simmons, 1983: 26.
81. Simmons, 1983: 22, 44. 45.
82. Simmons, 1983: 45.
83. See: gordons-gin.co.uk/about/facts-about-gordon's.

84. See: www.gordons-gin.co.uk/about.
85. Harvey, 1972: 38.
86. Conrad, 1995: 123; Sandham, 2012: 72, 73.
87. Noel Hume and Mytton, 2013: 10-11.
88. Dillon, 2002: 290.
89. See: www.gordons-gin.co.uk/about/gordon's-timeline.
90. Ebony, 1964: 127.
91. *The Statesman*, 12 September 1940.
92. See: www.ppd.com.hr/products/gin/gordons-dry-gin.
93. Pers. comm. Bill Lindsey, 19 May 2014.
94. *Gairsoppa* inv. no. TUR-12-90285-BE.
95. Burke, 1884: 479; see: www.hennessy.com/us/maison/history.
96. Faith, 2013: 74, 72; Newton, 2013.
97. Pers. comm. Bill Lindsey, 19 May 2014.
98. Conrad, 1995: 126; Taylor, 2002: 7.
99. Conrad, 1995: 126; Barnett, 2012; Spivak, 2012.
100. Conrad, 1995: 20-1, 22-4.
101. Black, 2010: 59.
102. Pers. Comm. Bill Lindsey, 17 May 2014.
103. Lockhart, 2012.
104. *The Statesman*, 13 September 1940.
105. Pers. comm. Bill Lindsey, 29 June 2014.
106. Brander, 1996: 97.
107. Hamilton, 114: 1961; Arthur, 2008: 58.
108. Gerth, 2006: 55.
109. See: www.sha.org/bottle/wine.htm#Hock or Rhine shape.
110. *Gairsoppa* inv. no. TUR-12-90133-BE.

6

THE ROYAL MAIL AT SEA

CHRIS TAFT

Beginnings

The SS *Gairsoppa* was nearing the end of its voyage from India to Britain when she sunk. Amongst its cargo were bundles of letters destined for all over Britain and for onward transmission to the United States of America. The postal system was a vital lifeline for people separated by distance and at times of war this need to communicate became even more important. The postal system had a strong association with the sea and mail as carrying cargo on ships had been happening even before the formalisation of the postal system in Britain.

The fifteenth century saw the formalisation of a state run postal system. Under the reign of Henry VIII the position of Master of Posts was established to take control of the running of the royal messenger system. Brian Tuke was the first person appointed to this new role and one of the first things he initiated was to formalise and control the key routes post travelled over. Post Roads from London were established, linking the capital with key parts of the kingdom. This road network, which built in some cases on the earlier Roman roads, also went on to become the basis of the trunk roads in Britain still used today. The first two routes established were to the north and south of London. The south route, vital for the continental mails, follows almost exactly what is today the A2 linking London and Dover. Henry VIII's troubled history with mainland Europe meant the postal link to France and onward to Rome was key. Tuke therefore ensured this route was working most efficiently and the Dover Road became the most important in the country.

The priority of the Dover Road in the very earliest days of the formalised postal system showed the importance of seaborne mail. Dover obviously offered the shortest and quickest route to France. However, it was not the easiest route at times. Dover was Britain's main sea port and there was therefore a lot of competing demands. The

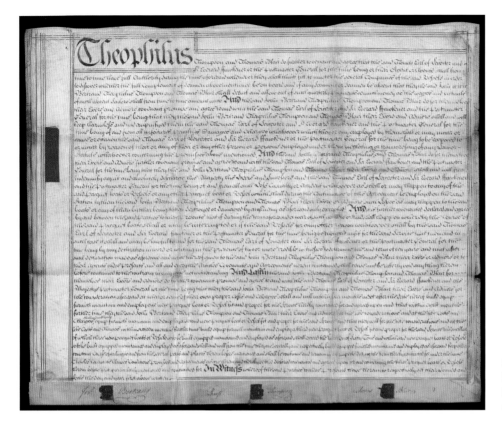

fledgling Royal Navy was obviously using it, as were merchant shippers. The postal service often found itself not a priority.

As trade with the known world began to expand, so too did the need for a reliable system of sending mail by sea. In 1688 the post office established a base at the small town of Falmouth to establish a packet boat service. Falmouth was a sparsely populated town free from the commercial and military use of some of the more established ports on the south coast. The post office hired two packet boats from Daniel Gwyn, who was paid a salary of £70 per annum for providing this service. Falmouth's location in the far southwest gave it quick and easy access to the Atlantic and it quickly expanded following the post office's arrival. In 1688 the main trade was with Spain and the packet boat service established regular journeys to the strategically important port of A Coruña in the north of the country. By 1707 packets from Falmouth were established to Barbados, Jamaica and certain southern states of North America. Falmouth, after the arrival of the post office, quickly became the most important port of the packet boat service.[1]

Packet services to Europe and the West Indies were obviously key for trade and international relations, but arguably even more important were services needed to interconnect the British Isles. The first packet station established by the post office, even before Falmouth, was at Holyhead in the sixteenth century for mail to Dublin. This was later supplemented by services from Milford Haven to Waterford and Portpatrick in Scotland to Donaghadee.

These services were operated under contract with private companies providing the vessels. The Postal Museum holds one such contract dated 15 December 1748 between the Postmaster General and John Bertrand, Theophilus Thompson and Thomas Blair for three vessels called the *Earl of Leicester*, the *Fawkener* and the *Wyvill*. The contract offered payment of £900 per annum and required a service three times a week.[2]

In the early nineteenth century, as the industrial revolution began to transform and speed up industry across the country, the subsequent rise in steam power meant a greater number of faster vessels began to emerge. This led to an increase in companies offering carriage across the seas and meant private companies were beginning to unofficially offer services to carry mail. This infringement of the Post Office's monopoly led to a number of changes in management of the postal system and for the carriage of mail by sea, causing the Post Office to control its own steam packet ships, the *Meteor* and *Lightning*. The *Meteor* first sailed from Holyhead on 31 May 1821.[3] By running its own ships, the Post Office hoped to bring down the costs associated with the service.

By 1836, twenty-six steam packet ships were in operation around the coast, including from Dover, Milford Haven and Liverpool. Despite a rise in operational complexity and the start of the Post Office's own ships, the organisation was not really well prepared for managing maritime business. In 1790 an Inspector of Packets was introduced to try and improve the system, but by 1823 some Falmouth packet services were being taken over by the Admiralty. After a series of government enquiries, in 1837 all packet operations were handed over to the Admiralty until 1860.

Under Admiralty control more contracts were let to private commercial shipping companies for the carriage of mail. When control of the packet service was handed back to the Post Office in 1860, the practice of using commercial companies was expanded. The government, however, maintained control over the arrangement and from 1860

6.2. A ship letter of 1822 from Calcutta to England, transhipped to Madeira, stamped 'India Letter. Plymouth Dock'.

6.3. A ship letter of 1840 for Malta sent via Falmouth.

VOICES FROM THE DEEP

6.4. Memorial in Falmouth to the Packet Boat Service.

6.5. One of the first two Post Office owned steam ships, the *Lightning*, launched in 1821.

all the contracts that were let for conveyance of mail by sea needed the approval of the House of Commons.[4]

From 1860 onwards the Post Office began issuing a number of contracts to commercial shipping companies for the conveyance of mails to ports around the globe. The Postal Museum holds examples of these and from them it is possible to trace the expansion of trade with countries worldwide as more and more contracts were let. The first contract held in the Royal Mail Archive with the British India Steam Navigation Company (BISN) – which later operated the *Gairsoppa* – is dated 20 December 1872 and was for the conveyance of mails via Aden and Zanzibar and onward to London.[5] Whilst the contracts were overseen by Parliament and operated by private companies, it was very much the responsibility of the Post Office to manage the schedules for the service; indeed this was the case even prior to 1860 while the Admiralty had control.

The schedules were set by the Post Office to fit with the requirements and volumes of post on route. On 23 October 1876, the Postmaster General wrote to the directors of the BISN to agree a new timetable from Aden to Zanzibar. The shipping companies maintained logs of their journeys and submitted abstracts of these to the Post Office for review. On 9 February 1876, for example, the Post Office wrote to the Director of BISN to query why the hour of departure from Aden was omitted from the abstract for the ships *Punjab* and *Akola* and to request that these logs be resubmitted.[6]

Ships carrying mail under contract to the Royal Mail were entitled to use the designation RMS, generally referring to Royal Mail Steamer or Royal Mail Ship. The designation was introduced in the nineteenth century, but was not granted to all ships that carried mail, only those specifically contracted.[7] The *Gairsoppa* was a general cargo vessel and never officially designated as an RMS ship and thus would not have carried the Royal insignia or flown an RMS flag. Flags were used even before the introduction of the RMS designation to show that a vessel was carrying mail, and not on war service, to try and avoid being attacked. A flag known as the 'Post Boy Jack' was used, which featured the Union Flag alongside an image of a post boy on horseback.

The Peninsular and Oriental Steam Navigation Company (P&O) was the first to be granted contracts for the carriage of mail to India around 1815.[8] The earliest contract for mails to India held by The Postal Museum, however, dates later to 18 March 1887.[9] P&O became the principal contractor operating on the Indian routes and in their initial contract provision was made for the company to provide accommodation and food for postal sorters who were provided by the Post Office and employed to sort and prepare the mail on route. The contract awarded P&O £265,000 per year, but very tight penalties were in place for any failings, including lateness.

The contract noted expected journey times on the Bombay to Brindisi (Italy) route. The route, via the Suez Canal, was expected to take 392 hours during the monsoon season. Outside of that period it was reduced to 344 hours. This included an allowance for stopping at Aden and thirty hours for getting through the Suez Canal. Whilst the contracts were very specific in their nature, they did build in a certain allowance for changes that were at times necessitated. Brindisi, for example, could be substituted for Salonica, although only with six months' notice to the government.[10]

The London and Zanzibar mail contract, awarded to the British India Steam Navigation Company, even specified the desired speed, this being not less than 10 knots.[11] In the ensuing years the number of contractors operating over the different routes changed and new routes were established as necessity demanded. The opening of the Suez Canal in 1869 greatly sped up logistics and opened the market to even more contractors.

The postal business was expanding rapidly in the nineteenth century thanks in large part to the postal reform of the 1830s. Social mail was on the increase and was now forming a part of the cargo for ships, rather than business mail that dominated before then. Social mail going abroad reached its peak at times of war.

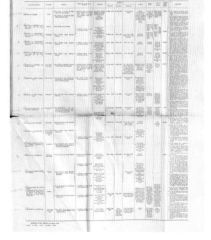

6.6. Reproduction of a design for a 'Post Boy Jack' flag flown by Royal Mail ships.

6.7. Abstract of mail contracts with shipping routes c. 1897.

VOICES FROM THE DEEP

Going To War

During the Boer War postal staff were sent to help establish postal services in South Africa, so that troops fighting abroad could correspond with home. By the outbreak of the First World War in 1914, the importance of mail for soldiers, sailors and airmen reached a completely new scale. Mail was so important for troops' morale, as well as ensuring loved ones at home could hear from those fighting abroad and know they were safe. The logistics associated with sending mail was an incredible task. Whilst the 1914-1918 war is seen perhaps as a fairly static affair, in reality troops were regularly moving around. The war was global, with much of it fought from ships. It was impossible, therefore, for those at home to always know where their family members were serving. Not only did people move regularly, but the importance of safeguarding military strategic knowledge meant people could not include details of their locations within letters. It was up to the post office to attempt to get mail to a moving target.

The system that was established during the First World War was later built on for the Second. During World War I people writing from home to those at war would send their letters addressed to the name, rank, number and regiment of the recipient at the GPO London. The GPO (General Post Office) established a postal depot purely to deal with the mail to theatres of war. Initially this depot was within the existing postal building in London, but such was the expansion of the volume of letters sent that bigger and bigger premises were needed and the final option was to create a purpose built temporary sorting office. The Home Depot, as it was known, was built in The Regent's Park, London, and at the time was the largest wooden building in the world. At the peak of the First World War around 1917, the Depot handled around 12 million letters a week. Within the Home Depot, postal sorters held highly sensitive information on the latest position of military units and ships. They would then determine the location letters and parcels would be sent to in order to reach their recipients. Throughout the war this system was gradually refined and so by 1939 the basis for an efficient system was already in place.

World War II

During the Second World War the logistical exercise was arguably even greater as more theatres of war opened up on an even wider scale and the war became faster paced and embraced more developing technology. The Post Office, however, had the benefit of experience and on declaration of war immediately began to put into place plans drawn up beforehand.

With war looming on 23 August 1939, a section known as the Home Depot was opened at Mount Pleasant designed to operate much as the Depot in Regent's Park had in the

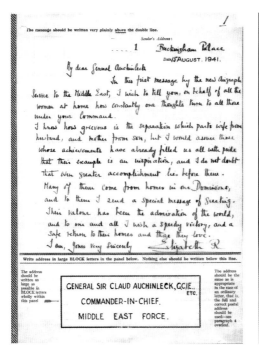

6.8. Inaugural Middle East airgraph sent by Queen Elizabeth II, August 1941.

6.9. Airgraph advertising poster, 1943.

first war. It was rapidly apparent that there was insufficient space at Mount Pleasant and on 16 September, shortly after the war started, the Home Depot was moved to Reading. This office, however, was also too small and the GPO then suggested two alternative sites, one at Nottingham and another at Bournemouth. Bournemouth was selected due to its proximity to the south coast port of Southampton and its Home Depot was opened on 1 December 1939.

After the fall of France in 1940, the value of the suddenly far more dangerous south coast channel ports was lessened for postal ships and Glasgow and Liverpool become the main ports used for the dispatch of mails and other cargo to the war. With this shift, in May 1941 the Home Depot moved once more, this time to the alternative site offered in 1939 at Nottingham. The Depot then remained there, although it continued to expand until 1948, being renamed the Home Postal Centre in 1942. Eventually the Depot occupied over 140 buildings in Nottingham.[12]

The logistical operation for sorting the mail was not dissimilar to the First World War, only on a larger scale, as by now more ports were being used. The post office produced what was known as the 'Daily List'. As the name suggested, these were issued each day and listed the destinations, the routes ships would take, the name of the ship, the 'outport office of exchange' and the latest time for post to reach the office of exchange before a ship would sail. From the Home Depot the mail would be sorted as to world destination and the Daily Lists consulted to determine the office of exchange. By way of example, mail for India would usually sail from Liverpool. The Daily List would indicate which ship would next be sailing for India and would state the time mail needed to arrive at the office. An office of exchange was effectively a GPO sorting office that acted as the final handover point for mail from the Post Office to the shipping company.[13]

The information contained within the Daily List was obviously highly confidential and a very closely guarded secret. Before the war the name of the ship the bags of mail were destined for was written on a label tied to the neck of the bag. However, in war this practice was discontinued and instead that information was sent by coded telegram. An entire language of code was developed for the postal service to ensure information about ship movements and destinations did not fall into enemy hands. Each port had a code name: Dover was 'LAPSUS' and mail being sent by train was marked 'FIAT', while 'BELLA' was used to indicate 'Mails For'. 'BELLA LAPSUS' therefore was 'Mails for Dover'.[14]

The global reach of the war and importance of letters meant that as much effort as possible was taken to get mails onto any ship possible. Wherever there was space, mails would be loaded and it is in this role that the *Gairsoppa* would have taken mail as she was never designated as a formal Royal Mail Ship. Such was the importance of the mails getting through, however, that every opportunity was seized.

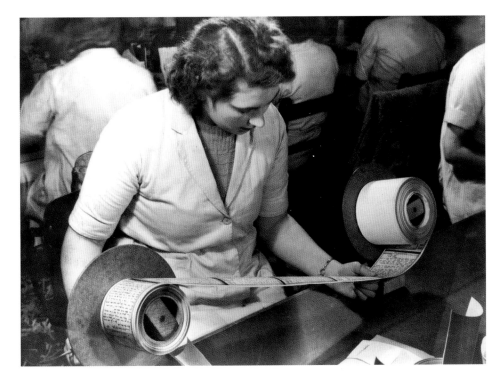

6.10. Airgraph film being processed at the Kodak Factory, 1940s.

The biggest change, and the one that had the greatest impact for mails by sea in World War II, was the routes they were forced to take. The opening of the Suez Canal in 1869 offered a massive saving of time from the previous route of sailing around the Cape of Good Hope. The war, however, took away the option of using the Mediterranean and so once more ships carrying post had to make the much longer journey around the Cape. This is the route that was taken by the *Gairsoppa* on its final voyage and the one used throughout the war by all mail ships. While a safer route in respect of attack, it significantly increased the time it took to move the mail. Transit times for mail ships from India to Britain taking this route were seventy-six and a half days. Airmail, though, was not much quicker at fifty-four days because as well as often flying complex routes, mail had to compete with other airborne cargo.[15]

Mail also took up a lot of space in aircraft and at time of war this proved problematic. Consequently, during the war a new way of sending letters was found that relieved the pressure both on aircraft space and also offered a much quicker alternative to ships. The Airgraph was a new technology introduced in January 1941. Rather than sending traditional letters, correspondents would write their letter onto specially provided forms. These forms were then photographed to microfilm and transported as reels of film to their destination, where they were developed before being delivered to the recipient. This saved a huge amount of space and weight on aircraft and meant letters could now be sent via the much speedier air routes. The transit time for an airgraph from India was fourteen and a half days. Some 1,600 letters on a reel would weigh just 5oz, compared with 50 lbs for the same number of written letters. In the four years of the airgraph service, 135,224,250 airgraphs were sent. The service ended on 31 July 1945.[16]

Despite the advantages of the airgraph, however, many ships continued to carry post as well, such were the volumes being sent. Ships had been the primary means of carrying mail for over 500 years and only once airmail began to become a viable alternative in the 1930s did its use properly begin to decline. Mail by sea, therefore, has always been a vital part of the story of Britain's postal service.

Just how much mail the *Gairsoppa* carried in December 1940 remains a mystery. British India Steam Navigation Co. records carefully listed the number of sacks of mail and packages travelling on their vessels to and from India. She turns up transporting mails from Madras to Rangoon on 12 August 1940. Strangely, the case of the *Gairsoppa*'s last voyage is mute, however: she is omitted from BISN paperwork, presumably due to intelligence restrictions around her silver cargo.

During the war, the BISN ship the *Strathallan* left Calcutta for the UK in 1940 via the Cape on 7 September with 130 bags of mail and 172 bags of parcel post, while the *Narkunda* sailed on the same route on 17 September 1940 carrying 191 bags of mail and 238 of parcel post. The *Somali*, which on its next voyage out transported a second cargo of 3 million ounces of silver ordered from India at the same time as the *Gairsoppa* in November 1940, took on board just thirty-two bags of mail and thirty-three of parcel post on 12 October.[17] Close to the date of the *Gairsoppa*'s final voyage, the *Theseus* left Africa for the UK on 8 November with 145 bags of mail and seventy-four of parcel post.

As one of the last BISN ships to leave India for Britain before Christmas 1940, perhaps the *Gairsoppa*'s hold included a little more mail than normal as writers made a last attempt to post home before the year's end.

Notes

1. Norway, 1895: 1-8.
2. The Postal Museum, London: POST 12/1. Contract to build, supply, equip, maintain and operate three packet boats.
3. The Postal Museum, London: POST 4/30. Holyhead Packet Station: Steam Packet Stores: The Agent's Monthly Record of Expenditure.
4. The Postal Museum, London: POST 114/56. United Kingdom & Foreign & Colonial Mails by Sea.
5. The Postal Museum, London: POST 51/51. Copies of Contracts between Postmaster General, The British India Steam Navigation Company and the Secretary of State for India in Council.
6. The Postal Museum, London: POST 48/309. Contract Packet Letter Book.
7. The Postal Museum, London: POST 122/2066. Royal Mail Pennant: Design and Regulations for Use.
8. Robinson, 1964: 108.
9. The Postal Museum, London: POST 114/56. United Kingdom & Foreign & Colonial Mails by Sea.
10. The Postal Museum, London: POST 114/56. United Kingdom & Foreign & Colonial Mails by Sea.
11. The Postal Museum, London: POST 114/56. United Kingdom & Foreign & Colonial Mails by Sea.
12. Proud, 1982: 29.
13. The Postal Museum, London: POST 56/81. Notes on the conveyance of mail by sea during the war.
14. The Postal Museum, London: POST 56/81. Notes on the conveyance of mail by sea during the war.
15. The Postal Museum, London: POST 47/1024. Army Postal Service Suring the Second World War: Collected Papers.
16. The Postal Museum, London: POST 50/18. Airgraph Service. A History 1945.
17. National Maritime Museum, Greenwich, BIS/7/115. Correspondence regarding mail contract, British India Steam Navigation Company Ltd 1938-46.

7

FROM MUSH TO MIRACLE: CONSERVING THE GAIRSOPPA POST

GRETEL EVANS & NATALIE MITCHELL

Introduction

It was the end of the day in the summer of 2013 when a call came through to the conservation laboratory at AOC Archaeology in Edinburgh – an urgent request for us to take receipt of a large consignment of marine artefacts arriving the next day. Fortunately, we were primed as we had space in our cold storage facilities, the conservation expertise and the freeze-drying equipment to ensure we could deal with the waterlogged assemblage.

The arrival of five large plastic tubs of shipwreck finds in seawater was accompanied by an unforgettable pungent odour. Any aroma of the sea was overpowered by the sulphurous eggy smell emanating from the black murky water that held the artefacts. It was vital to keep the finds wet and prevent them from drying out, which would lead to rapid decay.

Once they were safely stored in cold conditions to prevent microbial growth and slow down any deterioration, the first and foremost job was to carry out a conservation assessment. This would seek to establish what objects were present, the condition of the material, and allow us to develop the most appropriate conservation treatments to stabilise the objects while extracting the maximum amount of historical information from them.

Delving in to the filthy, foul-smelling water to dig out the finds was not a pleasant task, but it was balanced by the wonderful experience of pulling surprises from the depths. Personal belongings were common with leather shoes, wallets, books and even a lady's compact present – this gave an eerie aspect to the assessment, as these were once people's possessions, who were now no longer here. Four small tins provided

7.1. Opening letters and cards from the wreck of the *Gairsoppa* at AOC Archaeology, Edinburgh.

excitement as they appeared to still house their original contents, although the labels were barely legible. A handful of Indian copper coins would provide their own evidence of their original home. There was even a roll of 16-millimetre camera film, tangled but tempting for the possibility of what images it might reveal. Other objects indicated the more commercial nature of the shipwreck's contents: a roll of tartan cloth, samples of mica from the cargo and a large roll of paper plans.

And then there were the bundles and bundles of mush... sludgy black bundles of slimy paper, not nearly so exciting as the objects – or so we thought at the time.

Preservation

The condition of the artefacts was quite surprising given that they had lain on the seabed at a depth of 4,700 metres for over 70 years. Except for the roll of paper plans, which had already dried out, all the artefacts were waterlogged and most covered in black slimy deposits. There was little corrosion of the metal items, the organic materials such as the textiles and leather were in reasonable condition, and although staining from the corrosion of iron components was evident, it was not surprising. The reasonable condition of much of the material may be attributable to the depth at which they were immersed. Below 4,000 metres the marine environment is dark, and low temperature with reduced oxygen levels leads to a slowing of the chemical processes involved in degradation. The material in worst condition were the nineteen bundles of paper items. Many were extremely degraded and fragile, others retained their form better and could be seen to be legible. All were covered in the black slime from the deep, and it was this that created the stench of bad eggs – most likely the result of sulfate-reducing bacteria, which oxidise organic compounds while reducing sulfate to hydrogen sulfide, so producing the smell of rotten eggs.

The initial stage of conservation for all the material was the same: desalination was required to remove as much of the damaging salts from the objects before they were dried out. Salts can be particularly destructive to many materials such as metals, stone and organic materials. If not removed completely, salts will promote the degradation of materials over time. The desalination technique involved soaking the objects in successive changes of fresh water to remove the concentration of salts in the materials by the action of osmosis. It is a slow process taking weeks and months depending on the volume of material and other factors, such as temperature and agitation of the water. Its progress can be measured by testing the conductivity of the wash water because the conductivity reduces when the water becomes purer as it contains less salt.

To give an example, the conductivity of the water holding the objects when they arrived for conservation measured off the scale of the conductivity meter (over 1,999 µSiemens/cm), whereas the conductivity of tap water in Scotland can be around 70 µSiemens/cm and deionised water lower than 1µSiemens/cm. Desalination of the finds also offered the opportunity to carry out gentle cleaning to remove soiling and the black slimy deposits from the bacteria.

7.2. Tartan textile samples and 'Made In British India' labels posted via the *Gairsoppa* (TUR-13-00059).

As part of the conservation process the metal artefacts underwent x-radiography to reveal further information. Investigation aimed to reveal the presence of contents in the small tins, the construction of the lady's make-up compact and legends on the coins.

Once desalination of the artefacts was complete and the majority of the salts removed, conservation treatments aimed at stabilisation were undertaken. Metal items were dried using organic solvents to reduce the possibility of rusting. Leather items were stabilised using a freeze-drier, a machine which removes free water under low-temperature vacuum by the process of sublimation, so preventing shrinking and damage to the leather, which may occur through natural air-drying. The cloth was unrolled, sponged down and air-dried to reveal a collection of samples of different tartans – most fitting that they should end up in Scotland.

Conservation of the roll of paper plans revealed designs for a large hotel on Bahrain, drawn up by BAPCO (the Bahrain Petroleum Company), together with weather charts relating to the area.

At this stage in the conservation programme, the many bundles of paper items were still undergoing desalination. The volume of the material, and the tightly packed nature of the bundles, necessitated a longer desalination period compared to the rest of the assemblage.

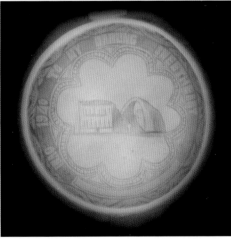

7.3. A lady's compact engraved with the initials 'VH' on the front. On the other side, x-ray revealed the text 'Iraq. 1940. To My Darling Sweetheart' (TUR-13-00065, Diameter 6.2cm).

Conserving the Post

The original treatment plan for the bundles of mushy paper was freeze-drying, which initially appeared to be the most appropriate way to process such a large volume of degraded material. There was a large volume of material – nineteen bundles, around 10 centimetres in depth, a mix of letters and documents – in effect hundreds of individual items. However, during discussions with paper conservator Helen Creasey it was suggested that there may be another way to process them, the advantage being that they could be opened up, unfolded and read. The feasibility of this needed to be explored and so Helen demonstrated a technique that might work.

7.4. A batch of business and personal letters en route to Boston and New York, before conservation (TUR-13-00078).

The basic method involved 'floating' a letter open, using a water bath to support the weight of the fragile paper as it was removed carefully from its envelope. The folded letter was then teased open in the water using a layer of Bondina (a non-woven polyester material) as a support, which then aided the removal of the fragile unfolded letter from the water bath; letters and envelopes were then air-dried and pressed flat under a weight for a period of time.

Good results were achieved with the trial experiments, but the technique was time-consuming and needed to be scaled up to process such a large volume of material. The technique was refined and developed to allow the hundreds of letters to be processed. Practical considerations, such as the amount of space needed to process and dry large volumes of this material in a busy conservation laboratory, together with recording, photographing and tracking each individual piece of paper, presented challenges. A numbering system was developed which would allow the various components of each letter to be recorded individually, but also to relate them to each other. One item could comprise an envelope, stamp(s) and several individual leaves of paper; every individual component was photographed. It was a large and logistically complex treatment, but the results were astonishing. The majority of the correspondence was clearly legible, addresses on envelopes were clear, even images on postcards and some photographs were visible.

Working on the conservation of the material evoked strong physical and emotional responses. One conservator recalled the sulphurous smell and the gelatinous texture

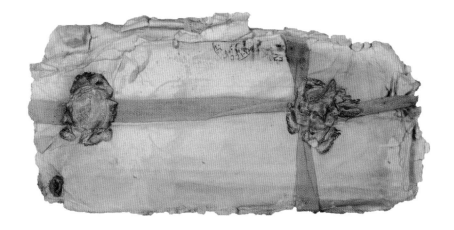

7.5. Letters from the Tata Iron & Steel Co., Tatanagar, Jamshedpur to New York, after conservation (Letters TUR-13-00079-42).

of the mushy paper. The degraded cellulosic slime, which covered a bundle when first extracted from the desalination bath, was most unpleasant. When this was washed away, the blackened surfaces of the compacted bundles were revealed and the painstaking process to separate the letters began. The outer letters in a bundle were usually in such poor fragmented condition that they could not be saved. But on separating the papers, and leaving them overnight in a final rinse water bath, the blackened surfaces reduced to reveal the historical handwriting and secrets of the past.

The feelings one conservator experienced when working on the personal correspondence are captured below:

> I remember opening each letter being like developing a photo you haven't taken. Not knowing what to expect as the blackened surfaces lightened before our eyes, very gently at first, to the extent you could blame the experience on a trick of the light. Over several more minutes the faintest inked writing would begin to appear. It was always exciting to return the next day to see the letters for the first time, our curiosity peeked by what we had seen the day before had now turned into pages of beautiful calligraphy, exotic postcards of India, Christmas cards, photographs and more.

> But this was also the first time anyone had seen these letters since the day their envelopes and fate were sealed and excitement for seeing what had appeared turned into reflection on the people involved, the letter almost secondary to this. As you read a letter intended for a loved one, a Christmas card or party invitation, it was impossible not to think about the person sending it. Who were they? What were they doing at the time? What were they feeling? And who was this person they were sending it to? What was the outcome of their letter never being received? It felt like snooping at times – seeing these personal documents, even though a lot of the letters had actually already been snooped on, the 'Opened By Censor' stamps still intact. With the high volume of letters to process, we kept the reading of them minimal, focusing on the task at hand. Taking a professional approach somehow made for a more sympathetic one.

Each letter carefully looked after, each postcard or Christmas card joyfully appreciated but not overstepping our familiarity with the material and devouring its contents.

The emotional engagement experienced while conserving the assemblage of artefacts salvaged from the SS *Gairsoppa* was felt by all who came in to contact with the project. It was a privilege to be involved in revealing the secrets held by the deep-sea shipwreck, told through the personal letters and belongings preserved below the waves.

7.6. Rolls of the British India newspaper *The Statesman* posted on the *Gairsoppa*.

8

VOICES FROM THE DEEP. DAILY LIFE, GOD & COUNTRY

SEAN KINGSLEY

*Out here we feel rather that we are fiddling while Rome is burning –
as we lead such normal & undisturbed lives.*

– Elizabeth and Henry Willmartt, Indian Civil Service,
Ranikhet to Betty McArdle, Exeter, 6 November 1940

In a slower age before smart phones, the Internet and the bustle of FedEx, millions of letters criss-crossed the world's oceans every month. Steel hulls were the only efficient means of mass communication between the world wars. For all this human endeavour, the 717 pieces of written correspondence recovered from the wreck of the *Gairsoppa* are the only collection of letters lost at sea to surface since antiquity.[1] Stowed alongside the Indian silver, tea and iron so desperately needed by war-torn Britain, seven decades late the *Gairsoppa*'s letters are the wreck's real treasure.

The forgotten voices from the deep, bundled up by the Royal Mail for delivery in London, southwest England, Edinburgh and California, range from dignitaries to the man on the street. At the bottom of the sea the words of the Maharajadhiraja Bahadur of Burdwan, Captain H.G. Quaritch Wales, a former advisor to the royal court of Siam and a pioneer in the history of Southeast Asia, and British army majors intermingled with the voices of soldiers, government officials, their wives and children, teachers, missionaries and businessmen. The shifting tide of war and the final years of empire are captured in these intimate words as the resourceful Raj stood at a crossroads between the old world and modernity.

The *Gairsoppa* post covers the full compass of the human spirit – fear and tragedy, hope, humour and love – at a time when emotions were particularly tender. Christmas 1940 was just three weeks away when the steamship left Calcutta on 5 December. "Amidst the gloom and anxiety of the War one must not forget to send good-wishes to one's friends during Christmas and the coming year", the Maharajadhiraja Bahadur of Burdwan (Sir Bijay Chand Mahtab) wrote to various friends.[2] "At this time of Storm and Stress, I wish I could know where you are and how you do. Please send me a line in reply", N.G. Kurien asked the Reverend John Perret at Staunton City Warren Rectory in Highworth, Wiltshire.[3] Between the lines all the writers fought valiantly to keep a stiff upper lip, insulating as far as possible families, friends and loved ones from pain and suffering. Many failed.

The letters' contents are described in two chapters through the key themes around which the correspondents' words gravitate: daily life, love, faith, war and business. Their words are faithfully reproduced using the post's precise language, grammar and direct quotes. Names and abbreviated addresses of senders and recipients are included where possible, with full references given in the end notes. In many cases these details are partial due to the realities of underwater preservation.

Slow Post

At the end of 1940 fear of an unknown future was prevalent. The combination of all-out war on myriad fronts and Government news censorship starved India from fully understanding Britain's plight. The imagination worked overtime in the idle hours.

Sea post took between two and four months to find a ship and reach its destination and air mail six weeks. Many of the *Gairsoppa*'s letters were posted from England between 24 and 30 September, others as early as 5 September, and were delivered around 20 November.[4] As Private W. Walker of the 1st Wiltshire Regiment in Allahabad wrote to his mother, Mrs A. Walker in Cold Ashton, Wiltshire, "I'm afraid we must all put up with stale news these days… we are lucky to get any letters at all".[5]

The mail was so erratic that numerous correspondents constantly feared the India-bound mail had been sunk. Confirmation to the contrary was joyfully received. Major K. Guy of the Rajputana Rifles was relieved to learn that his son, "My Dear old Porker", safely received his birthday present after three months "rather than feeding the fishes somewhere between here and England!"[6] Kitty Jenkins, teaching at St Agnes' U.P. School in the jungle of Ranchi, admitted finding it "difficult to write to loved-ones in England, nowadays, as we do not know when or how letters will arrive, nor under what circumstances you will be in when the letters do arrive".[7] To make matters worse, and added to the uncertainty of sea mail, was the rising cost of postage. From 1 December

1940, a heavier rate was introduced in India,[8] so that sending a letter to England went up by 1 anna to 3½ annas, the equivalent of 4d.[9]

Even after the mail got through, the blinkered reality was anguishing. Writing about the particulars of war was forbidden and risked falling foul of the censor's beady eye. "One must not discuss anything regarding war that would be useful to the enemy", Mrs E. Melbourne emphasized from the Royal Hotel at Barrackpore in Bengal. From Jubbulpore, Sgm. Wills also advised "My Darling Adorable Precious Little Shop Girl Wife" in Plymouth, Devon, that he had not written much because he did not want the censor reading his private thoughts.[10] Most of the mail to England, however, travelled unopened and marked on envelopes 'Passed By Censor'. Letters to Scotland and America, by comparison, were 'Opened By Censor'.

8.1. A Christmas card from John David and the boys, Calcutta to Mr and Mrs Park, Exmouth (Letter TUR-13-00088-39).

8.2. Anonymous Christmas card (Letter TUR-13-00088-38).

Eager recipients at least felt relieved by the simple news that a loved one was bearing up, but were otherwise left grasping at straws, reading between the lines. Posting photos to England was prohibited as well.[11] Most writers fortunately ignored the rules and wrote passionately about life in India and their feelings of war and life, even sending photos, which in cases – worn and eroded – survived beneath the Atlantic's waves.

Out in India British expats read the papers, but mostly crowded around the wireless for daily news. Newspapers arrived as irregularly as the post. Both Bandsman Fred Manning with the Devonshire Regiment in Waziristan and Sergeant Wills in Jubbulpore managed to secure an overseas *Daily Mirror* once a month.[12] Dorothy Matheson was delighted to receive an overseas *Daily Mail*.[13] Papers that did get through were emblazoned with terrifying photographs of buildings reduced to rubble by Nazi air raids, but for the sake of national security the bombed-out cities were not named. Relations a world away feared the worst.

"I have never felt the distance of separation as much as I do now", wrote Dot from her Mission in Bihar to May Newnam in Salisbury, closing that "I'm glad our parents have passed on... it would have been awful for them to endure for a second time. This time much worse so."[14] Radio reception could be hit and miss too: up in Shillong "atmospherics and interference" interrupted the wireless from London.[15] Kitty Shaw in Imphal, Manipur State, acknowledged to Mrs M. Luffman in Cludleigh, Devon, that even when you could hear the radio, little true information could be gleaned of bombing back home.[16]

British citizens stationed across the globe in India not only found themselves looking on helplessly as Hitler blitzed England from the air, but felt guilty when they were slow to respond. "The news from home is too dreadful & out here with the exception of war parties... it is difficult to realize the existing horrors in other parts of the world", a letter to Kewman Melville in Edinburgh clarified.[17] An anonymous writer expressed fear at what his family, Mrs Hay and daughter in Edinburgh, would say when they finally received his late letter: "Auntie will probably call me a 'two-timing' chisler and Chris will probably think of a far worse name..." The author had travelled in South Africa, Arabia and India, but hesitated from describing his experiences – "well girls, you would not want me to give away official secrets (Oh, fie, fie!)".[18]

Posting in hope, rather than certainty of a letter reaching its destination, defined the spirit of much mail. Aunt Vi told 'Minnie' Marshall in Burnham-on-Sea in Somerset that she was growing old, finding writing letters more and more difficult and was now merely "hoping this may get to you some day".[19] "All your news is really terrible", Agnes of Oxford Houses in Shillong replied to Maggie Browning in Budleigh Salterton, Devon, before remembering that "When this comes you will be in January, & who knows what will have happened."[20] Working for the SPG Mission in Ranchi, Dot asked dear May "However are you existing under these present awful conditions... I fear that even your – once secluded – little town must be having a bad time also. In fact it seems as if no place in England is safe".[21]

Daily Life

The cycle of life from boat to foreign shore with its novel existence is captured in the letter's lines. Most found the sea voyage to India an adventure. An engineer in Calcutta described his two-month trip from Liverpool to Bombay for Harry and Norah Wills of Dumfries in Scotland. "No doubt you will have been wondering if we are in India yet, or at the bottom of the sea", he opened. Despite some very narrow squeaks with U-boats and raiders, the voyage was nevertheless very pleasant, not least because so much food was available that no one could have imagined a war was raging. Once the ship safely left the very dangerous area – no doubt the northwest Atlantic where the incoming *Gairsoppa* would later be sunk – the crew "erected a swimming pool on one of the well decks, and it was my favourite place for most of the days. The black out at night was the great discomfort, as of course we dare not show a light of any description, not even navigation lights; and the heat in the cabins with the port holes and ventilators clamped down was unbelievable in the tropics. We slept on deck in the finish."[22]

Patricia Anderson from Shillong relayed to Miss F.L. Huth of Edgcott, Somerset, how she recently travelled on the *Stratheden* from Capetown to India under convoy, a beautiful ship with a telephone in the First Class cabins and a very posh band. "We had a raider on our tail, for several nights, and had to zig-zag the whole time", she wrote, adding that "A great many practical jokes were played by use of those telephones. One morning I was awoken by a gramophone record played down the earpiece."[23]

The weary traveller freshly docked in India was typically in for a rude awakening. M. Hammaker from Sholapur told Mrs Frank A. Kirstein in Los Angeles that since arriving on 6 September 1940, after a seven-week journey, no letters from home had arrived and "I really felt quite bewildered and dazed for some time!" His wife, Miriam, had come down with a temperature, while the writer succumbed to malaria and gall stones. "The food here has been a business", the correspondent complained, adding stoically that he had decided "I would live one day at a time and try to see what God's will was for me".[24]

On reaching Calcutta on the SS *Rampontari*, a man working for the Office of the Executive Engineer, Western (Electrical) Division in Bengal, found it strange how the natives slept at night wherever they happened to be when tired, "on the foot paths, road, gutter, on refuse heaps, in fact anywhere. Cows and bulls, which are sacred, also wander wherever they choose." Meanwhile, taxis "dash about 40 M.P.H. together with native carriages, stock carts, donkeys, wandering cows, goats and God knows what", he told Harry and Norah Wills in Dumfries, Scotland.[25]

C.H. Roiddulph, an engineer with the South Indian Railway at Trichinopoly, complained to his daughters, Miss Joan and Daphne Roiddulph at Southlands School in Exmouth, Devon, about recuperating in a rest house for two days. "I have had fever & pains all over the body due to my throat being inflamed", he explained, the malady caused by so much dust in the dry months "and it finds its way down ones throat to the tonsils". The doctor advised that the engineer's liver was not working well.[26]

Because correspondents were so wary of letting secrets slip and censorship, many opening paragraphs toyed with the art of talking about something and nothing, primarily the weather – a favourite British obsession. The days were generally like English

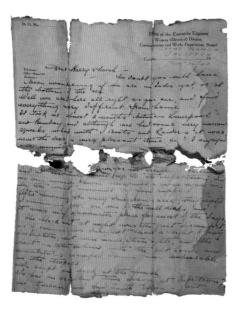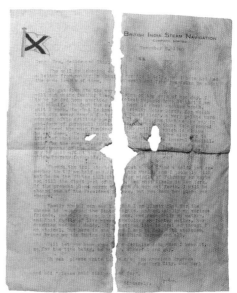

8.3. From Calcutta, a Western Electrical Division employee described his adventurous voyage from Liverpool to Bombay (Letter TUR-13-00043-1).

8.4. John Allen of the California Arabian Standard Oil Company looked forward to getting home to America (Letter TUR-13-00084-11).

summers, but cold at night. From Calcutta, Harry and Flo reported to Father Akell, Bev and Lile in Ash Thomas, Devon, that "While it is bleak & cold home, the sun is shining out here all day through Nov: Dec: Jan: Feb."[27] C. Prior's news from the Oxford Mission in Calcutta to Ottery S. Mary, Devon, recorded how September had been cool, October dry and November warm, which was good for the crops, but so hot that "some wasps wanted to make a nest inside my umbrella."[28]

In Assam the climate was "delightful", basking in about 80 degrees Fahrenheit by day and cold at night.[29] In Barisal in east Bengal, Sister Mary told Arthur E. Eastwood in Taunton how she too was revelling in the beautiful weather, although the thermometer plunged from 89° during the day to 66° at night, perfect for the writer's potted chrysanthemums being watered by dew on the veranda.[30]

In Kashmir the perfect weather was gradually dropping to about 8° Fahrenheit at night with frost and thick ice, G.A. Ostler told his mother in Bath, Somerset, but was still up to 60° – cloudless sunshine – from 8am to 5pm by day, so he could still enjoy an occasional day picnic. The high price of petrol limited distances driven, however.[31] A soldier writing to Mrs George in Kilmington, Devon, was concerned that prices in India had gone up by about 20% since before the war and predicted a minor financial crisis before the end of December 1940.[32]

In Darjeeling for a fortnight, Bill and Mabel Murray confirmed the weather had been grand, but now a thick mist had rolled in. "Must now close, my hands are so cold. I can hardly hold the pen", Mabel ended.[33] Down in Nilgiri in southern India, the monsoon had started and steam and "mist enveloped one".[34] In Valparai to the south of

VOICES FROM THE DEEP

India, heavy afternoon rains had damaged the Ghaut Road and washed away bridges on the Pollachi Road, but otherwise "There have been no scandals."[35] Lines sent to Weeke Barton, Devon, again mentioned the appalling rain in southern India, where the causeway of the Punajur river had been swept away and plague set in.[36]

Just like in Britain the question of what food and stores were available and their cost during war was a major conversation point in the *Gairsoppa* letters. Most correspondents found the way of life cheap. Taxation was considered higher than the cost of living.[37] "Postage & income tax gone up other wise you would hardly know there was a war", Mrs Hélène Maltby informed Mrs Fox near Taunton in Somerset from Calcutta, adding that "One seems to get nearly all the English Stores one wants & I gather we should go on using them to keep the Export trade going."[38]

Other than "much enhanced prices, we have not shared in anything", Mrs E. Melbourne wrote from the Royal Hotel in Barrackpore, Bengal. Rice was plentiful and "cases & cases of stuff have arrived for Xmas" with the slogan "Britain delivers the food".[39] M.S. Murray in Gorakhpur managed to buy 150 cheap oranges in Darjeeling.[40] A correspondent in Champaran, by contrast, told Mary Hudson in Cheltenham how disease had attacked her sugar cane crop, resulting in low prices at market. She was now busy planting for the next two months despite the feeling that "This war is spoiling everything."[41]

Exceptions included alcohol. In Calcutta beer cost "2,2" a bottle, so "we don't have much at the price", Mr and Mrs Bayly in Amesbury were informed.[42] The war of course changed food habits, as Mrs Melbourne's newspaper clippings home show. By the end of November 1940, the Colonial Office had banned banana imports as a non-essential bulky cargo. Another clipping, entitled 'Food Situation In Britain', advised that "Despite shipping losses from enemy action there is no cause for alarm about Britain's winter food situation", but that "The people of Britain must change their habits for the rest of the war… to give up the luxury of fruits like apples, apricots, grapes and bananas", whose space on ships was needed for meat.[43] All in all, "We out here must consider ourselves lucky. With the exception of higher market prices & now an increase in income tax, we hardly realize that a war is in progress", Kitty Shaw admitted to Mrs M. Luffman in Cludleigh, Devon, from Imphal in Manipur State.[44]

Despite feeling very cut off in Shillong due to weeks without letters, anonymous mail posted to the Reverend H.C. Barlow at Plymtree Rectory in Cullompton, Devon, described a father's life in Assam with his children, Philippa aged nine and Caroline aged five:[45]

> And here they are with ample food & no bombs or black-out. The feeling we
> all have out here is that it feels all wrong to be in peace & safety when our
> friends & relations are going through hell… Life is fairly humdrum here, but not
> 'as usual'. India is making a great war effort of which I actually can't tell you
> anything. Gandhi is being merely ridiculous & is ordering all ex-Ministers of

Congress governments to conduct technical offenses & get sent to jail. It was great fun being a minister, but there is not much enthusiasm for martyrdom!

Not everyone felt so splendidly isolated. Elizabeth and Henry Willmartt of Ranikhet felt strange living so quietly, while "England is fighting for her life, in London at any rate". The Indian Civil Service employee and wife reported to Mrs Betty McArdle in Westhay, Exeter, that despite lots of troop movements and Red Cross activities the mountainous districts where Henry was based were particularly cut off from the real world.[46]

In the cities the immediacies of war through threats of a Japanese invasion or air raids were felt more urgently than in the countryside. In Calcutta Tessa told Mr H. Fowler from Tupsley, Hereford, about a five-hour blackout planned from 7pm till 4am and was working out how to screen her drawing room windows with thirty yards of curtains.[47] A black out was also signalled on Willingdon Island on the southwest coast of India for an hour and a half from 9.30pm, after which Harry Cornish went down to check on the wharf as an ARP Warden, his wife in Middle Filham, Devon, learnt. Harry was greatly looking forward to sailing home the month after next because "all good things come to an end they say, but this will be… bad ones".[48]

Working for the British India Steam Navigation Company, D.N. Gill shared these reflections, informing his Darling Mater that he hoped to get home to Paignton, Devon, by the end of February 1941: "I am absolutely fed up with this place. Nothing to do & all day to do it in. Money is a bit short too. It goes nowhere these days."[49] Living an hour away from Calcutta by fast train, Mrs Cathie Hoyle was relieved to have a garden because there was nothing else to do stuck out in the sticks, she informed Auntie Edith Hoghtin in Fisherton, Salisbury. To make matters worse, "There is electricity out here, but no sanitation, i.e. we have thunder boxes." When Cathie did make it to the big city, she was nonplussed: "I find Calcutta very dirty, my hankies are like London, and I can't keep my hands & nails clean five minutes".[50] Sergeant Wills in Jubbulpore found the absence of telephone boxes in India strange.[51]

John A. Allen of the California Arabian Standard Oil Company on Bahrain Island in the Persian Gulf seemingly travelled to India on a British India Steam Navigation Company Ltd liner, but was now looking forward to starting home for America in a month and a half, he explained to Mrs LeRoy Seiler in San Francisco. Allen was plenty glad for the chance to see friends and acquaintances again. "I sometimes like to feel as though I am stoical", he shared, "but here is one time I say to Hell with stoicism, and bring on the States with the Third Termer and all."[52]

The Adorers in the Bishop's House at Ramna in Bengal, generally against a third presidential term but not yet anti-Roosevelt, prayed impartially that America would get the better man.[53] In the American election of 5 November 1940, President Franklin

L. Roosevelt broke with tradition to run for a third term in the shadow of the great depression and the world war and won. A year later he steered the United States into World War II after Japan bombed Pearl Harbour on 7 December 1941.

After Hours

For many correspondents, oblivious to the war or choosing to look on the bright side of life, wartime India was an exotic adventure played out against a backdrop of cheap and plentiful food, fine weather, endless outdoor pursuits and comparative peace far removed from war-ravaged Europe. "There are heaps of things being done out here, Cinema, Shows, Dances, Whist, Bridge & Mah Jong [charity] Drives, as well as Concerts, all for the War Fund", Emma McMullan wrote home. Town and country were a relaxed stage for polo, tennis, golf, football matches, squash, swimming and walking. Familiar relaxation saw writers head to the greyhound races in Bombay or Calcutta to place a bet.[54] Botanical gardens and river boat trips soothed mind and soul in Calcutta.[55]

After recently reaching Shillong on the SS *Stratheden* from Capetown, Patricia Anderson was learning golf and squash from a twenty-four-year-old acting major known as Popeye from the Gurkha Regiment. The hill station of Shillong was pretty gay with cocktail dances and horse races twice a week, learnt Miss F.L. Huth of Edgcott in Somerset, though the jockeys fixed beforehand who would win. Patricia found her 50 rupees a month allowance, excluding club bills, did not go far. She was rehearsing to act in the play 'Elsee Comes to Stay'.[56]

Newly arrived in India to work for Lloyd's Register of Ships, Jock described Bombay to Auntie Maggie Baxter in Edinburgh as a large and rather beautiful city with plenty of open spaces, trees and good shops. Social convention required him to join the golf course 14 miles away, as well as one or two clubs.[57] Mrs F. Brown of Calcutta was a member of the Ladies Golf Course and told her darling

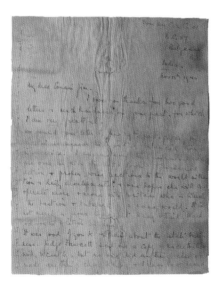

8.5. Barbara in Belgaum told cousin Jim Copp in Los Angeles about running a dance band with her husband, Major 'Cockus' Cox (Letter TUR-13-00085-10).

8.6. A half-anna stamp for the Bombay War Gifts Fund (Letter TUR-13-00086-07).

boys in Beaworthy, Devon, how the coat she made for Kim in dark green wool looks "rather like a sausage", but fitted him well.[58] R. Turner with the Devonshire Regiment stationed at the Jicca Barracks in Dalhousie took home a small cup after winning the final of a table tennis competition.[59] In Assam "Tennis is dead at the moment but we have a small golf course which is my first hobby", Jack B. Ronnlia in the employ of the Indian Foreign Service told Aunt Betty Hutchinson in Winscombe, Somerset. "I am golf secretary at the moment and annoying everyone by putting in new bunkers to catch [them out]", he added mischievously.[60]

A soldier in Peshawur shared his physical pain with his son in Batheaston, Somerset, walking about like a very old man and "all bent and gone in the back" from rheumatism after playing squash. His Hindu cook tried to cure him: he "chants his prayers and benedictions over my back, and waves… a little brush to and fro; I am a little better but whether from the efforts of the Hindu Cook or massage, or the medicine I am taking, or just the passage of time, I do not know!"[61]

The expatriate community kept busy playing hard at clubs, parties and charity drives. A.E. Porter with the Home Department of the Government of Bengal told Mrs Porter of Woodchester, Gloucestershire, how "The season is getting into swing and I find engagements piling up… I drink cocktails with the Bakers on Thursday and I see 'Pinnochio' and dine afterwards with the Blanks".[62] Barbara, the wife of Major 'Cockus' Cox in Belgaum, described how the couple ran a small dance band in which Cockus played the lead saxophone and his wife led the rhythm section with a good American metal guitar played as a tenor banjo.[63]

A surviving programme for an event staged by the McCloysters on 15 November 1940, sent to Mrs G. Brown in Falkirk, included a musical selection by the Royal Berkshire Regiment, the sketch 'Lady Emily Talks Business', Indian Classical Dancing, a performance of the play 'Itch. Thea's Stamp' and ended in time-honoured tradition with God Save the King.[64] Elsewhere, R. Groves circulated an agenda for the Cabul River Lodge of Freemasons, notifying members of a meeting at Nowshera to be attended in evening dress or uniform.[65]

More often than not, social events were staged to raise funds for the war effort. At school at Bowden House (in Seaford), Lesley read how Jeanette was "going tap dance for soldiers and for many Charity entertainments".[66] Lomas of the Imperial Tobacco Co. Ltd of India had been asked to join a sub-committee on children's amusements, such as Punch and Judy shows, for a very big fair at the Baker Club in aid of the War Charities next month, he wrote to his parents, Mrs O. de la H. Moran in Cheltenham.[67] Mrs. J. Mitchell, the wife of a man working for the Attack Oil Co. in Rawalpindi, was waitressing at a Christmas Fair in aid of the Red Cross.[68]

Mr and Mrs McMullan were told how Emma's charity work managed to make 300 rupees from table donations, and 900 total, in a recent event, and how she was knitting for the merchant men and sewing for the Women's Guild. At last Friday's sale of work, opened by Lady Lumly, Emma's children's stall took over 400 rupees and the whole fete earned 3,300 rupees and was reported in the local paper. Along with trips to the Taj Mahal, a focus on charity kept her mind off her husband's failing parcels business.[69]

At Kohar, Mrs Detsulls's letter from the Brigade House to Mrs C. Mackeer in Thorverton, Exeter, announced a tremendous drive taking place to raise funds for aeroplanes and the war generally, although she did not feel people were doing half enough. The chrysanthemum show brought in 300 rupees, half of which went to the Governor's aeroplane fund. Back home the writer hoped "you managed to eat Carol's pudding & didn't get indigestion after it".[70]

From the Mosaboni copper mines in Jharkhand, Ronald told Mr R. Williams of Redruth, Cornwall, how very hard he was working to get the ore out, so had little time to write or feel tired. He was doing his bit, however, having recently played football at Jatanagar for the war fund "and we all had a grand time". He lost four goals to nil to a first-class team and failed to win the big cup, almost 18 inches high and costing 95 rupees, presented by the steelwork manager's wife. On Saturday week he was off to a cricket match against a team from Zatanggar with proceeds again going to the war fund.[71]

Profits from the sale of several Christmas cards among the *Gairsoppa* post were "devoted to Red Cross War Fund for the Alleviation of Distress & Suffering caused by the war", while others decorated with a spitfire went to the East India Fund for British War Services.[72] Three spitfires soaring across half anna stamps issued by the Bombay War Gifts Fund were entitled "Buy This And Help The RAF".[73]

Cinemas were a welcome light relief. The front page of the English language India newspaper *The Statesman* ran 'On The Screen This Week' editorials surrounded by adverts announcing the latest screenings. *Gairsoppa* letters spoke enthusiastically about Shirley Temple's *Blue Bird*,[74] the comedy *Let George Do It* with George Formby,[75] and *I Take This Woman* by Spencer Tracey ("the best actor in Hollywood").[76] A soldier with the 9th Gorkha Rifles regiment and his wife enjoyed in one week *The Middle Watch*, "as funny a film as I've seen… and it did us good to have an uproarious laugh", although Pattie had to shut her eyes to avoid the horrors in the thriller the *Cat and the Canary* so often that she hardly got her money's worth.[77]

A.E. Porter, employed by the Home Department of the Government of Bengal, similarly watched two films in one week. *Hold My Hand* was "a farcical thing that made us laugh a great deal though afterwards when we thought it over there did not seem to be anything much to laugh at", while *All This and Heaven Too*, a leisurely film, was "perhaps a bit long and in places just a bit mawkish, but enjoyable".[78] Major Gerald Lecoss, by comparison, left *Gone with the Wind* in Delhi "not too impressed, and it is far too long".[79]

Animal Friends

Tales of the British love of animals loom large among the *Gairsoppa* mail. From the Exchange in Simla, Peg told Jane how she owned one and a half dogs, the half taken up by one so tiny that it only measured fifteen inches from nose to tail.[80] A letter from the Honnametti coffee estate in south India, heading to Weeke Barton in Devon, described the writer's adorable golden and white cocker spaniel and another golden retriever called Floogee. The writer also befriended "a squirrel which is nearly as much a nuisance as Miowlie, but not so terrifying!"[81] Writing on headed notepaper of her husband's regiment, the Inniskilling 27 at the Haig Barracks at Malappuram, Mrs Boyle told Mrs Lindsay in Edinburgh about her little pet mongoose.[82] A soldier's child in India shared with dear Alma Jack amazement at a parrot's clever tricks at a tea party.[83]

A father staying at the Hotel Cecil, Delhi, repeated a rhyme he heard from old man Jacocks with Darling Cilla Covell in Newquay, Cornwall:[84]

> There was a dachshund once, so long
> He'd not the slightest notion
> [the] time it took to notify
> His tail of an emotion.
> And so it was that while his eyes
> Were full of woe and sadness
> His little tail went wagging on
> Because of previous gladness.

Tessa from Magdala House in Calcutta described a trip with her children to see the sloths, elephants and hippopotamus in

8.7. A Christmas card sold for the East India Fund, British War Services. Sent to Mrs Templer, Edenderry, Chudleigh, Devonshire (Letter TUR-13-00083-18).

8.8. From Nowshera, Dot Matheson told her father and mother, Lady Tweedie at Wraxall House, about fattening turkeys for Christmas and planning to buy a fur coat in Peshawar (Letter TUR-13-00071-43).

VOICES FROM THE DEEP

the zoo. "We had a long chat to the kangaroos – who are very tame & come right up to the bars for monkey nuts", she told Mr H. Fowler of Tupsley, Hereford. "One has a baby in its pouch – the most adorable little thing. If it wiggles about too much & makes mother uncomfortable – she gives it such a slap & pokes it back into the pocket. Pauline thought it very funny".[85] A letter from Darjeeling to Dear Old One looked forward to taking the children to a camp with elephants, despite amused "visions of the children being carried off by man eaters".[86]

Jack B. Ronnlia, busy arranging war supplies in Assam for the Indian Foreign Service, wrote to Aunt Betty Hutchinson in Winscombe, Somerset, about happy plans to take his daughter Jacqueline, a pretty child with flaxen hair and blue eyes devoted to her brother and all animals, on her first elephant ride. After poor old Peter the spaniel had died, the family got a new pet black and white pup called Leon to live alongside their two hill ponies, Punch and Tolery, and eight Rhode Island red chickens, which had just reared seven chicks and laid eight eggs.[87] Parents Mr and Mrs Oakey of Swindon, Wiltshire, meanwhile, learnt from Gladys Clapp in Ootakamund that "My chicken are still off laying – what can be wrong with them perfectly healthy and full of beans, eggs have gone up too from 6 as to 7 as".[88]

On struck-through headed notepaper of the 10th Battalion the Sikh Regiment, Nowshera, Dot Matheson sent news to her mother, Lady Tweedie at Wraxall House, Somerset, of her five dogs and how "We bought a pair of turkeys a few days ago and I have to keep chasing them off the bed… I have just distracted them with a cabbage. We are fattening them for Christmas."[89]

Outward Bounds

India's fine climate and rolling countryside were a wonderful backdrop for an outdoors life that was unimaginable home in dreary Britain. Mrs Cassidy of Ichapur in the Bengal told her father, Commander S.W. Cornish in Trebetheric, Cornwall, how "We still keep the boys tethered for some of the day… but they fairly [run] around when loose".[90] A letter from someone running a hotel, Flagstaff House in Dehra Dun, 8,000 feet above sea level on top of a mountain, spoke of taking the children to the River Song for their first fishing lesson using bamboo poles, "but they soon bored of that as they did not manage to fool any fish".[91]

On holiday from teaching in Simla, Peg told dearest Jane of a trip to Kashmir, where she stayed on a houseboat at a lake with other girls and enjoyed surf-riding behind a motorboat. Despite India being "a hopeless place because distances are so great and it is impossible to meet people except once in a blue moon", Peg hoped to return to Kashmir for a proper trek with friends in the Liddar and Sind valleys.[92]

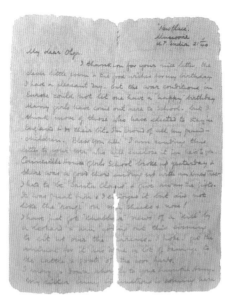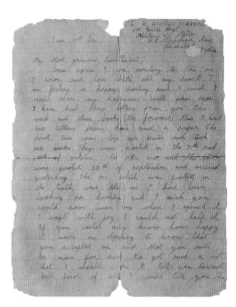

8.9. From Mussoorie, a grandpa planned to hunt a rampant leopard (Letter TUR-13-00083-53).

8.10. Pete Walker with the 1st Wiltshire Regiment in Allahabad wept for joy when Phyll Aldridge of Devizes agreed to marry him (Letter TUR-13-00071-24).

Henry Willmartt, an Assistant Commissioner in Ranikhet, and his wife Elizabeth, recalled for Mrs Goodman in Exeter a trek in September 1940 to the Pindari glacier at the foot of Narda Deri, which leads over the mountains to Tibet. "The scenery was magnificent – very steep mountain sides with rushing rivers in the valleys and shining waterfalls from hanging valleys on either side", they wrote, "then all the trees were taking on their golds & reds for autumn". The local water source was venerated.[93]

Mavis Bass in Durfai Fort, Nowshera, found India a small world by comparison. She wrote with great enthusiasm to Mrs R.C. Edge in Cheltenham of an unexpected encounter and started by thanking her for a cheque, "terribly sweet of you", as a wedding gift. Mrs Bass had been on honeymoon after marrying in a beautiful little church in Naini Tal, motoring to Delhi and Lahore and spending two weeks on a houseboat in Kashmir. Now at Nowshera heading back to the fort, Mavis was out walking one day with Mrs Walker when she spotted a large dog swimming in a river against the current. The newly wed was just about to jump in when a "very nice looking man" rushed up and said the dog was alright, he always does that. After talking, Mrs Walker asked me if he might be a gunner. Mavis felt sure the man was Sylvia Edge's brother because both shared the same mannerisms and speech. Mrs Walker thought she was mad. A few days later at a tennis tournament, Mavis was standing by the umpires table when the same man walked up and said "I am Edge, what do I have to do?" "Life is full of surprises", she concluded.[94]

Dot Matheson excitedly told her mother, Lady Tweedie in Wraxall, Somerset, how the previous Sunday she went to Peshawar in the North-west Frontier for the day and "had the most enormous & marvellous lunch & very nearly bought me a fur coat – the most lovely coats, they come from Russia and are frightfully cheap being duty free." Dot hoped

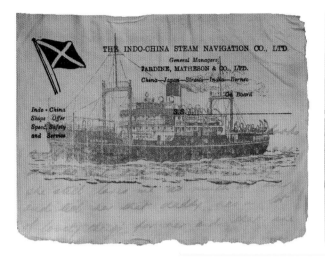

MATRIMONIAL-
HUSBANDS WANTED

WANTED husbands for five young and pretty sisters. (aged 16 to 24). One is daring. One is alluring. One is coy. One is wild. One is wise. You can have your pick. Apply with one anna stamp to Box PAP C|o Daily Gazette for Photo and full particulars of the girls. P. S. Can't afford any dowry.

Their youth and beauty will compensate you for it.

C12

8.11. Sailor Joe Moolem looked forward to his wife's cooking in San Francisco (Letter TUR-13-00084-25).

8.12. Joe Moolem joked whether his wife still loved him or if he should answer an Indian advert for husbands (Letter TUR-13-00084-25(3)).

to buy one the following Sunday on her way to tea at Bara Fort, an outpost miles from anywhere in tribal territory. Her husband Michael, a military officer, was very well and taking years off his life running all over the hills with his men before breakfast and bursting into his wife's room when she was still "fugging in bed and very dim from sleep."[95]

A soldier with the 9 Gorkha Rifles at Ambala in northern India told his mother, Mrs George of Kilmington, Devon, of finding a good new ride for cantering, which left Pattie out of breath from screaming. The couple rode a long way into the country and "the old woman and I could almost imagine the hound hunting." In other news, his garden was full of cornflowers in bloom, crysanths and the carrots, beet and spinach were doing well. In the kitchen, Pattie had baked some scones "which are not so good… I suspect they will become a classic as did a sponge cake you over made in Ragleth House!", the husband signed off.[96]

A grandfather in Mussoorie wrote to Olga of just hearing news of a kill by a leopard and "am going out this evening to sit up over the carcass. I hope I get the animal for it has done a lot of damage to the cattle & goats of the poor herds".[97] Arthur T. Taylor found that the "country around Calcutta is getting very built over and one has to go further afield to get decent jungle rides", and asked Maurice C. Houlder of Wheddon Cross, Somerset, whether Pam was still keeping the Quarme Harriers going "to help hunt down the stray parachutists who may land" and whether the Worcester Park Beagles (running team) were finished because of the war.[98]

Love in A Hot Climate

Keeping old and forging new relationships so far from home took much effort to fill the distance and loneliness in an age of uncertainty. Love blossomed amidst the *Gairsoppa*

BETTE DAVIS

DOROTHY BELLE DUGAN

MYRNA LOY

8.13. Photos of famous female film stars posted from India (Letter TUR-13-00079-39A).

letters. Sheer exuberant joy was felt by Pete W. Walker of the 1st Wiltshire Regiment stationed at Allahabad, who had proposed to Miss Phyll Aldridge in Devizes, Wiltshire, and waited over two months – nervously on tenterhooks – for a reply. Eventually the answer from "My Most Precious Sweetheart", sent on 30 September 1940, reached the soldier on 30 November:[99]

> I wept for joy, I could not help it. If you could only know how happy it made me darling to know that you accepted me and that you will be mine for ever… I felt the happiest man in the world. The other fellows must have thought I'd gone mad… There was no one in the room so I just let myself go. I wept with joy, I laughed, I shouted… I've felt a different man since then dear. I've felt so happy that I have been singing most of the time… I wish I could be there to put the ring on for you… I love you with all my heart darling and I shall be yours for ever.

In a second letter to his mother, Mrs A. Walker of Cold Ashton, Wiltshire, Pete hoped cautiously that "you will not be mad at me for becoming engaged but I had to do something for my darling's 21st birthday". The newly engaged soldier had recently been to another fellow's wedding, to whom he gave a blue and gold cruet set, but "I wish it had been my own… God grant that we shall all be spared to see the day when we get married."[100] Patricia Anderson had also attended a wedding in Shillong, where the police and the padre put up a notice with two L's (for learners) and "England Expects" written on it, so she wrote to Miss F.L. Huth in Edgcott, Somerset.[101]

From camp in Jubbulpore, Sergeant Wills and "My Darling Adorable Precious Little Shop Girl Wife", Mrs D.B. Wills of Plymouth, posted lengthy love letters across the waves. In his response to the wife's forty-one-page letter, the soldier detailed returning from the workshops the night before at 7pm, when one of the lads shouted about two letters waiting on his bed. He dived into its contents, started reading from the back and went to the Mess Hall, but was so excited he could not eat dinner, so came back to the bed "and looked up at your smiling face on the wall and started to read it from beginning to end".

Wills asked what his wife's shop dress was like before advising her to be moderate with her make-up and not to wear high heels because her feet would get sore. He warned against the reputation of Jack Baker, who had stopped to speak to her, before cryptically reminding his wife, "Yes darling I am still a wicked boy and I also know now what you are capable of doing, plus of course the noise you can make". In India, however, Wills was on his best behaviour. He had only drunk three glasses of alcohol since reaching the country and promised not to fall into heavy drinking.

At a recent Signals dance he had two waltzes and a foxtrot with the sergeants' wives, "so everything above board & proper." The bold vanity of 90% of the women being "open" by showing their painted toenails surprised Wills, who noted, "take out the

Half-casts & you would have thought you were back in Blighty". The husband drank two small bar shandies with a corporal and sergeant and "I was in bed by 2-15 coming straight back alone as a true Husband should", when he realised it would be 10am at home, so husband and wife would be praying for each other at the same time "many many miles apart". Wills closed his letter with seven lines of kisses.[102]

From Bombay, en route by sea to China, Joe Moolem managed to compose twenty-eight sides of a letter to his wife in San Francisco on Indo-China Steam Navigation Co. Ltd. notepaper. The sailor looked forward to getting home to America, "definitely before the end of January", not least because "I have been starved for over a year with the terrible cooking on board the ship. I have not tasted meat for months since I have come to India and with rotten cooking it is making it worse". Despite pulling out a tooth, a wisdom tooth from his lower right jaw, forcing him to eat slops, and losing two fingernails, Joe found he had nothing really to complain about.

For a lark, he attached a newspaper clipping from the *Gazette* to his wife advertising:

> Matrimonial Husbands Wanted. Wanted husbands for five young and pretty sisters (aged 16 to 24). One is daring. One is alluring. One is coy. One is wild. One is wise. You can have your pick. Apply with one anna stamp to Box PAP C/O Daily Gazette for Photos and full particulars of the girls. P.S. can't afford any dowry. Their youth and beauty will compensate you for it.

"What do you think about it? Shall I apply for one of them or do you still love me still?", the husband cheekily asked his wife, who had expressed concern in an earlier letter about putting on weight. Better to be a little overweight than underweight, Joe sweetly added, "and as I always say there is always a little more of you to love. I am longing for your love & kisses… Every day that passes brings me nearer to you, my love".[103]

Recuperating from his skin graft operation in the British Military Hospital in Rawalpindi, Rupert Searle told Kath Moon how "I can guess what it is like, these long and dark lonely evenings, with no one to keep you company and love you a little bit in and out. I only wish I was their [sic]… we shall have to make up for it when we are together and burn the lamp light." On the back of his envelope Searle wrote 'SWALK' – Sealed With A Loving Kiss.[104]

In a few lines from Delhi, Major Gerald Lecoss promised his wife in Braunton, Devon, that he will "write to you when I get to Nowpur, in fact I write to you very day, because our love is the only thing I value in the world, & I think of you the whole time".[105] Another soldier told his beloved, Miss M. Thorburn in Edinburgh, that he had spent an hour of thinking of something to say: "oh darling, every letter you send seems to make me want you more and more… all I can say is I love you, that's all I seem to think of maybe its because it's all that matters… and I always shall."[106]

8.14. An Indian water carrier card sent by Sally, Phil and Barbara to the Canadian Bank of Commerce, Los Angeles (Letter TUR-13-00079-18B).

8.15. An Indian snake charmer card sent to San Francisco by the Phelps's (Letter TUR-13-00079-15B).

Far from home, several correspondents shared scandals. A letter signed "Your old pal", working with the Royal Army Medical Corps, defensively asked Ruby Phillips in Bream, Gloucestershire, whether "You have no doubt heard of the local scandal by now of the flirtation concerning Mrs Cumin & myself, well she can go to hell… At the moment women are out of the question".[107]

From the Honnametti coffee estate in southern India, a heart-wrenching letter was winding its way on the *Gairsoppa* to Weeke Barton in Devon, telling a friend that "My dear, I'm afraid there's now little question of me getting engaged or married before you". The writer had left England with a week's notice, only just enough time to get a visa and sailing permit, and spent six weeks travelling by boat to Mumbai, where she was happier than ever before. Now with a broken heart, and nobody to confide in, she poured out her feelings about falling for a naval officer who she met on the ship and spent three days with in Bombay:

> This is the most desperate feeling, & it really is desperate, because its quite hopeless. He's married. Do you think I'm terribly abandoned? I'm not, I promise you, because I haven't hurt anybody, least of all his wife… He was pretty miserable at leaving his wife… I don't see how I can exist the rest of my life without him. He was just perfect for me in every way. He was my ideal of a man to marry. We were so happy together, and so young & gay, and I do so miss being made love to!! I shall never think about caring for anyone else unless I find a man as attractive and charming & thoroughly good... Please don't say a word about this to anyone. Especially your granny… I wish so much I hadn't left England. I wish I was with you all to share in the bombing and everything – Except that if I did I wouldn't have met… I must say all this unhappiness is worth it for all the incredible happiness we had when we were together.

As quickly as it started, the affair ended. "God knows where he is now", the writer admitted. Now she was stuck in a place where she did not know a single soul and everyone had left, except the instructors in an enormous cadet school, but even the cadets worked too hard to be of much use to a girl.[108]

On rare occasions writers shared cynicism at young love. Gladys Clapp in Ootakamund had just learnt with surprise that Eric was getting married back home. "Rather sudden what", he asked, adding "yes it must be very heart breaking when ones family after all one has done for them this life take wings & fly away. I suppose my day will come too. I remember an old lady on the boat, when I returned with June, telling me that it was one of the saddest things in life." The writer offered her mother in Swindon, Wiltshire, optimism at gaining a daughter and to "be thankful… she might have been a typical 'Miss Modern'."[109]

God & Country

Away from the cities, travelling among the distant interior and hills, the missionaries doing God's work were particularly isolated from home news. As C. Prior working with the Oxford Mission in Calcutta admitted to Ottery St Mary in Devon, "I take it on trust that there is a war on, as the newspapers speak of it. We are not conscious of it in any other way out in these villages".[110] The old ways were slow to change in the countryside and working conditions were harsh.

To their immense credit the men and women spreading the Gospels rarely complained despite fighting often hostile communities and, at times, extreme weather. "This is the season for dust storms", a newsletter written in the A.P. Mission Hospital at Kasganj explained in May 1940. "Frequently we look out towards the west and see a very black cloud level with the horizon; it is approaching rapidly… Once it blew in a perfectly good glass pane in our operating room window… At times the wind blows furiously, the dust fills the air and makes us grit our teeth".[111] From a mango grove in Jalegaon, Marthena Ransom told her folks in Los Angeles how she travelled 7 miles to work with village women and children, who were horrified to learn she was not married, but otherwise prayed it would not rain since "we are on earth here, which gets just like glue when it is wet. We would be stuck here forever and age if it would storm."[112]

Ester Page in eastern Bengal explained how the natives followed her in curiosity as she travelled upstream, apparently never having seen a white person before.[113] Sister Gwendolen with the House of the Epiphany in Barisal was worried about the leeches and fish ending up in her bath along with the water carried up from the Banaripara River.[114]

Rural poverty made illness and disease rife. In the Bengal the jute crop, though really good, yielded a very poor price, "scarcely half the cost of growing and curing it".[115] A cholera outbreak at Hazaribagh had to be countered by thousands of injections,

Do You Know?

A newsletter written by the Mahoba-Rath Mission in November 1940 and sent to Los Angeles laid bare the hardships of native life in India.[132]

Every 1 in 5 people in the world are Indian; one million of its people are totally blind and three million partly blind according to Red Cross reports.

An old woman was buried alive to save one of her two sons who had leprosy. Her last request was "put the dirt in gently."

The Land of Nepal has 2,700 Tantric temples of which one missionary wrote, "Their Scriptures are a guide to atrocious and unnatural sins."

In Baroda, rainfall has been almost nil for three years in some areas. In Kathiawar State, 40,000 cattle died in one week, first going blind, then starving. Last year the Government spent Rs. 18 million on Famine Relief alone.

In Bombay, a year ago the city formally renounced a tax yield of more than one million rupees a year by going dry. Now the Courts have declared the Prohibition law unconstitutional "and to the distress of many, and the open joy of the rest, Bombay is again a 'wet' city."

In Pauri a freak calf is kept in a temple for worship because it was born with a leg with three hoofs on its neck. It is worshipped as a revelation of God's power.

At Patna, the discovery of images of the Hindu god Vishnu and a Hindu goddess when digging a Muslim cemetery caused "serious communal tension". The Hindus threaten to excavate the whole graveyard, while the Mohammedans are ready to fight. The images have been set up for worship in the village centre.

The holy city of Benares has seen a spate of suicides on account of food scarcity. One entire family committed suicide after not eating for three days. Thousands of corpses are thrown into the Mother Ganges, but worshippers still drink the water as an act of worship as the corpses float by.

SIGNED BY THE KENNEYS, V. FRANDSEN, M.H. COWDEN,
D. JACOBSEN, A. BRATAAS AND THE MCKELVEYS

although most locals were too busy harvesting to be ill or cured.[116] Bettie Williamsen with the London Mission in Kaurapukur told her parents in Durley, Gloucestershire, that the locals were living on the starvation line, which "shows in weakened bodies and a greater prevalence of disease than ever".[117]

An Idyllic Mission

A newsletter written by the A.P. Mission Hospital in Kasganj U.P. on 15 May 1940 waxed lyrical about the area's natural beauty.[118]

At the Mission, "the red bougainvillea is still beautiful climbing up over the porch and over the arch out on the lawn. The golden mohur is beginning to blossom out in huge bunches of scarlet flowers... As the hot season comes on full blast, the little lizards come out from their hibernation from behind the pictures on the walls and play around the lights devouring the insects. The toads hop in the dead leaves near the house. They even come up to the porch and try to get in. Both the toads and lizards are quite harmless but the former tend to attract snakes, so are not very welcome guests.

Speaking of snakes, everyone loves a snake story. Sunday morning, while we were making rounds in the hospital before going to Sunday School, a man was brought in who had been bitten... To the average Indian every snake is very poisonous and black, so this one may or may not have been a cobra... The man had been bitten on a toe and his friends had improvised a tourniquet by tying a tight cord above the bite. He was brought in on a cot, pale and semi-conscious. All his friends and relatives had come with him as they feared he would die. While the nurse gave Anti-venom serum the doctor cut the wound and cauterized it. The relatives kept saying, 'Only save his life, use any expensive medicine you wish and we'll pay for it...' By evening the man was well enough to go home. We asked for Rs. 5-0-0. ($1.50) to pay the cost of the serum. It took an hour of arguing to get that much from them. The people were Mohammedans and said that we had done nothing, that God cured him. They believe that whatever happens is God's will. Fatalism."

Charles and Mabel Benfield and David Evangeline thanked Mrs Young in Los Angeles for her $35 and were happy to report that now the mission had opened its plague hospital, cures were starting among the locals toiling in Latur in the cotton, ground crops and pressing mills.[119] Some married catechists in the Bengal were working for as little as 7 rupees ($2) a month, Father Young explained. Most staff took double duty, but funds remained low; "if I cut salaries their families will starve", he warned.[120] Still, wonderful cases of healing were witnessed in Bangalore: four children of whooping cough and a Mohammedan of fever, while "One man was very sick with cholera, and the Lord healed him completely and then saved his soul."[121]

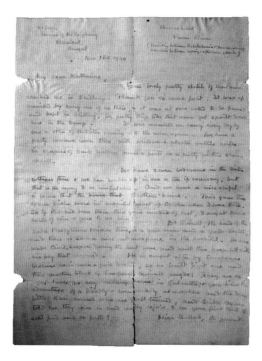

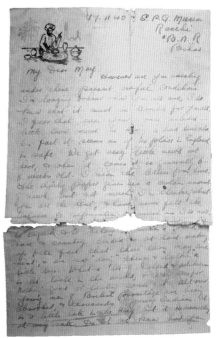

8.16. Natural wonders described by Sister Gwendolen of the House of the Epiphany on a houseboat at Barisal. To Miss M.K. Martin, St Cross, Streatham Rise, Exeter (Letter TUR-13-00083-03).

8.17. Dot Ruth from the SPG Mission in Ranchi was glad her parents did not live to endure a second world war (Letter TUR-13-00081-16).

A newsletter distributed by the Mission House at Hamirpur laid bare the hardships confronted in rural India, where an Indian Rajah (princely ruler) had just died, leaving behind eighty-five children, one million Indians were totally blind and an old woman was buried alive to save her sons from leprosy.[122] Mrs Browne with the D.H. Mission in Hazaribagh had attended a birth at "Almost the poorest hovel I've been in, the 3 starvings standing about with nothing on & completely silent – but mama as proud as punch at having pulled it off yet again & produced a son at least 2 inches long!... Oh these people! So many of them nowadays ask me in a whisper for 'medicine' to stop more babies coming."[123]

A letter from the formidable Isabel Frodsham with the Crescent Lodge in Mysore City, usually too busy to write from the villages with only a hurricane lamp for evening light, spoke of struggling to overcome village men and boys tearing up and burning the Gospels given to their women. She had recently been reading the St John's Gospel with a Muslim village doctor, whom the local Mohammedans tried to dissuade from Christianity. However, "at present he has forsaken BOTH and is dipping deeply into Philosophy, saying he is not 'SATISFIED' and must STUDY all points of view."[124]

With war squeezing pockets and portfolios, inadequate finances were a constant worry in the missionaries' letters. A high-ranking clergyman living in the Bishop's House in Ramna, Bengal, responsible for the Associates of Mary Queen of Apostles, a Dacca Diocesan Sisterhood, and the missionaries of the Holy Cross, admitted that the stoppage of the subsidy from the Sacred Congregation de Propaganda Fide hit hard.

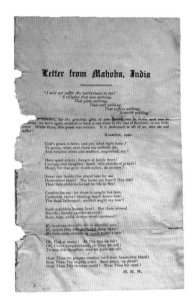

A VILLAGE SCHOOL IN EAST BENGAL.

8.18. A newsletter posted by J.H. Kenney from the Mission House in Rath (Letter TUR-13-00085-07D).

8.19. A photo showing a village missionary school in East Bengal. Sent by C. Prior of the Oxford Mission, Calcutta to Margaret in Ottery S. Mary, Devon (Letter TUR-13-00071-41C).

His female missionaries were especially important because "No man who is not of the family circle, may speak to a Hindu or Mussulman woman."[125] The fifty intentions received the previous evening from Father Goodall of the Bengalese Church (Brookland DC) "are a godsend to us, as since the War began our benefactors have forgotten us, except the chosen few whose charity is proof against the waywardness of the times."[126]

The A.P. Mission Hospital in Kasganj's Model A 1931 car had seen better days because "As you know, our Board is often embarrassed for lack of funds." The mission asked for $1,000 for a new Ford, the funds to be sent to the Board of Foreign Missions of the Presbyterian Church at 156 Fifth Avenue, New York.[127] Doing the Lord's work 76 miles north of Bangalore, among a Catholic community of a thousand souls, paid so low that most families could not support themselves, the Reverend J.M. Pinto confessed. His Diocese had received no donations in 1940 and his church badly needed a bell, priced £30, because the congregation found it difficult to recognise the time for Sunday mass and evening catechism class.[128]

Despite the trials and tribulations confronted every day by missionaries, the cause progressed. In Bangalore, C. Swinfen Eady felt that "the time is very short now. Surely world events all spell that 'the cometh of the Lord draweth nigh'... We are constantly getting into fresh villages, and preaching the wonderful message of salvation of the people... once again we commemorate the wondrous birthday of the king of Kings. Perhaps before another Christmas Day dawns, HE may be here for his own".[129]

The most poignant lines among the *Gairsoppa* missionary mail accompanied a newsletter from the Mahoba-Rath Mission posted by J.H. Kenney from the Hamirpur district to the Reverend and Mrs L.F. Turnbull in Los Angeles. Kenney had only returned to Bombay from abroad on 12 November 1940. Resting in the cool of their tents in Kashmir, the clearly overwhelmed missionaries, contrasting home with the here and now, wrote poetically how:[130]

God's peace is here; and yet, what right have *I*
To peace, when over there the millions die,
And helpless wives and mothers anguished cry?…
My Brothers they who die in dreadful pain!
My sisters they who weep and weep again!
My little ones, screaming 'neath battles rain!

A few shipwrecked letters touched upon both India's struggle for independence and the country's Muslim community. Mail from a high-ranking clergyman living in the Bishop's House in Ramna, Bengal, was bemused how Gandhi's exclusive weapon was "Satyagraha or soul-force" and reported how in October 1940 the leader sought permission from the Viceroy of India to preach non-cooperation by the people of India in the European war:[131]

The Viceroy, with infinite patience, would make a distinction. Conscientious objectors, His Excellency explained, would not be obliged to engage in war-like activities, but he could not permit these to preach non-cooperation. This did not satisfy "the Saint". He regarded it as a denial of freedom of speech. He did not, however, know what next move to make. At the time, he had no inner inspiration from God to enter a fast unto-death tactic in order to obtain light for the Viceroy to see things in the Gandhian way. The holy man expressly says that he will do nothing unless the inspiration comes, unless the Inner Voice speaks.

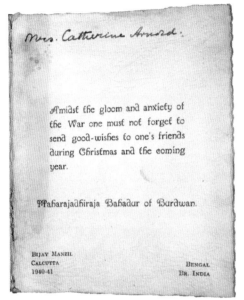

8.20. Christmas greetings from the Maharajadhiraja Bahadur of Burdwan to Catherine Arnold at the Royal United Hospital, Bath (Letter TUR-13-00088-42).

8.21. A Christmas card from Edie Moore, Darjeeling to Ethel Mann, Ashburton (Letter TUR-13-00088-46).

8.22. A Christmas card from Sister Agnes of the Oxford Mission, Barisal to Haggie Browning, Budleigh Salterton, Devon (Letter TUR-13-00071-37).

8.23. A Christmas card from Mary to her father, Weston-Super-Mare (Letter TUR-13-00071-63D).

8.24. A Christmas card sent by Felix Moorat of the Queen's Regiment in Razmak to Lucy and Cecilia Moorat (Letter TUR-13-00079-07).

8.25. A leopard card sent by A.E. Porter of the Indian Civil Service, Calcutta to his son in Woodchester, Gloucestershire (Letter TUR-13-00083-46G).

8.26. A Bombay greetings card from Igor to Miss Marian Johnson, San Francisco (TUR-13-00084-13).

8.27. A greetings card of a boat carrying clay cooking pots sent to Miss Callow in Cirencester (Letter TUR-13-00081-12).

8.28. An anonymous card, boat on water (Letter TUR-13-00081-10).

8.29. A personalised Christmas card sent to Miss V. Martin in Mortehoe, Devon (Letter TUR-13-00081-23).

8.30. Mr Fitch photographed at Radal-Pinal with a pal from Haddenham in Cambridgeshire. To Mrs J.W. Fitch, 117 Milton Street, Higher Brixham, Devon (Letter TUR-13-00079-02F).

8.31. An anonymous season's greetings card (Letter TUR-13-00086-11).

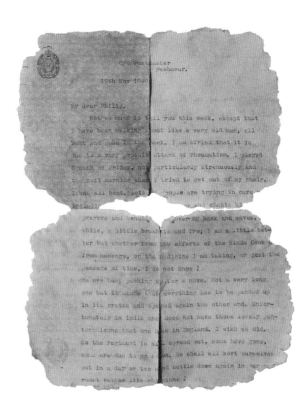

8.32. From Peshawur, a Hindu cook chanted prayers to cure a soldier's back, bent from rheumatism after playing squash (Letter TUR-13-00079-01).

8.33. Mac in Shillong sought guidance in preaching the teachings of Islam (Letter TUR-13-00083-46).

8.34. A season's greeting card sent by Jack Alleman of the Catholic Mission in Patna to Mrs H. Lohrum in Los Angeles (Letter TUR-13-00084-29).

8.35. A card of an Indian temple sent by Kamal to his grandparents (Letter TUR-13-00086-34).

8.36. From camp in Jubbulpore, Sgm. Wills posted love letters to his "Darling Adorable Precious Little Shop Girl Wife" in Plymouth (Letter TUR-13-00071-29).

8.37. An envelope from The Crown Engineering Works in Lahore to Messers Frazar & Co. Ltd. in San Francisco (Letter TUR-13-00084-35).

VOICES FROM THE DEEP

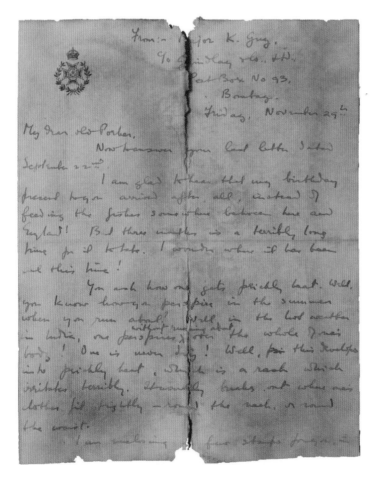

8.38. Major K. Guy of the Rajputana Rifles in Bombay sent his son an envelope returned from German-captured Paris & covered with curious stamps (Letter TUR-13-00088-20).

8.39. A photo of "Christopher Michael Aged 1 Year" sent by Miss Joan & Mr Herbert in Imphal on 4th Assam Rifles notepaper (Letter TUR-13-00081-29).

8.40. A photo of N. Templar sent to Mr & Mrs Boubia in Teignmouth, Devonshire (Letter TUR-13-00083-15).

8.41. A photo of "Dmr Bradley at Solon" sent by Drummer H. Reeves of the 2nd Worcestershire Regiment at Sialkot to his parents (Letter TUR-13-00088-06).

8.42. From Rajputana, D. Sikar sent a photo for his student diploma to the Hollywood Radio & Television Institute in Los Angeles (Letter TUR-13-00080-07).

Notes

1. The *Gairsoppa* Postal Archive consists of 1,256 items: 246 personal letters, 343 business letters, 88 Christmas cards, 40 postcards, 15 cheques, 444 envelopes and 80 miscellaneous items (string, fabric sample, newspaper clippings, newsletters, party invitation, photographs, stamps).
2. Letter TUR-13-00088-42. Maharajadhiraja Bahadur of Burdwan, Bijay Manzil, Calcutta, Bengal, Br. to Mrs Catherine Arnold, Royal United Hospital, Bath.
3. Letter TUR-13-00071-45, 28.11.40. N.G. Kurien, Eraviperoor, Tiruvalla, Travancore to Rev. Father John Perret, Staunton City Warren Rectory, Highworth, Wilts.
4. Letter TUR-13-00086-43. A Father, Lahore to G.J. Coleen (?), c/o Mrs Walker (?), Moray Place, Edinburgh, Scotland. Letter TUR-13-00083-16, 25.11.40. Bill and Mabel Murray, Bungalow 18, Gorakhpur, BNW to Burt and Grace Lee, Lower Blagdon Farm, Blagdon Hill, Nr Taunton, Somerset.
5. Letter TUR-13-00071-55B-E, 1.12.40. Pete W. Walker, 5569374, 1st Wiltshire Regiment, Military W/T Stn, HQ Allahabad Area to Mrs A. Walker, Cold Ashton, Nr Marshfield, Chippenham, Wiltshire.
6. Letter TUR-13-00088-20, 29.11.40. Major K. Guy, Kohat, Rajputana Rifles, c/o Grindlay & Co. Ltd, Post Box No. 93, Bombay to Master John Guy, Dorset House School, 90 Woodleigh Hall, Cheriton Bishop, Near Exeter, Devon.
7. Letter TUR-13-00083-41, 24.11.40. Kitty Jenkins (?), St Agnes' U.P. School, Itki, Ranchi Distr., BNR to Mrs Maggie Mason, 10 Seaton Place, Ford, Plymouth, Devon.
8. Letter TUR-13-00088-52, 1.12.40. Pam, Hotel Imperiel, Queensway, New Delhi to Tim G. Preedy, Bryne House, College Road, Cheltenham.
9. Letter TUR-13-00088-54, 25.11.40. Je----da, Berhampore to Nellie and Winnie Barney (?), Bath, Somerset. Letter TUR-13-00071-15, Advent Sunday 1940. Mrs Browne, D.H. Mission, Hazaribagh, Bihar to Rev. Eliott Keworthe Browne, Darnford Vicarage, Nr Salisbury.
10. Letter TUR-13-00071-29, 29.11.40 to 1.12.40. Sgm: Wills R., 2592258, R., STC(I), Jubbulpore, to Mrs D.B. Wills, Plymouth, S. Devon.
11. Letter TUR-13-00071-47, 2.12.40. Neil (?), The 9 Gorkha Rifles, Ambala to Mrs George, Kilmington, Axminster, Devon.
12. Letter TUR-13-00071-42, 26.11.40. Bandsman Fred Manning, Devonshire Regiment, Waziristan to Mr and Mrs S. Manning, Ewhurst, Barton Close, Okehampton, Devon. Letter TUR-13-00071-29, 29.11.40 to 1.12.40. Sgm: Wills, 2592258, R., STC(I), Jubbulpore to Mrs D.B. Wills, Plymouth, S. Devon.
13. Letter TUR-13-00071-43. Dot Matheson, 55 The Mall, Nowshera, NWFP to Lady Tweedie, Wraxall House, Wraxall, Somerset. On headed notepaper of 10th BN The Sikh Regiment, Nowshera.
14. Letter TUR-13-00081-16, 17.11.40. Miss Dot Ruth, SPG Mission, Ranchi, Bihar to Mrs May Newnam, 12 Devonshire Road, Salisbury, Wilts.
15. Letter TUR-13-00088-50(6), 2.12.40. Godfrey, Headquarters, Eastern Bengal & Assam Area, Shillong, Assam to Mrs Hylie (?), 30 Chatsworth Drive, Cheltenham, Gloucestershire.
16. Letter TUR-13-00081-05, 15.11.40. Kitty Shaw, Imphal, Manipur State to Mrs M. Luffman, Cludleigh, South Devon.
17. Letter TUR-13-00086-19. Aunt Peg (?), Hotel Imperial, New Delhi to Kewmure Melville Esq, 2 Church Hill, Edinburgh, Scotland.
18. Letter TUR-13-00086-16, November 1940. Bombay to Mrs Hay and Daughter, c/o Farrer, 7 Manor Place, Edinburgh.
19. Letter TUR-13-00088-40, 25.11.40 and 28.11.40. Mrs Vi Lanlager (?), Nerooklyu (?), Yercaeel (?) PO, S. India to Mrs C.G. 'Minnie' Marshall, Burnham-on-Sea, Somerset.
20. Letter TUR-13-00071-37, 1.12.40. Agnes, Oxford Houses, Shillong to Mrs Maggie Browning, Stoneborough House, Budleigh Salterton, Devon.
21. Letter race, 17.11.40. Miss Dot Ruth, SPG Mission, Ranchi, Bihar to Mrs May Newnam, 12 Devonshire Road, Salisbury, Wilts.
22. Letter TUR-13-00043-1, 16.11.40. Office of the Executive Engineer, Western (Electrical) Division, Communications & Works Department, Bengal (in pencil: 8 Lyons Range, Calcutta) to Mr and Mrs Harry and Norah Wills, Cassalands, Dumfries, Scotland.
23. TUR-13-00081-18, 15.11.40. Miss Patricia Anderson, Pasveni Institute, Shillong, Assam to Miss F.L. Huth, Edgcott, Exford, Somerset.
24. Letter TUR-13-00084-17, 18.11.40. M. Hammaker, Harding House, Sholapur to Mrs Frank A. Kirstein, Los Angeles, California.
25. Letter TUR-13-00043-1, 16.11.40. Office of the Executive Engineer, Western (Electrical) Division, Communications & Works Depart-

ment, Bengal (in pencil: 8 Lyons Range, Calcutta) to Mr and Mrs Harry and Norah Wills, Westfield, Cassalands, Dumfries, Scotland.

26. Letter TUR-13-00088-14. C.H. Roiddulph, c/o the Chief Engineer, South Indian Railway, Trichinopoly to Miss Joan Roiddulph, Southlands School, Exmouth, Devon.

27. Letter TUR-13-00083-19, 18.11.40. Harry and Flo, Calcutta to Mrs T. Williams (Senior), Gatehurst, Ash Thomas, Nr Tiverton, Devon.

28. Letter TUR-13-00071-41, 29.11.40. C.E. Prior, Oxford Mission, 42 Cornwallis St, Calcutta to Miss Margaret Kelvyn (?), Minnamore, West Hill, Ottery S. Mary, Devon. Calcutta.

29. Letter TUR-13-00083-47, 24.11.40. Jack B. Ronnlia, I.F.S. (Indian Foreign Service), Ganhale, Assam to Miss Betty Hutchinson, Yeofuld, Winscombe, Somerset (My Dear Aunt Betty).

30. Letter TUR-13-00083-29, 23.11.40. Sister Mary, St. OMSS, Barisal, E. Bengal to Arthur E. Eastwood Esq, Haigh Court, Taunton.

31. Letter TUR-13-00071-35, 29.11.40. George A. Ostler, Srinagar PO, Kashmir to Mrs Ostler, Bath, Somerset.

32. Letter TUR-13-00071-47, 1.12.40. Neil (?), 9 Gorkha Rifles, Ambala to Mrs George, Kilmington, Axminster, Devon.

33. Letter TUR-13-00083-16, 25.11.40. Bill and Mabel Murray, Bungalow 18, Gorakhpur, BNW to Burt and Grace Lee, Lower Blagdon Farm, Blagdon Hill, Nr Taunton, Somerset.

34. Letter TUR-13-00079-09, 18.11.40. Miss Sampson, Hihew High School, Gomoor, Nilgiri, S. India to Mrs G. Privey (?), 63 -------ax Place.

35. Letter TUR-13-00088-24, 29.11.40. Cicely E. Smart (?), Pachamallai, Valparai PO, S. India to Mrs Katharine Dea---, Wadebridge, Cornwall.

36. Letter TUR-13-00088-19, 28.11.40. Honnametti Estate, Altilean-Nuypas PO (?), S. India to Week Barton, Nr. Tawton, Devon.

37. Letter TUR-13-00083-25, 24.11.40. Lomas, c/o Imperial Tobacco Co of India Ltd., 37 Chuoreughie (?), PO Box 89, Calcutta to Mrs O. de la H. Moran, Cheltenham.

38. Letter TUR-13-00088-48, 1.12.40. Mrs Hélène Maltby, 10 Cavalry Lines, Delhi to Mrs Fox, Rumwell Hall, Nr. Taunton, Somerset.

39. Letter TUR-13-00071-23, 2.12.40. Mrs E. Melbourne (British), Royal Hotel, Barrackpore, Bengal to G. Carpenter, 32 Cumber-

land Rd, Swindon, Wiltshire.

40. Letter TUR-13-00083-16, 25.11.40. Bill and Mabel Murray, Bungalow 18, Gorakhpur, BNW to Burt and Grace Lee, Blagdon Hill, Somerset.

41. Letter TUR-13-00071-16, 1.12.40. Puckrie, Barashakia PO, Champaran to Mrs Mary Hudson, Cheltenham.

42. TUR-13-00083-48, 25.11.40. Kathleen, 11 Suite, 53 Chouringhee Road, Calcutta, to Mr and Mrs Bayly, Alluhera, Salisbury Road, Amesbury, Wiltshire.

43. Letter TUR-13-00071-23, 2.12.40. Mrs E. Melbourne (British), Royal Hotel, Barrackpore, Bengal to Gerald Carpenter, 32 Cumberland Rd, Swindon, Wiltshire.

44. Letter TUR-13-00081-05, 15.11.40. Kitty Shaw, Imphal, Manipur State to Mrs M. Luffman, Cludleigh, South Devon.

45. Letter TUR-13-00088-34, 29.11.40. John ?, Stonylands, Shillong, Assam to the Reverend Cedric Barlow (?), Plymtree Rectory, Cullompton, Devon.

46. Letter TUR-13-00088-45, 6.11.40. Elizabeth and Henry Willmartt, c/o Asst. Commissioner ICS (Indian Civil Service), St Albans, Ranikhet, UP to Mrs Betty McArdle, c/o Mrs Goodman, Westhay, Streatham Rise, Exeter.

47. Letter TUR-13-00083-44, 23.11.40. Tessa, Magdala House, Hastings, Calcutta to Mr H. Fowler, Tupsley, Hereford.

48. Letter TUR-13-00088-22, 27.11.40. Mr J.H. Cornish, Willingdon Island, Cochi State to Mr and Mrs Cornish, Middle Filham, S. Devon.

49. Letter TUR-13-00071-28, 27.11.40. Letter: D.N. Gill (?), The Muriel Club, Kidderpore, c/o Mackinnon Mackenzie & Co, BISN Co., Agents, Calcutta to Mrs Reell (?), Rohna, Murliton Hill (?), Paignton, S. Devon.

50. Letter TUR-13-00083-45, 24.11.40. Mrs Cathie Hoyle, 2/4 Harrighi Street, Calcutta c/o Lloyd's Bank, Chowrenghe, Calcutta) to Mrs Edith Hoghtin, 4 St Paul's House, Fisherton, Salisbury.

51. Letter TUR-13-00071-29, 29.11.40 to 1.12.40. 2592258, Sgm: Wills, R., STC(I), Jubbulpore, C.P. to Mrs D.B. Wills, 4 North Hill Terrace, Tavistock Road, Plymouth, S. Devon.

52. Letter TUR-13-00084-11, 8.11.40. John A. Allen, c/o C.A.S.O.C. (California Arabian Standard Oil Company), Bahrein Island, Persian Gulf to Mrs LeRoy Seiler, San Francisco, California.

53. Letter TUR-13-00078-15, 6.11.40. Bishop's House, Ramna, Dacca, Bengal to Very Reverend Father.

54. Letter TUR-13-00086-33. Bombay Club to Mrs A.F. Chard, 33 Sciennes Rd, Edinburgh, Scotland.
Letter TUR-13-00088-33. Tracy ?, Lloyds Bank Limited, 101/1 Clive Street, Calcutta to Mrs Janet Pincher (?).
55. Letter TUR-13-00083-44, 23.11.40. Tessa, Magdala House, Hastings, Calcutta to Mr H.M. Fowler, 28 Church Road, Tupsley, Hereford.
56. Letter TUR-13-00081-18, 15.11.40. Miss Patricia Anderson, Pasveni Institute, Shillong, Assam, India to Miss F.L. Huth, Edgcott, Exford, Somerset.
57. TUR-13-00086-27, 26.11.40. Olive and Jock, Lloyd's Register of Ships, Exchange Bld., Bombay to Mrs Maggie Baxter, St Margarets, 31 Templeland Road, Edinburgh.
58. Letter TUR-13-00071-10, 3.12.40. Mr. F. Brown, 2 London Court, Moira St, Calcutta to Master L. and P. Brown, Hydneye House, Witherdon, Beaworthy, Devon.
59. Letter TUR13-00088-08. R. Turner, 5615497, Devon Regt, Jicca Barracks, Dalhousie to Miss Joe Webber, Royal Devon & Exeter Hospital, Exeter, Devon.
60. Letter TUR-13-00083-47, 24.11.40. Jack B. Ronnlia, I.F.S. (Indian Foreign Service), Ganhale, Assam to Miss Betty Hutchinson, Winscombe, Somerset.
61. Letter TUR-13-00079-01, 20.11.40. Peshawur to Miss Rich, Brook Lodge, Batheaston, Somerset.
62. Letter TUR-13-00083-46, 24.11.40. A.E. Porter, ICS, Home Dept, Government of Bengal to Mrs Porter, Highcroft, Woodchester, Stroud, Gloucestershire.
63. Letter TUR-13-00085-10. Mrs C.L.C. 'Barbara' Cox, Belgaum, B.P. to Andrew J. Copp, 937 Consolidated Building, 607 South Hill St, Los Angeles, California.
64. Letter TUR-13-00043(10). Event Programme. 'The McCloysters. 15th November, 1940'. To Mrs G. Brown (?), 10 Watling Drive, Camelon, Falkirk.
65. Letter TUR-13-00079-05. R. Groves, Secretary to A.E. Joyce, Lounluce, Grove Road, Nr. Curlea (?).
66. Letter TUR-13-00088-11. Mummy, James Finlay & Co. Ltd., Calcutta to Miss Lesley.
67. Letter TUR-13-00083-25, 24.11.40. Lomas, c/o Imperial Tobacco Co of India Ltd, 37 Churoroughie (?), PO Box 89, Calcutta to Mrs O. de la H. Moran, Cheltenham.
68. Letter TUR-13-00086-03, 25.11.40. Mrs. J. Mitchell, Attack Oil Co., Rawalpindi Rd., Rawalpindi, Punjab to Mr(s)? Porter, 7 Blinkbonny Cres., Blackhall, Edinburgh.
69. Letter TUR-13-00086-09, 24.11.40. Emma ----ffaus (India) Ltd, ----wich Gate, Bombay to Mr and Mrs McMullan, 1a Ashton Villas, Brumstane Road…
70. Letter TUR-13-00088-15, 29.11.40. Mrs Detsulls, Brigade House, Kohar to Mrs C. Mackeer, Brook Lodge, Thorverton, Exeter, Devon.
71. Letter TUR-13-00071-52. Ronald, Mosaboni Mines, India to Mr R. Williams, Lower Hill Farm, Redruth, Cornwall.
72. Letter TUR-13-00081-01. Herbert, Joan & Christopher Michael to Miss F. Grimes, c/o Miss Errington, Clarence Villa, Gloucester Road, Cheltenham.
73. Envelope TUR-13-00079-27A, 20.11.40. National Bank of India Limited Bombay to Canadian Bank of Commerce, San Francisco.
74. Letter TUR-13-00083-44, 23.11.40. Tessa, Magdala House, Hastings, Calcutta to Mr H. Fowler, Tupsley, Hereford.
75. Letter TUR-13-00086-03, 25.11.40. Mrs. J. Mitchell, Attack Oil Co., Rawalpindi Rd., Rawalpindi, Punjab to Mr(s)? Porter, 7 Blinkbonny Cres., Blackhall, Edinburgh.
76. Letter TUR-13-00086-28, 23.11.40. RHQ Squadron, 3rd Carabiniers, Sialkot to Miss M. Thorburn, c/o Rendall, 16 Wardieburn Pl. West, Granton, Edinburgh.
77. Letter TUR-13-00071-47, 1.12.40. Neil (?), The 9 Gorkha Rifles, Ambala to Mrs George, Kilmington, Axminster, Devon.
78. Letter TUR-13-00083-46, 24.11.40. A.E. Porter, ICS, Home Dept, Government of Bengal to Mrs Porter, Highcroft, Woodchester, Stroud, Gloucestershire.
79. Letter TUR-13-00088-49(5), 1.12.40. Major Gerald Lecoss (?), Maiden's Hotel, Delhi to Mrs Lecoss (?), c/o Mrs Phillips, Four Winds, Braunton, Barnstaple, Devon.
80. Letter TUR-13-00045, 24.11.40. Peg, the Exchange Simla to Jane.
81. Letter TUR-13-00088-19, 28.11.40. Honnametti Estate, Altilean-Nuypas PO (?), (?), S. India to Week Barton, Nr. Tawton, Devon.
82. Letter TUR-13-00086-08. Mrs Boyle, 'Inniskilling 27', Haig Barracks, Malappuram, S. Malabar to Mrs Lindsay, 5 South Learmonth, Edinburgh.
83. Letter TUR-13-00084-24. 1 Hidrib Cafe?, The Mall, Dalhousie to Dear Alma Jack.
84. Letter TUR-13-00071-04. Father, Hotel Cecil, Delhi to Cilla Covell, Eliot Hotel, Newquay, Cornwall.
85. Letter TUR-13-00083-44, 23.11.40. Tessa, Magdala House, Hastings, Calcutta to Mr H. Fowler, 28 Church Road, Tupsley, Hereford.

86. Letter TUR-13-00081-26, 17.11.40. Chevremont II, Darjeeling to Mrs Opeshire (?), Cheddar, Somerset.
87. Letter TUR-13-00083-47, 24.11.40. Jack B. Ronnlia (?), I.F.S. (Indian Foreign Service), Ganhale, Assam to Miss Betty Hutchinson, Winscombe, Somerset.
88. Letter TUR-13-00088-25, 28.11.40. Gladys Clapp, 'Idalia', Ootakamund to Mr and Mrs Oakey, 39 Corby Avenue, Swindon, Wiltshire.
89. Letter TUR-13-00071-43. Dot Matheson, 55 The Mall, Nowshera, NWFP to Lady Tweedie, Wraxall House, Wraxall, Somerset.
90. Letter TUR-13-00083-10, 23.11.40. Mrs Cassidy, 8 The Park, Ichapur, Nawabganj, Bengal to Commander S.W. Cornish Rh, Staithe, Trebetheric, Nr. Wadebridge, Cornwall.
91. Letter TUR-13-00086-01. Flagstaff House, Dehra Dun, UP to Mary.
92. Letter TUR-13-00045. Peg, the Exchange Simla to Jane.
93. Letter TUR-13-00088-45, 6.11.40. Elizabeth and Henry Willmartt, c/o Asst. Commissioner, ICS (Indian Civil Service), St. Albans, Ranikhet, UP to Mrs Betty McArdle, c/o Mrs Goodman, Exeter.
94. Letter TUR-13-00071-48, 30.11.40. Mrs Mavis Bass, c/o MNAR Walker, 39 Dufferin Rd, c/o Nepalese Cont., Durfai Fort, Nowshera, NWFP to Mrs R.C. Edge, Eastlands, 190 Leckhampton Road, Cheltenham, Glos.
95. Letter TUR-13-00071-43. Dot Matheson, 55 The Mall, Nowshera, NWFP to Lady Tweedie, Wraxall House, Wraxall, Somerset.
96. Letter TUR-13-00071-47, 2.12.40. Neil (?), The 9 Gorkha Rifles, Ambala to Mrs George, Kilmington, Axminster, Devon.
97. Letter TUR-13-00083-53, 21.11.40. 'New Place', Mussoorie, U.P. to Olga.
98. Letter TUR-13-00081-08, 16.11.40. Arthur T. Taylor, 2b Dalhousie Square, Calcutta to Maurice C. Houlder Esq, Wheddon Cross, Somerset.
99. Letter TUR-13-00071-24, 1.12.40. Pete W. Walker, 5569374, 1st Wilts Regt, Military W/T Stn, HQ Allahabad Area to Miss P. Aldridge, 21 Roseland Avenue, Devizes, Wiltshire.
100. Letter TUR-13-00071-55, 1.12.40. Pete W. Walker, 5569374, 1st Wilts Regt, Military W/T Stn, HQ Allahabad Area to Mrs A. Walker, Cold Ashton, Nr Marshfield, Chippenham, Wiltshire.
101. Letter TUR-13-00081-18, 15.11.40. Miss Patricia Anderson, Pasveni Institute, Shillong, Assam to Miss F.L. Huth, Edgcott, Exford, Somerset.
102. Letter TUR-13-00071-29, 29.11.40 to 1.12.40. 2592258, Sgt Wills, R., STC(I), Jubbulpore, to Mrs D.B. Wills, Plymouth, S. Devon.
103. Letter TUR-13-00084-25. Joe Moolem (?) to Mrs J. Moolem (?), 2910 Fulton Street, Apt No. 8, San Francisco, California.
104. Letter TUR-13-00071-14, 17.11.40. Rupert Searle, HQ Devonshire Regiment, B.M. Hospital, Rawalpindi to Miss Kath Moon, 26 Higher Lux St., Liskeard, Cornwall.
105. Letter TUR-13-00088-49. Major Gerald Lecoss (?), Maiden's Hotel, Delhi to Mrs Lecoss (?), c/o Mrs Phillips, Four Winds, Braunton, Barnstaple, Devon.
106. Letter TUR-13-00086-28, 23.11.40. RHQ Squadron, 3rd Carabiniers, Sialkot to Miss M. Thorburn, c/o Rendall, 16 Wardieburn Pl. West, Granton, Edinburgh
107. Letter TUR-13-00071-19, 1.12.40. 1366744 (?), L/C Pedmore (?), Royal Army Medical Corps, BM Hospital, Jubbulpore to Ruby Phillips, Whitecloft Road, Bream, Nr Lydney, Glos.
108. Letter TUR-13-00088-19, 28.11.40. Honnametti Estate, Altilean-Nuypas PO (?), S. India to Week Barton, Nr. Tawton, Devon.
109. Letter TUR-13-00088-25, 28.11.40. Gladys Clapp, 'Idalia', Ootakamund to Mr and Mrs Oakey, 39 Corby Avenue, Swindon, Wiltshire.
110. Letter TUR-13-00071-41, 29.11.40. 29.11.40. C.E. Prior, Oxford Mission, 42 Cornwallis St, Calcutta to Miss Margaret Kelvyn (?), Minnamore, West Hill, Ottery S. Mary, Devon. Calcutta.
111. Missionary Newsletter TUR-13-00084-14, 15.5.40. A.P. Mission Hospital, Kasganj U.P.
112. Letter TUR-13-00079-03, 22.11.40. Marthena Ransom, Mission House, Amravati, Berar to Mrs Mary S. Ransom, 3435 Lee St., Los Angeles, California.
113. Letter TUR-13-00081-09, 10.11.40. Ester Page, c/o W. Duncan, Godenare, Karayanganj, Eastern Bengal to Mr(s) Weeks, Barcombe Road, Paignton, Devon.
114. Letter TUR-13-00071-38, 30.11.40. Sister Gwendolen OMST, House of the Epiphany, Barisal, Bengal to Miss Chanipernowure, 8 Queens Terrace, St. David's Hill, Exeter.
115. Letter TUR-13-00078-15, 11.11.40. Bishop's House, Ramna, Dacca, Bengal to Dear Reverend Father.
116. Letter TUR-13-00071-15, Advent Sunday 1940. Mrs Browne, D.H. Mission, Hazaribagh, Bihar, to Rev. Eliott Keworthe Browne, Darnford Vicarage, Nr Salisbury.

117. Letter TUR-13-00081-17, 17.11.40. Bettie Williamsen, London Mission, Kaurapukur, Tollygange P.O., Calcutta to Dr and Mrs Williamsen, Toney Cottage, Durley, Gloucestershire.

118. Letter TUR-13-00084-14, 15.5.40. A.P. Mission Hospital, Kasganj, U.P

119. Letter TUR-13-00085-15. Charles and Mabel Benfield and David Evangeline, Latur, BL Rly, Nizam's Dominions to Mrs Edwin D. Young, the Southland Hotel, Flower at Sixth, Los Angeles, California.

120. Letter TUR-13-00078-15, 11.11.40. Bishop's House, Ramna, Dacca, Bengal to Dear Reverend Father.

121. Letter TUR-13-00085-3. Constance Swinfen Eady, 10 Harris Road, Bangalore, S. India to Mr and Mrs R.T. Teviotdale, 7912½, South Vermont, Los Angeles, California.

122. Letter TUR-13-00085-07D-E, November 1940. J.H. Kenney, Mission House, Rath, Hamirpur Dist., UP to Rev. & Mrs. L.F. Turnbull, 1108 N Carnado Terrace, Los Angeles, California.

123. Letter TUR-13-00071-15, Advent Sunday 1940. Mrs Browne, D.H. Mission, Hazaribagh, Bihar, to Rev. Eliott Keworthe Browne, Darnford Vicarage, Nr Salisbury.

124. Letter TUR-13-00071-11. Isabel Frodsham, Crescent Lodge, Idgah, Mysore to Mr Butler, Arden, Fleseleny Rd (?), Bede, Cornwall.

125. Newsletter TUR-13-00078-15(3), 11.11.40.

Bishop's House, Ramna, Dacca, Bengal to Dear Reverend Father.

126. Letter TUR-13-00078-15(5), 19.11.40. Bishop's House, Ramna, Dacca, Bengal to Rt. Rev. and Dear Msgr.

127. Newsletter TUR-13-00084-14(3-5), 15.40. A.P. Mission Hospital, Kasganj U.P.

128. Letter TUR-13-00085-18. Rev. J.M. Pinto, Byndoor, SR, Holy Cross Mission, Byndoor, S. Kanara, British India to Mr Louis Hess, 4327 Walton Ave., Los Angeles, California.

129. Letter TUR-13-00085-3. Constance Swinfen Eady, 10 Harris Road, Bangalore, S. India to Mr and Mrs R.T. Teviotdale, 7912½, South Vermont, Los Angeles, California.

130. Newsletter TUR-13-00085-07D-E. Mahoba, India. J.H. Kenney, Mission House, Rath, Hamirpur Dist., UP to Rev. & Mrs. L.F. Turnbull, 1108 N Carnado Terrace, Los Angeles, California.

131. Letter TUR-13-00078-15, 6.11.40. Bishop's House, Ramna, Dacca, Bengal to Very Reverend Father.

132. . Letter TUR-13-00085-07D-E, November 1940. J.H. Kenney, Mission House, Rath, Hamirpur Dist., UP to Rev. & Mrs. L.F. Turnbull, 1108 N Carnado Terrace, Los Angeles, California.

133. Letter TUR-13-00083-46H, 20.11.40. Mac, 'Pisgah', Nongthymmai, Shillong to Mr Porter, ICS, Home Dept., Government of Bengal, Calcutta.

9

WAR & WHEELS OF COMMERCE

SEAN KINGSLEY

Tides of War

Reading the *Gairsoppa* mail reveals how British India cobbled together a reasonable, though far from precise, impression of war at home and abroad through various sources – nuggets of information buried in inbound letters, newspapers and radio. The heroics of Dunkirk were still on many lips, while the horrors of the Blitz and Mussolini's recent assault on Greece were major talking points.

Douglas, Dorothy, John and Jeremy in Upper Assam, for instance, were so glad to hear that Dick Fraser of Teignmouth, Devon, got back from Dunkirk "alright", even without his kit.[1] A clipping from the British India newspaper *The Statesman*, folded into one letter, vividly recalled the 'Epic of Dunkirk':[2]

> So long as the English tongue survives, the word Dunkirk will be spoken with reverence. For in that harbour, in such a hell as never blazed on earth before, at the end of a lost battle, the rags and blemishes that have hidden the soul of democracy fell away… Men died so that others could escape… It was the common way of the free countries, rising in all his glory out of the mill, office, factory, mine, farm and ship… This shining thing in the soul of free men Hitler cannot command, or attain, or conquer… It is the great tradition of democracy. It is the future. It is victory.

Various writers brought up the effects of the Blitz. The papers had reported that Liverpool had it "very hot" last Thursday,[3] while Pam told Tim Preedy in Cheltenham how she understood that "Bristol has been having a hard time the last week with the raiders".[4] On the whole the papers did not give specifics, but spoke in general terms about the likes of the bombing of a "west of England Cathedral town."[5]

Kathleen in Calcutta commented to her parents, Mr and Mrs Bayly in Amesbury, Wiltshire, that "with no home with half or hole [sic] family killed what a terrible sight

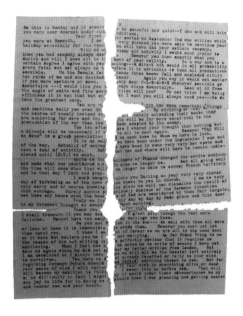
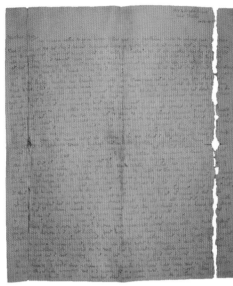

9.1. John Bunce pleaded with his wife Jilian in Taunton Heath to beware falling bombs (Letter TUR-13-00083-33).

9.2. Major Cleane in Allahabad complained about the lack of beef and hoped Mussolini harbours rats in his vitals (Letter TUR-13-00088-47).

it must be. I do hope this war will end soon".[6] An anonymous writer from the British Military Hospital in the Lahore Cantonment expressed relief to Miss M. Russell in Coxley, Somerset, that Glastonbury had not been hit, wondered how many planes had passed over her way and hoped the Germans did not kill any cows.[7] Numerous friends had fled the Blitz. "I am ever so pleased you are far away in Paignton & out of the danger zone", a soldier wrote home to Bernice McTyner.[8]

Others were not so fortunate. From the Brigade House in Kohar, Mrs Detsulls sympathised with Mrs C. Mackeer in Thorverton, Devon, about "What a time you are having the Grannies. Lucky you've got Sybella there to help – how awful about the house she had been living in in London being completely wrecked."[9] "London is no safe place for anyone who can avoid it", Sister Mary in Barisal agreed with Arthur E. Eastwood in Taunton.[10]

The knowledge that loved ones were possibly being pounded from the air magnified many writers' anxiety about their safety and welfare and left Brits in India feeling helpless. "Hope the air raids are not terrifying your news too much", enquired Kitty Shaw. "It must be deadly, especially at nights with little or no sleep & constant noise".[11]

From afar in India, "in some very very hot spots" where three bombs had exploded within 10 yards of him and one decidedly closer, John pleaded with his wife, Jilian Bunce in Taunton Heath, Devon, to take the utmost precautions from falling bombs. "P-L-E-A-S-E whenever possible go downstairs - - - I would like you always to sleep downstairs", he advised. "Look at it from the angle of exits and fire possibilities will you? Do not think I am being officious it is not that but only that I want you [to know

I] will always need you - - - So do take the greatest care." To the recent news that the family church had been hit, John replied that "Surely anyone previously dubious of the Germans intention now knew any house even the house of God are considered by them fair targets. Truly we live only day by day by God's grace and this dear is my foremost thought on awakening each morning."

In hindsight, John reminisced that perhaps building an air raid shelter would have been wiser than buying a new suite, although no one could have foreseen the collapse of France. The husband advised his wife to keep a memo of her insurance policies safe in case of fire and to remove as much as possible from the top rooms, especially anything flammable, because incendiary bombs do not penetrate far. The letter ended with the anguishing thought of "How I hate to know you're in danger - - - But oh how I will hate and try to avenge if anything happens to you my beloved, my A-L-L." Mr Bunce, meanwhile, found it hard to grasp the immediacies of war in England, unlike in India where "my only complaint is the mosquitoes and every and apparently the attention of every conceivable insect that flies".[12]

On headed notepaper of the Bengal Club in Calcutta, Tom's reply to a letter from Miss C. Hubweir in Bath, who wrote about light damage to Ross Road, practically replied that "It isn't much good putting the windows back as they may go out again."[13] Captain G.C. Monchton in New Delhi summed up the general malaise: "What a business it all is, but I hope the Hun flames have been nowhere near you all, and as you know you are all constantly in my thoughts and prayers. There is always a silver lining to every cloud, and it is good to know that the vile dagoes are really having a bad time of it now, and it would be no surprise to me if they suddenly collapsed."[14]

Italy's unprovoked attack on Greece on 28 October 1940 – against Hitler's own military plans – was on the minds of many letter writers. The ancient home of democracy was an obstacle to Mussolini's ambitious imperial policy to revive the Roman Empire by extending the territory under his control across the Mediterranean to the Near East.[15] After the first major Greek counter-attack across the Macedonian front on 14 November, Il Duce's forces were forced to retreat back to Italy-occupied Albania.

"The Greeks are making a wonderful stand & the British Navy is living up to its wonderful tradition – but how one wishes it did not involve such suffering & murder", Sister Gwendolen of the House of the Epiphany in Barisal, but currently on a houseboat down the Pasu River, shared with Miss Katharine Martin of St Cross, Exeter.[16] John's letter to Jilian Bunce in Taunton Heath, Devon, felt that the collapse of France changed the whole outlook of the war by bringing danger to a former safe area. Elsewhere in the northern Mediterranean, he wrote:[17]

The news from Greece continues to be exceptionally good and even the Italians are admitting serious losses. This wonderful achievement against overwhelming odds is ample proof dearest God is on our side. Long may the Greeks continue their wonderful work which must pass down in history and certainly give the average Frenchman (never to blame for his country's collapse) a deal to think about… There is a great deal of truth in the saying 'Things at the worst will cease, or else climb upward' and I do believe the climb upward has commenced… Surely Mussolini must now realise what determination [there is] even in a small nation. I am convinced he has not the Italian nation behind him and the defeats his army is now experiencing are but a result of disinterestedness and lack of unity of purpose. But there I go again the war is a topic to be avoided.

A note from Assam agreed that things looked "blue when France went down & it looked to me as if Britain would follow suit, but what a recovery she has made thanks to the navy & RAF. The tide is now turning the other way… & now Italy is getting Hell" after attacking Greece.[18]

From news heard on the wireless direct from London, Denis Pudlay wrote enthusiastically to Mary Hudson in Cheltenham how "it looks to us as if Hitler has no more cards to play and we are getting stronger day by day."[19] Gladys, another keen radio listener – "what a boon indeed that we possess one" – wrote passionately about her sense of the war's direction to her parents, Mr and Mrs Oakey, in Swindon, Wiltshire:[20]

England has defiantly turned the corner now without a doubt. Gallant little Greece has gone a long way to helping her. Italy has got what she deserved alright, and as Cyril Lakie on the radio in his talks says the moral value to all the wavering neutrals will be far reaching indeed!! Dear old England you have come thro the an [sic] awful lot. The pictorial page of the Madras Mail lies open before me and shows the awful wreckage of bombs on England. Oh dearest folks how nervous it does make me for your safety and I do pray God hourly to have you in His safest keeping. Looking out thro front room window as I sit writing this – blue skies and sunshine – quiet and peaceful – oh I do wish you were safe out of it all. Oh do pack up & come – but of course I know that the high seas are very dangerous too – still better that than not to know when a stray bomb may fall!

From the SPG Mission in Ranchi, Dot asked May Newnam in Salisbury however she was existing under the present awful conditions. On her side of the ocean, "India is at last waking up to the fact that their time may come next, & are now doing 'things' & 'talking' a little less. What a lot of hatred and wickedness is let loose in the world, & why ever for. Nothing good or lasting comes of it… All our young men of British parentage are being absorbed, and thousands of young Indians. It is a little late in the day but it is something at any rate".[21] Army call-ups were as visible in India as at home with the noose of world war tightening. Writing care of Whiteaway Laidlaw & Co. in Calcutta, Archie's office was short-handed because four of the European staff had joined up and another two were leaving shortly.[22]

Frontline

The soldiers serving with twenty-two regiments in India, whose conspicuous words and even occasional faces turn up among the *Gairsoppa* letters, generally kept a tight lid on their day jobs. Unlike letters dispatched to America and Scotland, however, whose envelopes were vividly stamped 'Opened By Censor', those addressed to England flew through the system unread, in cases leaving behind revealing snapshots of life fighting the border tribes in the northern frontier. The actions of the 1st Battalion the Devonshire Regiment in Waziristan are especially conspicuous.

9.3. Rupert Searle of the 1st Devonshire Regiment almost lost a leg from gangrene at the British Military Hospital, Rawalpindi (Letter TUR-13-00071-13).

9.4. Bill Wheeler of the Devonshire Regiment got over jaundice and was fighting the rotten tribes in Razmak (Letter TUR-13-00071-09).

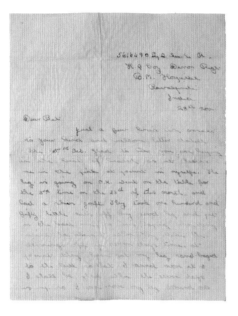
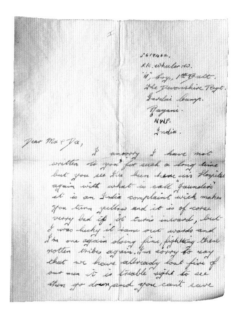

Most of the soldiers whose letters sank on the *Gairsoppa* were stationed on the remote edge of British India's North-west Frontier Province in modern Pakistan. This wild mountainous no-man's land linking Central and Southern Asia was the most strategically sensitive border in the Empire. Beyond here the limits of British conquest ended. In the same tough terrain where Western forces played a deadly game of cat and mouse for a decade with al-Qaeda and an elusive Osama bin Laden, Britain fought tribal guerrillas for almost a century and failed.

Leading up to World War II, Indian soldiers stationed in the Khyber Pass, the Kurram Valley and Waziristan served a two-year tour of duty and British infantry units one year. Along this front line the army and RAF tested mountain warfare strategies, trained new troops and fine-tuned tactics. In late 1936, 61,000 troops were deployed to the North-west Frontier to put down an insurrection inflamed by the holy Muslim priest Mirza Ali Khan, better known as the Fakir of Ipi – the Osama bin Laden of the age

– and cross-border attacks by Wazirs, Mahsuds, Bhittanis and Afghans. By April 1937, four more brigades were needed to reinforce the garrison at Razmak, where several *Gairsoppa* correspondents were stationed. The 1936-1939 Waziristan Campaign ended in the killing of 245 British Indian soldiers, while another 684 were wounded and seventy-three died from disease.[23]

9.5. Lance Sergeant Jack Bloomfield with the 1st Battalion Duke of Cornwall's Light Infantry at Lahore shared his daily routine (Letter TUR-13-00071-12).

When England declared war on Germany, the tribes were still running wild. British troops patrolled the long unruly lines of border communication, escorted convoys and supported road protection sorties with fire. An equally worrying concern was the possibility of attack by imperial Russia – friend or foe? – across the infamous Khyber Pass. By November 1939 the Commanding Officer of the Razmak Brigade reckoned he was losing more men than the army in France. Between February and May 1940, two brigades covered the construction of Frontier Constabulary posts in the Ahmadzai region, a jumping off point for tribal raids.

In early 1940 the British garrisons in the Khyber, Kurram and Tochi Valleys were rein-forced, equipment and ammunition brought in, concrete pill-boxes strengthened and gun-emplacements sprung up around the Khyber and the lower Kurram, Shinki and Shabur gorges of Waziristan. Overall, the frontier was comparatively quiet by autumn 1940, helped by 400 tribal leaders from the South Waziristan district signing at Peshawar expressions of friendship with the British-India Government and offering prayers for the army's wartime success.[24] But in late 1940 *lashkar* tribal militants led by Mahsud

Hayat Khan attacked the Tiarzha Narai and Ladha posts with cannon loaned by the Fakir of Ipi. In return, the RAF pounded Hayat's village and troops were sent in. When the 5/8th Punjab column lost contact with the main troops withdrawing on the night of 6-7 December 1940, sixty-six of the regiment's soldiers died and sixty-five were wounded.[25]

Capture by the local tribes could be horrifying: beheadings were common and on one occasion a British officer was castrated, flayed alive and his skin pegged out on rocks. The main agitator, the Fakir of Ipi, evaded capture despite more than 40,000 troops being sent to Waziristan. By 1943, fifty-seven British and Indian infantry battalions and four armoured car regiments were deployed in the North-west Frontier Province.[26]

Serving in northern India was as tough as it got, but such was the setting for many hardy soldiers' letters heading home on the *Gairsoppa.* Jack Butler from the 1st Battalion the Devonshire Regiment told his mother in Holsworthy, Devon, how his men had to be "on our guard every second because these cunning tribes are so keen on getting us in a trap" and was not expecting a good Christmas on the frontier. Jack had been in India almost four years, with two more to go, "perhaps more if this blinking war does not come to an end. God knows best though Mother".[27]

Bill Wheeler from the same regiment calmly explained to his mother and father in Peverell, Plymouth, that he had been in hospital with jaundice, "an India complaint that makes you turn yellow and it is of course very bad if it turns inward, but is was lucky it came out wards". Wheeler was now so fine that he was "fighting these rotten tribes again" in Razmak, where his regiment lost five men. Eight other boys were in hospital with wounds from attacks using 'dum dums' "made from old tins and stuff they manage to pick up anywhere on the Frontier, so you see we are having as bad a time as them poor devils in France or anywhere else." Wheeler shared how "it is a treable [terrible] sight to see them go down, and you can't save them". An enclosed sketch of a dum dum showed a bullet making a half-inch hole when entering the body and expanding to 8 inches when exiting.[28]

From the Orderly Room of the 1st Battalion Duke of Cornwall's Light Infantry regiment at the Napier Barracks in the Lahore Cantonment of the Punjab, Lance Sergeant Jack Bloomfield merrily shared his daily routine with his parents in Strete, Devon, and in a second letter, probably to his girlfriend, Miss M. Trembath in Breage, Cornwall. On the night of 30 November 1940, Bloomfield had participated in "a big Scheme", when the battalion advanced 30-35 miles during the Monday and Monday night, but "getting the worst of it" had to withdraw to a defensive position. On the Wednesday, Thursday and Friday the troops dug in, becoming "one of the very few battalions who have ever really dug the whole system of trenches, and communication trenches, etc." Bloomfield issued operations' orders, received and sent messages, but also rolled up his sleeves to share in the digging.[29]

Every day between 0545 to 0645 hours his soldiers stood to before heading to breakfast at 0700, sorting theirs kits and cleaning rifles. When standing to at reveille and retreat (dawn and dusk), the period when the enemy was most likely to attack, the soldiers "occupy a fire position in the trench and adopting a position of alertness." From 0800 to noon digging started, followed by lunch, rest and a shave from noon to 1400. Between 1400 and 1800 hours the troops returned to digging before break, supper and a smoke from 1800-2000. From 2000 to midnight they were back digging. "Should we ever have to enter the theatre of war I guess we would all be ready for it! It is damned hard work walking so far and then having to dig for 3 days", Bloomfield admitted. "I'd like you to have seen the whole completed affair – all the trenches as they actually are in real warfare, linked together so that we could travel to all our forward companies without being seen by the enemy", the Lance Sergeant enthused. "We have pass words and all the rest of the business".

"Both my feet and my hands were sore, not forgetting my back! (Tell Dad not to laugh too much)", he added, before ending "It will be nice to sleep in a bed again instead of on the hard ground with only one blanket and a great coat. The nights are as cold as Hell!" The troops bedded down under the stars in their shorts and shirts with just one blanket "to get tough all round". Although Bloomfield liked looking at the stars, he felt the work had broken his back and heart.[30] Bandsman Fred Manning with the Devonshire Regiment at Gardai Camp in Waziristan also felt the chill of the nights, telling his parents in Okehampton how "Its very cold here, and we're still under canvas... it will seem funny to be under a solid roof again."[31]

Also fighting with the 1st Battalion the Devonshire Regiment, Harry thanked Mary Hook in Darracott near Taunton for a scarf, which was just the thing he wanted "for its beastly cold here", and would welcome a woollen hat, "one of those that cover the face", if his girlfriend had the time. Harry had not seen barracks for ten months and had just returned safe and fit to camp, although "There are some that's been unlucky since we have been here. I must stop telling you too much about this place for I should be untrue to my Country if I were to carry on". Still wired from his patrols, the soldier added, "Take it from me Mary that it is the time when we must keep awake and keep our eyes and ears in working order with our brain for we are now fighting for Victory, and not in sport." On the front of his envelope the soldier scribbled in pencil "England For Ever".[32]

Private Bert Matthews of the 1st Battalion Queen's Royal Regiment at Razmak complained to his parents, Mr and Mrs J. Semmens of Penzance in Cornwall, how "I don't like it here, but I am like the others making the best of a bad job." Tribesmen raids had killed a few troops at Razmak the week before and while on Road Protection Matthews was twice under fire before three light tanks helped them withdraw.

The soldier's photos of his regiment patrolling the mountains, the Royal Artillery destroying a village, Coronation Camp and possibly enemy cannon were remarkably found preserved inside his letter home. Matthews was otherwise unimpressed by the lack of entertainment and female company in the countryside, but on the upside felt uplifted to "see the Royal Navy smashed up the Italian fleet, and that the Greeks are doing well. Gee I would like to be having a smack at them."[33]

From Campbellpur, Roy D. White with the Royal Artillery told his father in Warminster, Wiltshire, of his happiness in being given extra bedding and coal for the barracks room. A bit of fire made his digs feel "more like home". Otherwise White complained of nowhere to go except the pictures "and that is a pretty rough place." Life on the front line was otherwise very cheap, such as cigarettes and Woodbines costing the equivalent of about 2 pence farthing. A good feed could be got for about 6 annas (less than posting two letters home).[34]

R. Turner with the 1st Battalion the Devonshire Regiment stationed at the Jicca Barracks in Dalhousie, told his darling, Miss Joe Webber at the Royal Devon and Exeter Hospital, how there "are no amusements here at all alas" and that "I think we shall be the only white troops here, so things will be rather miserable." To cheer himself up, Turner was enjoying his three-week old puppy called James, who insisted on climbing all over the writing pad as the solider wrote.[35] C. Dunton Jnr of the 85/11 Field Regt Royal Artillery had been working at the Dulhatt hill station for a month as a clerk in the Department Quartermaster's office, where he had bad memories of his dog

9.6. Bert Matthews of the 1st Battalion Queen's Royal Regiment at Razmak described tribesmen raids (Letter TUR-13-00088-21).

9.7. Photos of the North-west Frontier sent home to Penzance by Bert Matthews: the Royal Artillery destroying a village; troops on mountain patrol (TUR-13-00088-21).

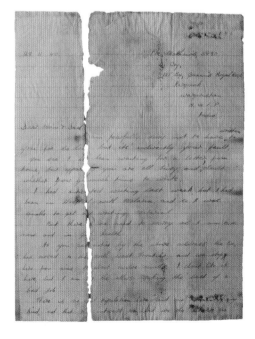

being shot. On this occasion, so he explained to his girlfriend Dorothy in Ironbridge, Wiltshire, he brought another dog up to the base for a pal in hospital, but a panther got it in the night as well.[36]

A breakdown of humour over living conditions loomed large in a letter sent home to Norwood in Gloucestershire by Major J.C.T. Cleane based in Allahabad. The major had recently been in the city of Simla, "all truly ghastly". During an air raid firing on the house he was in, the walls cracked and bricks fell round him. Cleane could not wait to get out of Dihra for Christmas, which would do his troops a power of good because most of the people were Hindus and a bit of beef could not be got. The Commander Officer had invited the major for dinner recently, but his wife forgot to tell the cook, "so I got no beef". The unfed major signed off, "To hell with the Pope. May Mussolini harbour rats in his vitals & Hitler – well I now sully the paper."[37]

In some lines home to Master John Guy at Dorset House School in Cheriton Bishop, Devon, Major K. Guy explained how the climate gave one prickly heat, "a rash which irritates terribly. It usually breaks out when one's clothes fit tightly – round the neck, or round the waist." The major was very busy getting to grips with a new subject, Air Defence, and was charged with a whole city's safety. He sent his stamp collector son, "My Dear old Porker", an envelope posted to Uncle B. in May 1940, but which "never reached him, as the Germans were in Paris first", having captured the city in June 1940. The letter was covered with a mass of stamps, including 'Opened By Censor' and 'Service Suspended. Returned To Sender'.[38]

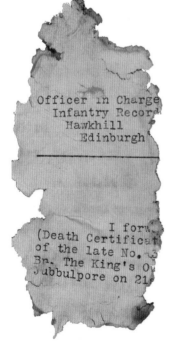

Casualties of the tribal war shared mixed fortunes. Rupert Searle of the 1st Devonshire Regiment informed his sister in Cornwall that he was in the British Military Hospital at Rawalpindi, where he was having a stem graft from his good to bad leg, which had gangrene.

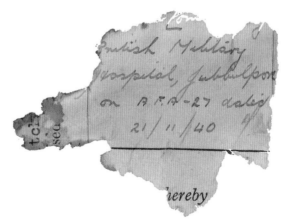

9.8. Scraps of death certificates sent by Captain J.D. Henson, the 2nd Battalion King's Own Scottish Borderers, Jubbulpore to the Officer In Charge, Infantry Record, Hawkhill, Edinburgh (Letter TUR-13-00086-44).

Military Regiment Writers in the *Gairsoppa* Letters

Assam Rifles – 2nd Battalion, 4th Battalion

10th Baluch Regiment – Air Headquarters, New Delhi

Band of His Excellency the Governor of Bengal

Border Regiment – Ghorpuri Battalion, Poona. 2nd Battalion

3rd Carabiniers – RHQ Squadron, Sialkot

Devonshire Regiment – 1st Battalion, 'C Company', 125 Battalion. Gardai Camp, Rayani, and Waziristan, North-west Frontier; Jicca Barracks, Dalhousie

Duke of Cornwall's Light Infantry – 1st Battalion. Napier Barracks, Lahore Cantonment, Punjab

9 Gorkha Rifles, Ambala

27th Inniskilling Regiment of Foot – Haig Barracks, Malappuram, S. Malabar

85/11 Field Regiment – Meerut

King's Own Scottish Borderers – Jubbulpore, Central Provinces

Queen's Royal Regiment – 1st Battalion, Razmak, Waziristan

Queen Victoria's Own Corps of Guides – Peshawur, North-west Frontier

Rajputana Rifles – Kohat, North-west Frontier

Royal Army Medical Corps. – Jubbulpore, Central Provinces

Royal Army Ordnance Corps.

Royal Artillery – Medium Battery, Campbellpur, North-west Frontier

Royal Indian Army Service Corps. – Chaklala, Rawalpindi

1 Signal Training Centre – Jubbulpore, Central Provinces

Sikh Regiment – 10th Battalion, Nowshera, North-west Frontier

Wiltshire Regiment – 2nd Battalion, Allahabad and Sialkot

Worcestershire Regiment – 2nd Battalion, Sialkot

A second operation on 26 November 1940, when 150 little cuts were taken from his good leg and grafted to his bad one, almost had his leg off. The prognosis was not good: "they said then the longest I would live was two days. I had to fight for it the second night it was touch and go… but I won in the end". Searle hoped one day to walk again, but expected to take Christmas dinner in a hospital bed.[39] In the British Military Hospital, Lahore Cantonment, the matron, W. Russell, had the sad job of telling Mrs Oates in Cornwall that her soldier son had been in hospital for three weeks in a critical condition and was too ill to write, but was getting everything he needed, feeling no pain, starting to sleep better and taking more interest in his food.[40]

Scraps of poorly preserved typed letters en route from Captain J.D. Henson via a military hospital in Jubbulpore in central India to the Infantry Record Officer of the King's Own Scottish Borderers in Hawkhill, Edinburgh, seemed to bear the worst news, containing the terms "I certify that the next of kin...", in one case naming a deceased soldier. At least one cause of death was malaria.[41]

The enemy was not just Indian tribes fighting the British Raj. An unnamed author wrote home from Moradabad to "Meine Liebe Ellen und Liebe Walter" about a trip to discuss with a Committee "the question of interment" of Mutti (mother), who was being held in a parole camp in the hills of Nairi Tal with about thirty others, no doubt due to her nationality. The writer explained that she was being looked after well amid views of Himalayan snows, but nevertheless "One dare not open the newspaper and think too much. The best is to just live in the present and not worry over the future. If only a British victory came soon."[42] A second letter by the same author, heading for Los Angeles, was written in mixed German and English.[43] Ted from the 85/11 Field Regiment in Meerut confirmed to his parents in Swindon, Wiltshire, that big prison camps for Germans had been built near Bombay.[44]

Wheels of Commerce

Much of the *Gairsoppa* post focussed on finding ways to grind out profits under conditions of war. The shipwrecked business correspondence covers a wide swathe of affairs from consumer to producer and everything in between. Updates of crops and accounts were dispatched to Devon and London from the tea estates of Bhatkawa, Darjeeling, Koomber and Rajahbhat in northeast India and Yellapatty to the southwest. Reminders of outstanding invoices and cheques were en route to Los Angeles, San Francisco and London.

Orders for medical equipment, rubber sheeting and bibles were shipped to London and Wiltshire. Tanners and exporters of calfskins and hides confirmed sales. Catalogues for watch making, pencils and postcard board samples were requested. Completed examination sheets for the long-distance learning of radio and television engineering were being returned for marking to the "Internationally Known Radio Home Study School", the Hollywood Radio & Television Institute in Los Angeles.[45]

9.9. Dadajee Dhackjee & Co. of Bombay enquired if Messrs. Marshall Dill in San Francisco could replace their lost $1 million annual business with F.G. Farben Fabrican Industrielle of Frankfurt (Letter TUR-13-00079-17).

9.10. J.P. Ghadiali & Co. of Bombay enquired if Messrs. West Coast Importing & Exporting Co. in San Francisco could bypass India's embargo on canned American products by re-routing via Canada (Letter TUR-13-00080-01).

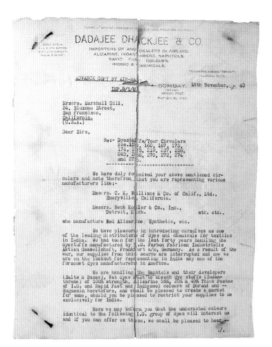

The war inevitably pinched the logistics of business, often requiring creative solutions. J.P. Ghadiali & Co. of Bombay was disappointed to be forbidden from importing tinned goods from Messrs. West Coast Importing & Exporting Co. However, if the San Francisco firm could bypass India's strict embargo on all canned American products by re-routing via Canada as the country of origin, Ghadiali & Co. could commit to substantial orders, including cold storage shipment of thirty cases of apricots, fifty cases of peaches, thirty cases of pears, a hundred cases of fruit salad, and ten cases of covering chocolate. Sausages, Viennas and Frankfurts, ham, bacon, pate, caviars, asparagus, peas, French beans, sauerkraut and cauliflower were also of interest.[46]

The T. Matandas & Co. of Karachi, by contrast, cancelled its former orders of fruit, although vegetable shipments were still allowed, excluding Tomato Catsup.[47] The tomato embargo was intensified by very severe storm damage to the tomato crop in the Bombay region.[48] The ketchup enjoyed in the *Gairsoppa*'s dining room (Chapter 5) was a rare commodity in World War II.

One of India's leading distributors of dyes and chemicals for textiles, Dadajee Dhackjee & Co. of Bombay, reached out to Messrs. Marshall Dill in San Francisco to fill the $1 million yearly void created by the loss of business with F.G. Farben Fabrican Industrielle in Frankfurt. The Indian company had worked with the Germans for the last forty years.[49] Wary of security when importing sulphur for bleaching and refining sugar, DAS & Company of Bombay warned Messrs. Stauffer Chemical Company in San Francisco that "Under any circumstances our name must not be written on any packages inside or outside."[50]

Shipped goods were subject to unexpected delays or acts of war. Many firms, including the Silver Java Pacific Line, had by November 1940 agreed to change a clause stamped on Bills of Lading, whereby "Carriers have the right to transship the cargo by port to a neutral or allied belligerent vessel however no responsibility can be accepted in the event of a neutral vessel becoming enemy after the vessel has been transhipped".[51] *The Statesman* for 25 October 1940, rolls of which were being sent to the UK on the *Gairsoppa*, also told its readers that henceforth for the P&O and British India Steam Navigation Co. Ltd., "All vessels may call at any ports on or off the route and the route and all sailings are subject to cancellation change or deviation with or without notice."[52]

On the plus side, war boosted many of India's industries, such as cloth manufacture, munitions and steel works (see Chapter 4).[53] The shipwrecked mail has left behind a healthy audit of the wide range of commodities bought and sold by India. The Malang Trading Co. of Madras sent tanned sheep and goat skins to Messrs. Gough, Kidston & Co. in London.[54] Pangda Tshang in Kalimpong shipped one hundred bales of light grey Tibet wool on the SS *Manipur*, valued at £1,433, to the Alexander Smith & Sons Carpet Co. in New York.[55] An invoice for 50,000 yards of burlap/hessian cloth in twenty-five bales, sent on the SS *Silver Yew*, was posted by Ramsahaimill More Ltd. to Stein Hall & Co. Inc. in New York.[56]

Equipment to test milk quality in the Imperial Dairy, Bangalore, was ordered from Tintometer Ltd. in London.[57] The Bengal Immunity Company Limited enquired from Messrs. New Chemical Corporation of America in New York about purchasing potent Vitamins A and D fish liver concentrates used in vegetable oils, as well as Thiamin Chloride and Riboflavin.[58]

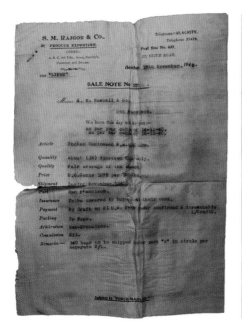

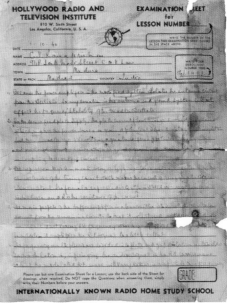

9.11. S.M. Rajgor & Co. of Bombay confirmed shipping tons of seeds to Messrs. H.M. Newhall & Co. in San Francisco (Letter TUR-13-00084-42).

9.12. Exam sheet from C.V. Ramakisman, 91A South Masi Street, CMV Lane, Madura, Madras to the Hollywood Radio & Television Institute, 810 West Sixth Street, Los Angeles (Letter TUR-13-00080-04D).

9.13. A National Bank of India cheque for £5 sent to Mrs Jessie Ridley in Paignton, Devon by Mr C.W. Morley at the Koomber Tea Estate, Cachar (Letter TUR-13-00088-26).

P.S.P. Kandasamy Nadar & Sons of Tuticorin reminded Messrs. N.E. Neter & Co. Ltd in London of a rare opportunity to send a Clan Line Steamer shipment of senna leaves and pods, crude drugs and spices.[59] An invoice for $361.90 for three cases of cardamoms sent out from Bombay on the SS *President Polk* steamer was posted to Messrs. D.M. Hutton & Co. in Los Angeles.[60] A combination of 25 tons of cuminseed, 5 tons of dill-seed, 3 tons of Indian nigerseed, 2 tons of celeryseed and 1 ton of white poppyseed was confirmed for shipping to Messrs. H.M. Newhall & Co. in San Francisco by S.M. Rajgor & Co. in Bombay.[61]

The Manufacturers Agents & General Merchants R. Rustomji & Co. of Bombay requested condensed milk and sardines from Messrs. Prince George Meskhi-Gleboff Inc. in Los Angeles. Subject to favourable rates, India could import 300 cases of sardines at a time, the fish packed 3½ ounces per tin and one hundred tins to a case. The firm also asked for quotes to import corn beef and thin crisp, corrugated, water clear Gelatine sheets of cheap quality toilet paper in bundles of about 1lb, wrapped with blue glazed paper printed with gold ink and packed about 112 packets to a carton.[62] Copies of life insurance documents held by Indian employees, on their way for rubber stamping by the Manufacturers Life Insurance Company in Toronto, would never reach Canada for approval.[63]

Notes

1. Letter TUR-13-00083-31, 24.11.40. Douglas, Dorothy, John & Jeremy Lappundy (?), Panitola PO, Upper Assam to Mrs H.R. Fraser, c/o Mrs Stayner, Llanstephan, Teignmouth, Devon.
2. Letter TUR-13-00083-39C.
3. Letter TUR-13-00071-58, 1.12.40. Prem Miwas, Pearey Ral Rd, Karol Bagh, Delhi to Mrs Gwen Lunham, 24 Northfield Square, Tuffley, Gloucester.
4. Letter TUR-13-00088-52, 1.12.40. Pam, Hotel Imperiel, Queensway, New Delhi to Tim G. Preedy, Bryne House, College Road, Cheltenham.

5. Letter, TUR-13-00071-38, 30.11.40. Sister Gwendolen OMST, House of the Epiphany, Barisal, Bengal to Miss Chanipernowure, 8 Queens Terrace, St. David's Hill, Exeter.

6. Letter TUR-13-00083-48, 25.11.40. Kathleen, 11 Suite, 53 Chouringhee Road, Calcutta, to Mr and Mrs Bayly, Allukera, Salisbury Road, Amesbury, Wiltshire.

7. Letter TUR-13-00088-13, 30.11.40. B.M.H., Lahore Cantonment, to Miss (?) M. Russell, Coxley, Somerset.

8. Letter TUR-13-00071-50, 28.11.40. 14/40 Civil Lines, Cawnpore to Miss Bernice McTyner, c/o Mrs Inwood, 25 King's Ash Road, Paignton, Devon.

9. Letter TUR-13-00088-15, 29.11.40. Mrs Detsulls, Brigade House, Kohar to Mrs C. Mackeer, Brook Lodge, Thorverton, Exeter, Devon.

10. Letter TUR-13-00083-29, 23.11.40. Sister Mary, Barisal, E. Bengal to Arthur E. Eastwood Esq, Leigh Court, Taunton.

11. Letter TUR-13-00081-05, 15.11.40. Kitty Shaw, Imphal, Manipur State to Mrs M. Luffman, Cludleigh, South Devon.

12. Letter TUR-13-00083-33, 18-25.11.40. John Bunce to Mrs Jilian Bunce, Taunton Heath, Taunton Braunton, North Devon.

13. Letter TUR-13-00083-42, 26.11.40. Tom to Miss C. Hubweir (?), 29 Forester Avenue, Bath.

14. Letter TUR-13-00088-53, 1.12.40. Captain G.C. Monchton, Marina Hotel, New Delhi to the Rev. J.F. and Freda Monchton, Penn House, Tivoli Road, Cheltenham.

15. Papagos, 1949: 80.

16. Letter TUR-13-00083-03, 18.11.40. Sister Gwendolen, House of the Epiphany, Barisal, Bengal to Miss Katharine Martin, St Cross, Streatham Rise, Exeter.

17. Letter TUR-13-00083-33, 18-25.11.40. John Bunce to Miss Jilian Bunce, Taunton Heath, Taunton Braunton, North Devon.

18. Letter TUR-13-00081-12, 15.11.40. Hensetea (?), Naffring (?), Assam to My Dear Betty.

19. Letter TUR-13-00071-16, 21.11.40-1.12.40. Embossed notepaper, Denis Pudlay (?), Puckrie, Barashakia PO, Champaran to Mrs Mary Hudson, --5 Lansdown Parade, Cheltenham.

20. Letter TUR-13-00088-25, 28.11.40. Gladys Clapp, 'Idalia', Ootakamund to Mr and Mrs Oakey, 39 Corby Avenue, Swindon, Wiltshire.

21. Letter TUR-13-00081-16, 17.11.40. Miss Dot Ruth, SPG Mission, Ranchi, Bihar to Mrs May Newnam, 12 Devonshire Road, Salisbury, Wiltshire.

22. Letter TUR-13-00083-34, 24.11.40. Archie, c/o Whiteway Laidlow & Co, Calcutta to Mrs Lilian Osborne, 3 Matford Lane, Exeter, Devon.

23. Moreman, 1998: 138, 163; Roe, 2010: 183.

24. *Express and Echo*, 2 October 1940.

25. Roe, 2010: 182-83.

26. Moreman, 1998: 179. Roe, 2010: vii, 21.

27. Letter TUR-13-00071-18, 29.11.40. Jack Butler, 5614903, 1st Battalion the Devonshire Regiment, Gardai Camp, Waziristan, NWF to Mrs S. Butler, Lower Village, Bradworthy, Holsworthy, Devon.

28. Letter TUR-13-00071-09. 5619462, R/C W. Bill Wheeler, A. Coy, 1st Batt., the Devonshire Regiment, Gardai Camp, Rayani, NWF to Mrs F. Wheeler, 30 Watts Pk Road, Peverell, Plymouth, Devon.

29. Letter TUR-13-00071-12. L/Sjt. Jack Bloomfield, Orderly Room, 1st Battalion Duke of Cornwall's Light Infantry, Napier BRS, Lahore Cantonment, Punjab to Mrs C. Bloomfield, Asherne Lodge, Strete, Nr Dartmouth, Devon.

30. Letter TUR-13-00071-40, 1.12.40. L/Sjt. Jack Bloomfield, Orderly Room, 1st Battalion Duke of Cornwall's Light Infantry, Napier Barracks, Lahore Cantonment, Punjab to Miss Margaret Trembath, Breage, Nr Helston, Cornwall.

31. Letter TUR-13-00071-42, 26.11.40. Bandsman Fred Manning, Devonshire Regiment, Gardai Camp, Waziristan to Mr and Mrs S. Manning, Ewhurst, Barton Close, Okehampton, Devon.

32. Letter TUR-13-00088-41. Harry, 5617785, 1th Buold, 'C' Coy, 1st Devons, Army Post Office to Miss Mary Hook, Darracott, Curry Road, Nr. Taunton.

33. Letter TUR-13-00088-21, 28.11.40. Private Bert Matthews 5980, D. Coy, 1st. Bn. Queen's Royal Regt., Razmak, Waziristan, NWFP to Mr and Mrs J. Semmens, 4 Colinsey Place, Trenear Estate, Penzance, Cornwall.

34. Letter TUR-13-00088-17, 29.11.40. Drv. Roy D. White 2620, Medium Battery R.A., Royal Artillery, Campbellpur, NWFP to Mrs A.J. White, Boreham Road, Warminster, Wiltshire.

35. Letter TUR13-00088-08. R. Turner, 5615497, Devon Regt, Jicca Barracks, Dalhousie, India, to Miss Joe Webber, Royal Devon & Exeter Hospital, Exeter, Devon.

36. Letter TUR-13-00071-22, 20.11.40. Charles Dunton Jnr, 85/11 Fd Regt RA, Meerut to Miss Dorothy Ford, Ironbridge, Wiltshire.

37. Letter TUR-13-00088-47. Major J.C.T. Cleane (?), Allahabad, UP to Mrs Cleane (?), Norwood, 39 Leckhampton Road, Cheltenham, Glos.

38. Letter TUR-13-00088-20, 29.11.40. Major K. Guy, Kohat, Rajputana Rifles, c/o Grindlay & CO. Ltd, Post Box No. 93, Bombay to Master John Guy, Dorset House School, 90 Woodleigh Hall, Cheriton Bishop, Devon.

39. Letter TUR-13-00071-13. 5616490, Rupert Searle, HQ Devon Rgt B.M. Hospital, Rawalpindi to Miss Bet Searle, Foster Kitchen Staff, E.M. Hospital, Bodmin, Cornwall.

40. Letter TUR-13-00071-39, 1.12.40. W. Russell, Matron, OHMS, British Military Hospital, Lahore Cant. to Mrs Oates, Clasewale (?), Cornwall.

41. Letter TUR-13-00086-44. J.D. Henson, Captain, 2nd Bn, King's Own Scottish Borderers, Jubbulpore to Officer In Charge, Infantry Record, Hawkhill, Edinburgh.

42. Letter TUR-13-00085-1, 24.11.40. Moradabad, U.P.

43. Letter TUR-13-00084-38. Moradabad, U.P. to Mary Harper?, ----- 55th Street, Los Angeles, California.

44. Letter TUR-13-00071-21. 834204, Ted, 85/11 Field Regt, Meerut to Mrs. T. Charleston (?), 61 Stafford St., Swindon, Wiltshire.

45. By example Letter TUR-13-00080-03. A.J. Powell, 2 Portuguese Church, George Town, Madras to Hollywood Radio & Television Institute, 810 West Sixth Street, Los Angeles, California.

46. Letter TUR-13-00080-01, 16.11.40. The Importers & Exporters Ltd Agents, J.P. Ghadiali & Co., Telegraphic Address 'Helio' Bombay, Post Box No. 446 to Messrs. West Coast Importing & Exporting Co., 25 California Street, San Francisco.

47. Letter TUR-13-00079-32B, 8.11.40. T. Matandas & Co., Post Box 25, Bunder Road, Karachi to Messrs: Liberty Gold Fruit Co., 310 California Street, San Francisco, California.

48. Letter TUR-13-00084-19, November 1940. Mather & Platt Ltd., Engineers, Bombay House, 24 Bruce Street, Fort, Bombay, Post Box 327 to Messrs. The Food Machinery Corporation of America, 70 Pine Street, San Francisco, California.

49. Letter TUR-13-00079-17, 18.11.40. Dadajee Dhackjee & Co., Motor Department, Shree Pant Bhuvan, Sandhurst Bridge, Bombay 7 to Messrs. Marshall Dill, 24 Bluxome Street, San Francisco, California.

50. Letter TUR-13-00084-28, 23.11.40. DAS & Company, 59 Apollo Street, Fort, P.O. Box No. 784, Bombay to Messrs. Stauffer Chemical Company, 624-638, California Street, San Francisco, California.

51. TUR-13-00084-42, 5.11.40. S.M. Rajgor & Co., Bombay 9 to Messrs. H.M. Newhall & Co., Newhall Building, San Francisco, California.

52. Letter TUR-13-00076-01-PC, 25.10.40.

53. Letter TUR-13-00079-42(3), 17.11.40. Tata Iron & Steel Co., Jamshedpur, Via Tatanagar, B. N. Ry. to Messrs. Tata Iron & Steel Co., 90 Broad Street, New York.

54. Letter TUR-13-00069-03, 22.11.40. Malang Trading Co., Tanners, Merchants & Agents, Periamet, Madras to Messrs. Gough, Kidston & Co., Chemical Manufacturers, 43 & 45 Great Tower St., London EC3.

55. Letter TUR-13-00078-03. Pangda Tshang, Tibet Wool Merchants, Kalimpong, Bengal to Alexander Smith & Sons Carpet Co., New York.

56. Letter TUR-13-00078-04(4), 11.11.40. Ramsahaimill More Ltd., Calcutta to Stein Hall & Co. Inc., New York.

57. Letter TUR-13-00069-05, 20.11.40. Adair Dutt Co. Ltd, Mount Road, Madras Office to London office.

58. Letter TUR-13-00078-06, 20.11.40. Bengal Immunity Company Limited, Manufacturers of Biological and Pharmaceutical Products to Messrs. New Chemical Corporation of America, 250 East 43 Street, New York.

59. Letter TUR-13-00069-10, 20.11.40. P.S.P. Kandasamy Nadar & Sons, Tuticorin, S. India to Messrs. N.E. Neter & Co. Ltd, 29 Mincing Lane, London EC3.

60. Letter TUR-13-00079-34C, 14.11.40. Invoice Chartered Bank of India, Australia & China to Messrs. D.M. Hatton & Co., Los Angeles.

61. Letter TUR-13-00084-42(2), 5.11.40. S.M. Rajgor & Co., Post Box No. 637, 22 Clive Road, Bombay 9 to Messrs. H.M. Newhall & Co., Newhall Building, San Francisco, California.

62. Letter TUR-13-00084-40, 22.11.40. R. Rustomji & Co., Manufacturers Agents & General Merchants, 31 Pitha Street, Fort, P.O. Box. No. 884, Bombay to Messrs. Prince George Meskhi-Gleboff Inc., 276 Chamber Commerce Building, Los Angeles.

63. Certificate TUR-13-00070-01. By example Policy No. 652,408. To the Manufacturers Life Insurance Company, Toronto, Canada.

10

CONCLUSION. FUTURE HORIZONS

SEAN KINGSLEY & NEIL CUNNINGHAM DOBSON

At the moment when the *Gairsoppa* sank, nobody could have predicted the fate of the free world. An Allied victory was far off and far from certain. Some writers among the shipwrecked mail prayed for a quick end to war in these days of uncertainty, while others wanted finality over several decades of German belligerence. Mrs J.S. Boodlen in Whitehaven, Devon, was told that "we do not want a patch up peace – we must beat the swine. And do it properly. Their women must feel it".[1]

Tom's opinion from the Bengal Club in Calcutta to Miss C. Hubwein in Bath optimistically believed that the war was "all working out nicely & Hitler will probably have started in the Near East by the time you get this & that is where he will meet his downfall. Russia comes in too & the final Armageddon takes place some time in the next year".[2]

Mrs Browne at the D.H. Mission in Hazaribagh, Bihar, by contrast, did not know what to expect. "What a world", she shared with the Reverend Eliott Keworthe Browne near Salisbury. "I suppose everyone's now waiting to know what Hit: has up his sleeve. While our RAF continue pounding away at his bomb factories he's bound to sit still. Meanwhile old Muss: is messing about in messing most things… It's simply amazing how England weather the summer's Blitzkrieg – and the threat of invasion… like that of Bonaparte".[3]

The highly experienced Major C.E. Cox, Companion of the Order of the Indian Empire, was confident that America was a crucial key, so he informed his wife's cousin Jim Copp and his wife Cora in Los Angeles:[4]

> I wonder what America will do in the end?… I well remember the day I went with
> you to that luncheon party of ex service men. Do you remember that & how

proud they were of what they had done in the last war? I often wonder what their feelings are now when they are so badly wanted for help in the present one & what they will do. I can never forget the magnificent men I met in California... one cannot believe that in the end America will not rally wholeheartedly to help destroy this menace to world peace... May this awful war come to a successful end as soon as possible but not before Hitler & all his devils have been put down for good & all. I only pray that America will come in eventually & help do this.

Three months later Major Cox's hopes began to be fulfilled as the Yankee tide turned. America signed the Lend-Lease Act in March 1941 to loan money, arms and food to the UK and on 8 December Franklin D. Roosevelt finally sent his country to war after the Japanese bombing of Pearl Harbour.

India's Legacy

India's vast reserves of raw materials and bottomless labour was another key player in the defeat of Hitler. As a newspaper clipping cut out of *The Statesman* of 16 November 1940 by Miss E.M. Ruth of the SPG Mission, Ranchi, and sent to Mrs E. Newnam in Salisbury, Wiltshire, accurately predicted, "As time passes and Britain and Germany destroy each other's industries more and more systematically, the difficulties will increase... In India there is safety and a vast reserve, both of recruits and of teachable labour".[5]

The loudest voices among the *Gairsoppa* letters were British citizens fighting, working and acting out a thoroughly Anglo-Saxon lifestyle in India. The Raj may have been on its last legs, but British India was still a colonial bastion of old empire. The officers on the *Gairsoppa* were British too, albeit supported by a crew of almost predomi-nantly Lascar Indians (Appendix 1). As the

10.1. Major C.E. Cox in Belgaum wondered when America will rally to help destroy the menace to world peace (Letter TUR-13-00085-10-E).

former First Lord of the Admiralty, Winston Churchill was fully aware of the Fourth Service's role in the war, which he acknowledged in his Victory in Europe broadcast of May 1945: "My friends, when our minds turn to the North-western approaches we will not forget the devotion of our merchant seamen… so rarely mentioned in the headlines."[6]

India was a very different prospect. Churchill had a nightmarish obsession with the country's growing wealth and Britain's impoverishment as a result of India's accumulation of sterling balances and debt in London.[7] The historical legacy of the last voyage of the *Gairsoppa*, its cargo and letters are a stark reminder that this shipwreck's story is conspicuously about the great debt of gratitude Britain owed the people of India for its wartime victory. It was Indian workers who toiled in the tea estates to bring brew to Blighty, choked in the iron mines and sweated in the furnaces of Bombay and Calcutta to melt silver into bars.

Alongside these vital industries, 50,000 soldiers swelled the Indian army each month, ultimately making up a fighting force of 2.5 million men and women: the largest volunteer body of its kind in the world. Its men fought with distinction in the Abyssinian Campaign, the Western Desert, Egypt, Africa, Greece, Italy, Germany and the Far East, Singapore, Malaya, Hong Kong and Burma. Another 8 million Indians toiled in auxiliary work for the armed forces and over 5 million were employed in war industries.[8] Little wonder Sir Jeremy Raisman, a finance member of the Government of India, acknowledged in somewhat understated fashion in February 1944 that "It will be sufficient to say that the trained soldiers and the stream of munitions and war stores poured out by India have been a most potent factor in the victories achieved in these theatres."

Future Horizons

As history unfolded, World War II marked a beginning, not an end. A united nations and united Europe became stronger. Back in India, the British India Steam Navigation Co. Ltd rebuilt and by January 1947 had twenty-four new ships back in service.[9] Maritime war risk claims at least gave the firm the finances to start again after fifty-one ships – half the BISN fleet – were destroyed and 1,083 officers and crew killed.[10]

The voices of the *Gairsoppa* recovered from the 4,700 metre-deep wreckage stand alone as the only significant cache of letters found beneath the world's oceans, but their discovery and remarkable preservation set a potential precedent for similar finds in the decades and centuries to come. How many lost mail bags lie in the icy cold, dark black depths nobody can say. Perhaps millions of letters, though, may survive below the world's waves – silent but now no longer forgotten.

Behind the cargoes, small finds and letters stands the memory of the brave few. The *Gairsoppa*'s crew was always ready to respond to attack, never went anywhere on the ship without a lifejacket, slept in clothes and kept the lifeboats at the ready, equipped with emergency rescue gear. Every merchant ship and every merchant sailor feared the fate of the *Gairsoppa*. Her memory can be honoured and her secrets revealed only due to the skill of state-of-the-art ROV (Remotely-Operated Vehicles) robots, tools and their expert operators, a new technological science that is opening up the great unknown of the deep.

The letters from the *Gairsoppa* are today housed at The Postal Museum in London alongside a rich collection illustrating the history of the UK mail service. From the safety of dry land, there they are available to chroniclers of World War II India and Britain of the future.

Notes

1. Letter TUR-13-00071-44B. Jim, Sapur Papuhies (?), Kothapetta to Mrs J.S. Boodlen, The Priory, Whitehaven, Tavistock, Devon.
2. Letter TUR-13-00083-42, 26.11.40. Tom to Miss C. Hubweir (?), 29 Forester Avenue, Bath.
3. Letter TUR-13-00071-15, Advent Sunday 1940. Mrs Browne, D.H. Mission, Hazaribagh, Bihar to Reverend Eliott Keworthe Browne, Darnford Vicarage, Nr Salisbury.
4. Letter TUR-13-00085-10, 26.11.40. Major C.E. 'Cockus' Cox, C.I.E., Belgaum to Andrew J. Copp, 937 Consolidated Building, 607 South Hill St., Los Angeles, California.
5. Letter TUR-13-00081-16(6-9), 17.11.40. Miss Dot Ruth, SPG Mission, Ranchi, Bihar to Mrs May Newnam, 12 Devonshire Road, Salisbury, Wilts.
6. Elphick, 1999: 10.
7. Voigt, 1990: 191.
8. Ahluwalia, 1949: 110, 113.
9. St George Saunders, 1948: 161.
10. Blake, 1956: 196

APPENDIX 1
GAIRSOPPA CREW LIST

The 86-person crew list for the SS *Gairsoppa*'s final voyage (5 December 1940 to 16 February 1941) includes names, ages (when known) and positions on the ship. Unless otherwise stated, all are identifiable as lascars and Indians of British India.

Abdul Aziz, 45, Tindal
Abdul Barik, 44, Seaman
Abdul Ghafur, 20, Trimmer
Abdul Hakim, 32, Fireman
Abdul Jabbar, 37, Seacunny
Abdul Karim, 45, Oiler
Abdul Karim, 33, Trimmer
Abdul Latif, 48, Trimmer
Abdul Majid, 39, Seacunny
Abdul Malik, 45, Tindal
Abdul Qudus, 41, Serang
Abdul Rashid, Seaman
Abdul Satar, 27, Fireman
Abdur Rashid, Trimmer
Ali Ahmad, 30, Seaman
Ali Ahmad, 31, Fireman
Amin Rahman, 44, Trimmer
Aqal Ali, 39, Seaman
Ayres, Richard, Second
Officer (British)
Caldeiro, L., 19, Cook
Cardoze, Pudade, 43, Cook
Carmichael, Andrew Parker, 32,
Third Engineer Officer (British)
Collaco, Joas Piadade, 43, Boy
Costa, Joaquim Maten, 22, Boy
Cummings, George, 37,
Chief Officer (British)
De Costa, F., 29, Boy
De Costa, Jose Antonio, 32, Boy
Dulla Mian, 30, Fireman
Dupuy, William Frederick, 26,
Purser (British)
Fazl Karim, 30, Fireman

Fernandes, Thomas Martino,
38, General Servant
Firoz Ali, 30, Donkeyman
Fyfe, Peter, 49,
Chief Engineer Officer (British)
Hafiz-Ur-Rahman, 40, Seaman
Hampshire, Robert, 18,
Radio Officer (British)
Hinton, William Thomas, 31,
Deck Hand (British)
Hyland, Gerald, 40, Master (British)
Illahi Bakhsh, 55, Winchman
Jabal Haq, 41, Seaman
Jalal Ahmad, 48, Oiler
Jetu, 36, Topass
Khalil Rahman, 75, Serang
Khurshid Mian, 40, Cassab
Khurshid Mian, 43, Seacunny
Kishori, 21, Topass
Lang, Robert, 44, Second
Engineer Officer (British)
Leong Kong, Carpenter (Chinese)
Lucas, Wilfred, 25, Junior
Engineer Officer (British)
Majib-Ul-Haq, 40, Seaman
Majid Mian, 29, Seaman
Mangal, 36, Topass
Maqbul Husain, Seaman
Maqbul Husain, 26, Trimmer
Morrison, Campbell, 24,
Third Officer (British)
Motihar Rahman, 41, Seaman
Muhammad, 50, Bhandary
Muhammad Harun, 28, Seaman

Muhammad Islam, 31,
Lamp Trimmer
Mulaqat Juma, 37, Fireman
Munir Ahmad, 29, Fireman
Murshid Mian, 33, Bhandary
Nazir Ahmad, 50, Tindal
Nisar Ahmad, 20, Trimmer
Nur Ahmad, 30, Fireman
Nur-Ul-Haq, 38, Seacunny
Odd, Hugh Henry, Fourth
Engineer Officer (British)
Pais, Acacio Rozario, 66, Butler
Price, William George, RM, 55,
Marine (DEMS Gunner) (British)
Raja Mian, 21, Trimmer
Rodrigues, 31, Boy
Rodrigues, C., 51, Baker
Rodrigues, E.C., 29, Pantryman
Rodrigues, Tiofilo, General Servant
Salamat Ullah, 38, Seaman
Sayid Ahmad, 36, Seaman
Sayid Rahman, 42, Cassab
Sheikh Kinu, 54, Boy
Sheraz-Ul-Haq, 42, Trimmer
Shujat Ali, 45, Oiler
Sikandar Badshah, 33, Seaman
Taz-Ul-Mulk, 40, Seaman
Thomas, Norman, 20, Deck
Hand/Gunner (British)
Tufail Ahmad, 23, Trimmer
Wali Mian, 36, Seaman
Wilayat Ali, 33, Fireman
Woodliffe, John Martin, 17,
Cadet (British)

BIBLIOGRAPHY

1. Introduction

Fleming, L., *Last children of the Raj. British childhoods in India, 1939-1950* (London, 2004).

Jog, N.G., *Will War Come To India?* (Bombay, 1941).

Longmate, N., *How We Lived Then. A History of Everyday Life During the Second World War* (Capetown, 1973).

2. British India Steam Power

Blake, G., *B.I. Centenary 1856-1956* (London, 1956).

Chakrabarty, D., *Rethinking Working Class History. Bengal, 1890-1940* (Delhi, 1989).

Churchill, W., *The Second World War, Volume 2. Their Finest Hour* (London, 1949).

Cunningham Dobson, N., *German U-boats of the English Channel & Western Approaches: History, Site Formation & Impacts* (OME Papers 35, Tampa, 2013).

Dobson, N.C., *Oral Testimony. An interview with Norman Walker Dobson on his work as a 2nd Radio Officer Aboard the British India Steam Navigation Company Cargo ship SS Urlana on her Final Voyage* (May 1996).

Doenitz, K., *Memoirs. Ten years and Twenty Days* (London, 2002).

Edwards, B., *Beware Raiders! German Surface Raiders in the Second World War* (Barnsley, 2001).

Elphick, P., *Life Line. The Merchant Navy at War 1939-1945* (London, 1999).

Hague. A., *The Allied Convoy System 1939-1945. Its Organization, Defence and Operation* (St Catharines, Ontario, 2000).

Halley, M.P., *An Ethnography of Marine Convoys During World War II* (University of Sheffield, 1995).

Howard, A.M., 'Freetown and World War II. Strategic Militarization, Accommodation, and Resistance'. In J.A. Byfield, C.A. Brown, T. Parsons and A. Alawad Sikainga (eds.), *Africa and World War II* (Cambridge University Press, 2015), 183-99.

Jackson, R., *Kriegsmarine. The Illustrated History of the German Navy in World War II* (London, 2001).

Kaplan, K. and Currie, J., *Convoy. Merchant Sailors at War 1939-1945* (London, 1998).

Keegan, J., *Battle at Sea* (London, 1988).

Kipling, R., *From Sea to Sea and Other Sketches. Letters of Travel* (London, 1900).

Koop, G. and Schmolke, K.-P., *Heavy Cruisers of the Admiral Hipper Class* (London, 2001).

Laxon, W.A. and Perry, F.W., *B.I. The British India Steam Navigation Company Limited* (Kendal, 1994).

Lloyd's War Losses, The Second World War – 3 September 1939 - 14 August 1945: Volume 1 (London, 1991).

St George Saunders, H., *Valiant Voyaging. A Short History of the British India Steam Navigation Company in the Second World War, 1939-1945* (London, 1948).

Schmalenbach, P., *German Raiders. A History of Auxiliary Cruisers of the German Navy 1895-1945* (Annapolis, 1977).

Smith, H., *Life of John Wilson. For Fifty Years Philanthropist and Scholar in the East* (Cambridge, 2012).

Spencer, G.T., *Journal of a Visitation-tour, in 1843-4, Through Part of the Western Portion of His Diocese* (London, 1845).

Stern, R.C., *Type VII U-boats* (London, 1998).

Tennent, A.J., *British and Commonwealth Merchant Ship Losses to Axis Submarines 1939-1945* (Stroud, 2001).

Von der Porten, E.P., *The German Navy in World War II* (New York, 1968).

Von Trapp, G., *To The Last Salute* (University of Nebraska Press, 2007).

White, D., *Bitter Ocean: The Battle of the Atlantic, 1939-1945* (New York, 2008).

3. Into The Deep. Diving the *Gairsoppa*

Bertke, D.A., Kindell, D., Smith, G., *World War II Sea War, Volume 3: The Royal Navy is Bloodied in the Mediterranean, Day-to-Day naval Actions October 1940 through May 1941.* (Lulu.com, USA, 2012).

Biological Activity Reaction Test, BART™ User Manual, 2004 (Droycon Bioconcepts, Canada, 2004).

Campbell, N.J.M., 'British Naval Guns 1880-1945'. In J. Roberts (ed.), *WARSHIP Volume 10, No 1* (Conway Maritime Press, 1986).

Cullimore, D.R., 'The Impact of Bioconcretious Structures (Rusticles) for the RMS *Titanic*: Implications for Maritime Steel Structures', *SNAME Transactions* 108 (2000), 179-95.

Cullimore, R., Pellegrino, C. and Johnston, L., 'RMS *Titanic* and the Emergence of New Concepts on Consortil Nature of Microbial Events', *Reviews of Environmental Contamination and Toxicology* 173 (2002), 117-41.

Cunningham Dobson, N., *German U-boats of the English Channel & Western Approaches: History, Site Formation & Impacts* (OME Papers 35, Tampa, 2013).

Hague. A., *The Allied Convoy System 1939-1945. Its Organization and Operation* (Chatham, 2000).

Halley, M.P., *An Ethnography of Marine Convoys During World War II* (University of Sheffield, 1995).

Hurd, A., *Britain's Merchant Navy* (London, 1943).

Life-saving Measures for Merchant Seamen in Time of War (Statement Prepared at the Request of the Joint Maritime Commission, Studies & Reports Series P (Seamen) No.4. Montreal, 1942).

Ransome-Wallis, P., *The Sea and Ships* (London, 1957).

Thomas, R.E., *Stowage, the Properties and Stowage of Cargoes* (Glasgow, 1945).

Williamson, G., *U-boats vs. Destroyer Escorts the Battle of the Atlantic* (Oxford, 2007).

4. Silver Waves. A Wartime Cargo

Accounts Relating to the Sea-borne Trade and Navigation of British India. For December 1940 (Department of Commercial, Intelligence and Statistics, India).

Ahluwalia, G.C., *A World in Conflict (World War II & India)* (Delhi, 1949).

Ally, R., 'Gold, the Pound Sterling and the Witwatersrand, 1886-1914'. In J. McGuire, P. Bertola and P. Reeves (eds.), *Evolution of the World Economy, Precious Metals and India* (Oxford University Press, 2001), 97-122.

An Analysis of the Sources of War Finance and an Estimate of the National Income and the Expenditure in 1938 and 1940 (London, 1941).

Awasthi, R.C., *Economics of Tea Industry in India* (Assam, 1975).

Barnett, C., *The Audit of War. The Illusion & Reality of Britain as a Great Nation* (London, 1986).

Boog, H., Rahn, W., Stumpf, R. and Wegner, B., *Germany and the Second World War. Volume VI: The Global War* (Oxford, 2001).

British War Production 1939-1945. A Record (The Times, London, 1945).

Chaudhuri, A., *Enclaves in a Peasant Society. Political Economy of Tea in Western Dooars in Northern Bengal* (New Delhi, 1995).

Collingham, L., *The Taste of War. World War Two and the Battle for Food* (St Ives, 2011).

Datta, S.B., *Capital Accumulation and Workers' Struggles in Indian Industrialisation. The Case of the Tata Iron and Steel Company 1910-1970* (Edsbruk, 1986).

Griffiths, P., *The History of the Indian Tea Industry* (London, 1967).

Hicks, J. and Allen, G., *A Century of Change: Trends in UK statistics since 1900* (House of Commons Research Paper 99/111, 1999).

Indian Tea Statistics. 1941 and 1942 (Governor-General in Council, Delhi, 1948).

Kharia, D.P., 'A Glimpse of the Tata Iron and Steel Company Limited, Jamshedpur'. In *International Symposium on Modern Developments in Steelmaking, February 15, 1981* (Jamshedpur, 1981), 28-37.

Lloyd's War Losses. The Second World War, 3 September 1939 – 14 August 1945. Volume I (London, 1989).

Longmate, N., *How We Lived Then. A History of Everyday Life During the Second World War* (Capetown, 1973).

McLaine, I., *Ministry of Morale. Home Front and the Ministry of Information in World War II* (London, 1979).

Misra, S.R., *Tea Industry in India* (New Delhi, 1986).

Mukerjee, M., *Churchill's Secret War. The British Empire and the Ravaging of India during World War II* (New York, 2010).

Rao, K.N.P., *A Brief History of the Indian Iron and Steel Industry* (Journal of Iron and Steel Institute Special Report 78, 1964).

Rothermund, D., 'The Monetary Policy of British Imperialism', *Indian Economic & Social History Review* 7.1 (1970), 91-107.

Smith, K., 'Maritime Powers in Transition: Britain's Shipping Capacity Crisis and the Mobilization of Neutral American Power, 1940-41'. In G. Kennedy (ed.), *The Merchant Marine in International Affairs 1850-1950* (London, 2000), 155-75.

Tennent, A.J., *British and Commonwealth Merchant Ship Losses to Axis Submarines, 1939-1945* (Sutton, 2001).

Tomlinson, B.R., *The New Cambridge History of India. III.3. The Economy of Modern India, 1860-1970* (Cambridge, 1993).

Voigt, J.H., 'India in the Second World War: a History with Problems', *Neue Forschungen zum Zweiten Weltkrieg* 28 (1990), 187-201.

Watson, E.A., 'The Tea Industry in India', *The Journal of the Royal Society of Arts* 84 (1936), 445-64.

Weir, E.M.K., 'German Submarine Blockade, Overseas Imports, and British Military Production in World War II', *Journal of Military and Strategic Studies* 6.1 (2003), 1-42.

Wickizer, V.D., *Coffee, Tea and Cocoa. An Economic and Political Analysis* (Stanford University Press, 1951).

5. Message In A Bottle

Arthur, H., *The Whiskey Companion. A Connoisseur's Guide* (Philadelphia, 2008).

Balch, P.A., *Prescription for Nutritional Healing. A Practical A-to-Z Reference to Drug-Free Remedies Using Vitamins, Minerals, Herbs & Food Supplements* (London, 2006).

Barnett, R., *The Book of Gin. A Spirited World History from Alchemists' Stills and Colonial Outposts to Gin Palaces, Bathtub Gin and Artisanal Cocktails* (Grove Press, 2012).

Black, R., *Alcohol in Popular Culture. An Encyclopedia* (Santa Barbara, 2010).

Brander, M., *Brander's Guide to Scotch Whiskey* (New York, 1996).

Britton, N., *HP Sauce. My Ancestors' Legacy* (Bloomingon, IN, 2013).

Buchan, W., *Domestic Medicine, or a Treatise on the Prevention and Cure of Diseases by Regimen and Simple Medicines* (New York, 1812).

Burke, B., The *General Armory of England, Scotland, Ireland and Wales. A Registry of Armoral Bearings from the Earliest to the Present Time. Volume 2* (London, 1884).

Burkitt, H. and Zealley, J., *Marketing Excellence. Winning Companies Reveal the Secrets of their Success* (Chichester, 2006).

Chynoweth, K. and Woodson, E., *Lemon. Growing, Cooking, Crafting* (San Francisco, 2003).

Collingham, E.M., *Imperial Bodies. The Physical Experience of the Raj, c. 1800-1947* (Malden, MA, 2001).

Colvard, R.E. *A World Without Drink: Temperance in Modern India, 1880-1940* (PhD Thesis, University of Iowa, 2013).

Conrad, B., *The Martini. An Illustrated History of An American Classic* (San Francisco, 1995).

Cumo, C., 'Lemon'. In C. Cumo (ed.), *Encyclopedia of Cultivated Plants: From Acacia to Zinnia* (3 Volumes) (Santa Barbara, 2013), 563-70.

Dillon, P., *Gin. The Much-Lamented Death of Madam Geneva* (London, 2002).

Donovan, T., *Fizz. How Soda Shook Up the World* (Chicago, 2014).

Dunkling, L., *The Guinness Drinking Companion* (Enfield, 1992).

Faith, N., *Cognac. The Story of the World's Greatest Brandy* (Oxford, 2013).

Gerth, E., *Bottles from the Deep. Patent Medicines, and Other Bottles from the Wreck of the SS Republic* (Shipwreck Heritage Press, 2006).

Hamilton, H., *The County of Banff. The Third Statistical Account of Scotland* (Glascow, 1961).

Hare, H.A. and Martin, E., *The Therapeutic Gazette. A Monthly Journal of General, Special and Physiological Therapeutics* XXIII (Detroit, 1899).

Harvey, R.W. (ed.), 'News Behind the Ads', *The Kiplinger Service for Families* 26.5 (May 1972), 37-8.

Hughes, D.A., *A Bottle of Guinness Please. The Colorful History of Guinness* (Wokingham, 2006).

Jurafsky, D., *The Language of Food. A Linguist Reads the Menu* (New York, 2014).

Lockhart, B., 'The Origins and Life of the Export Beer Bottle', *Bottles and Extras* (May-June 2007), 49-58.

Lockhart, B., Lindsey, B., Schriever, B. and Serr, C., 'Other 'A' Marks', *Historic Glass Bottle Information Website* (E-Published, August 2013).

Lundy, R., *In Praise of Tomatoes. Tasty Recipes, Garden Secrets, Legends & Lore* (New York, 2006).

McCallum, J.E., *Military Medicine. From Ancient Times to the 21st Century* (Santa Barbara, 2008).

Madden, D., *Ginger Beer* (National Centre for Biotechnology Education, University of Reading Science and Technology Centre, 2007).

Maiya, H., *The King of Good Times* (CreateSpace Publishing, 2011).

Mansfield, S., *The Search for God and Guinness. A Biography of the Beer that Changed the World* (Nashville, Tenn., 2009).

Meyers, H.M. and Gerstman, R., *The Visionary Package. Using Packaging to Build Effective Brands* (New York, 2005).

Neiberg, M.S., *Dance of the Furies. Europe and the Outbreak of World War I* (Harvard University Press, 2011).

Report of the Committee Appointed to Consider the Existing Conditions Under Which Canteens and Regimental Institute Are Conducted Together with Minority Report and Appendices (Papers by Command. Great Britain. Parliament. House of Commons) (Eyre and Spottiswoode, Printers to the King's Most Excellent Majesty, London, 1903).

Sandham, T., *World's Best Cocktails. 500 Signature Drinks from the World's Best Bars and Bartenders* (Beverly, MA, 2012).

Shimizu, H., *Japanese Firms in Contemporary Singapore* (National Press of Singapore, 2008).

Shurtleff, W. and Aoyagi, A., *History of Worcestershire Sauce (1837-2012)* (Soyinfo Center, 2012).

Simmons, D.A., *Schweppes. The First 200 Years* (London, 1983).

Smith, A., *Food and Drink in American History. A "Full Course" Encyclopedia* (Santa Barbara, 2013).

Smith, A.F. 'Cadbury Schweppes'. In A.F. Smith (ed.), *The Oxford Companion to American Food and Drink* (Oxford University Press, 2007), 80.

Spivak, M., *Iconic Spirits. An Intoxicating History* (Guilford, CT, 2012).

Taylor, D., *Martini* (London, 2002).

The Crown Cork Cap and Crown Soda Machine 1892 and 1898 (The Mechanical Society of Mechanical Engineers. ASME Region III Baltimore Section, 25 May 1994).

Tucker, B., 'The International Expansion of an Enterprise of the Semi-Periphery: South African Breweries Limited'. In M. Taylor and T. Thrift (eds.), *Multinationals and the Restructuring of the World Economy. The Geography of the Multinationals, Volume 2* (New York, 1986), 86-104.

Youngerman, B., *Global Issues. Pandemics and Global Heath* (New York, 2008).

6. The Royal Mail at Sea

Norway, A., *History of the Post Office Packet Service 1793-1815* (London, 1895).

Proud, E. (ed.), *History of British Army Postal Service Vol. III* (London, 1982).

Robinson, H., *Carrying British Mails Overseas* (London, 1964).

9. War & Wheels of Commerce

Moreman, T.R., *The Army in India and the Development of Frontier Warfare, 1849-1947* (Basingstoke, 1998).

Papagos, A., *The Battle of Greece 1940-1941* (Athens, 1949).

Roe, A.M., *Waging War In Waziristan. The British Struggle in the Land of Bin Laden, 1849-1947* (University Press of Kansas, 2010), 183.

10. Conclusion

Ahluwalia, G.C., *A World in Conflict (World War II & India)* (Delhi, 1949).

Blake, G., *B.I. Centenary 1856-1956* (London, 1956).

Elphick, P., *Life Line. The Merchant Navy at War 1939-1945* (London, 1999).

St George Saunders, H., *Valiant Voyaging. A Short History of the British India Steam Navigation Company in the Second World War, 1939-1945* (London, 1948).

Voigt, J.H., 'India in the Second World War: a History with Problems', *Neue Forschungen zum Zweiten Weltkrieg* 28 (1990), 187-201.

PICTURE CREDITS

INDEX